WATER WITCHING U.S.A.

A Vermont dowser searches for water. (Photograph by Verner Z. Reed)

WATER WITCHING U.S.A.

Second Edition

EVON Z. VOGT
and
RAY HYMAN

THE UNIVERSITY OF CHICAGO PRESS
Chicago and London

The University of Chicago Press, Chicago 60637
The University of Chicago Press, Ltd., London

© 1959, 1979 by The University of Chicago
All rights reserved. Published 1959
Second Edition 1979
Printed in the United States of America
86 85 84 83 82 81 80 79   54321

Library of Congress Cataloging in Publication Data

Vogt, Evon Zartman, 1918–
  Water witching, U.S.A.

  Bibliography: p.
  1. Divining rod. I. Hyman, Ray, joint author.
II. Title.
BF1628.V6 1979   133.3'23   79–240
ISBN 0–226–86297–6

Table of Contents

Preface to the Phoenix Edition

In the almost twenty years that have passed since the first edition of this book, much has happened. We describe some of the more relevant happenings in the world of dowsing in the Postscript we have written for this edition. Surprisingly, however, nothing has happened to change any of the basic conclusions we reached about dowsing in 1959. If anything, those conclusions are even more timely today.

In 1959 water witching was a widespread practice in rural America and was considered to be a practical tool for locating underground water. At times it was also employed to try to find other underground substances such as oil and metals. The rural American diviners, the number of whom we estimated to be approximately twenty-five thousand, were not generally concerned about how the technique "worked," nor did they think in terms of joining associations or societies with other diviners; and they showed no obvious tendencies to apply their technique to other uses.

As far as we know, this situation has not changed much among the rural diviners. However, since the first edition, we have uncovered a new breed—the urban dowser—who has made the practice part of the "occult explosion." Unlike his or her rural counterpart, the urban diviner employs the rod or pendulum to try to find a variety of objects and to attempt to answer all sorts of questions. This urban dowser tends to be involved with other occult arts and is much concerned with rationalizing the practice, usually in terms of "new forces" or "supernatural powers." It is the urban diviner, also, who has taken steps to create and join organizations to promote and protect the divining art.

We describe this new breed of diviner in the Postscript. We also look again briefly at some questions we posed in the first edition. No new evidence produced by the world of dowsing has been able to alter our basic conclusions.

EVON Z. VOGT
RAY HYMAN
October, 1978

Preface

The research for this book was initiated in the spring of 1955, when the two authors met at a dinner party in Cambridge and discovered they had mutual interests in water witching and related phenomena in American culture. Vogt had previously done anthropological field work on water witching in rural American communities; Hyman had been a professional magician and a member of the International Brotherhood of Magicians and the Society of American Magicians before he took his Ph.D. in psychology and began to teach social psychology and statistics at Harvard. These complementary interests and skills and a shared curiosity about water witching led to the organization of a small research project supported by grants from the Laboratory of Social Relations and the Department of Psychology at Harvard. We were ably assisted during 1955–56 by two graduate research assistants, Elizabeth G. Cohen (sociologist) and Peggy Golde (anthropologist), who contributed ideas, energy, enthusiasm, and more working hours to the enterprise than it was ever possible to pay them for.

At various stages of the research we profited from consultations with other members of the Harvard faculty, especially Professor L. Don Leet, who provided geological advice and information, Professor Fred Mosteller, who made important suggestions concerning the design of our sample survey, and Professors Gordon Allport, E. G. Boring, Jerome Bruner, Bernard Cohen, Sanford Dornbusch, Clyde Kluckhohn, Talcott Parsons, Samuel Stouffer, Philip Teitelbaum, and Gordon Willey, who all gave advice and encouragement. We also received valuable comments from Charles Nyquist and James Savage. We are especially indebted to the five hundred county agricultural extension agents whom we pestered with our questionnaires but who responded so generously with their time and information that we are dedicating the book to them.

Most of the book was written at the Center for Advanced Study in the Behavioral Sciences, Stanford, California, where Vogt was a Fellow during 1956–57 and where Hyman joined him for two months in the fall term. The Center administrative staff offered every possible encouragement and service, and other Fellows in our own and other fields contributed significantly to the book in the discussions that reverberated around the seminar rooms and coffee tables. There was hardly anyone at the Center who did not have something to say about the subject of water witching, pro or con, but we should like especially to acknowledge the assistance of Kingsley Davis, David Hamburg, Morris Opler, John M. Roberts, Richard Savage, Hans Speier, George Spindler, and Allen Wallis.

In its final stages of preparation the manuscript was greatly improved by the skilful and painstaking editorial work of Barbara Metzger, who served as our research assistant during 1957–58. We wish to thank Harriet Fraser, who typed the final copy for the publisher.

Many of the photographs on the techniques of water witching were taken by David DeHarport, and we should like to express our appreciation for permission to use them in the book. We are grateful to Verner Reed, Philip Dukette, Gaston Burridge, Jerry Smith, and Clarence V. Elliott for permission to use other photographs which add materially to the interest of the book.

Finally, we should like to thank Harold E. Thomas of the United States Geological Survey, who wrote Appendix II, "Water-Well Location by Scientific Divination," especially for this volume.

Evon Z. Vogt
Ray Hyman

CHAPTER 1

Why Water Witching?

Since this matter remains in dispute and causes much dissension among miners, I consider it ought to be examined on its own merits.

GEORGIUS AGRICOLA, 1556

"If we hadn't been so desperate for water, and could have thought the situation over more coolly, I don't suppose we'd ever have got involved in our curious adventure with dowsing, or water witching."

With these words Mrs. Nancy E. Bond begins her feature article on water witching in a recent issue of *Woman's Day* (Bond, 1956). Mrs. Bond details the plight in which she and her husband, an English instructor at Dartmouth, found themselves when their two wells ran dry. Despite a professed skepticism about water witching, the Bonds were persuaded to send a rough map of their property to Kenneth Roberts, the famous novelist and vehement champion of dowsing. Roberts put the renowned talents of Henry Gross to work, and Henry's divining rod located a well which supplied abundant water throughout one of Hanover's worst droughts. And, unlike the run-of-the-mill diviner, Henry located this well while he was a hundred and fifty miles from the site. On the basis of this one personal experience Mrs. Bond concludes, "I don't pretend to understand dowsing, but it saved the day for us, and I'm sold."

1

Mrs. Bond's story is an interesting, but isolated, incident in the lives of one American family. The story becomes more significant when we discover that the Bonds are not alone in appealing to water witching for help. In fact, they are but one of many thousands of families that today turn to the diviner when they need more water. The particular form of witching the Bonds employed—the long-distance location over a map (see Fig. 14)—is not typical of the pattern as it is generally encountered. More typical is the scene we are about to describe. You may come across a similar scene with slight variations on any day in any part of the United States (see Frontispiece).

Jeff Green seems like a man in a trance. His head is bent forward, and his eyes are focused upon the junction of the two forks of the peach limb that he holds in his hands. He clutches one fork of the branch in each hand in such a way that the junction points almost straight up in the air. For the past half-hour he has been pacing back and forth over Frank Brown's pasture. Suddenly the peach limb quivers, and, as Jeff moves forward a few paces, it twists in his hands and points downward with such violence that the bark peels off. Jeff looks up and smiles at Frank Brown. "Dig here," he says, "and you'll find the water that you need."

Jeff has just given an exhibition of the ancient art of water witching, otherwise known as "water divining," "dowsing," "smelling," "witch wriggling," and by a variety of other terms. His divining rod has just indicated a site at which Frank Brown hopes to find an adequate supply of underground water. Frank Brown is aware that the government men frown upon this practice. But he needs water desperately. When his two previous attempts to drill wells produced only dry holes, the county agricultural extension agent could respond with nothing more helpful than "Maybe you'll have better luck next time." So Brown, in desperation, sought the aid of a neighboring farmer and water diviner. Jeff Green was an old-timer in the county and had a reputation for successfully witching hundreds of wells. To call upon him seemed, under the circumstances, the sensible thing to do.

All over the country, rural people seek out the diviner in just such situations as these. So great is the demand for the services of the diviner that an estimated twenty-five thousand diviners are actively plying their trade in the United States today.

Water witching would be worth studying if only because of its widespread popularity among the rural population. But our curiosity is piqued by the additional fact that the practice is considered an outcast by orthodox science. Geologists, water engineers, government officials, and other scientists have opposed this unorthodoxy ever since it became popular some four hundred years ago.

We are interested in what happened to the Bonds, then, because in their experience we may find some clues to why water witching persists in the face of scientific opposition. And an understanding of the persistence of water witching may give us some insights into why other unorthodoxies still survive within a culture that prides itself on its scientific and technological advancement.

With these facts in mind, let us look again at the story of the Bonds to see what clues it may contain. We note that the Bonds regarded water witching as "a lot of superstitious nonsense." Under ordinary circumstances they never would have considered using it. But with no cash, two dry wells, a thirsty dog, and other immediate water needs, they finally turned to a diviner for guidance. We can judge the extent of their predicament when we find Harry Bond devoting over two hundred hours of hard labor to digging at a spot suggested by a man in whose abilities he had no confidence.

Having committed so much to the judgment of a forked twig, the Bonds experienced a tremendous sense of relief and satisfaction when their efforts were rewarded with water beyond their needs. They were thankful and expressed their gratitude openly. We can understand how this one experience converted the Bonds from skeptics to vociferous believers in the powers of the divining rod.

The conversion of the Bonds contains all the ingredients that led us to study water witching. The Bonds are well-educated and sensible people. They know that water witching is considered unscientific. Yet, when the chips are down and they have a lot at stake, they go against what their education and their reason tell them. Under conditions of extreme uncertainty and anxiety, they turn to the water witch. It is this aspect of water witching that caught our attention. Here is an apparent paradox. Here are people who ordinarily guide their lives by the latest scientific knowledge but who forsake science in their hour of need and resort to pseudo science.

To us water witching is a fascinating subject in its own right. But we see also in this practice one example of a more general phenomenon. We are interested in how people cope with the environment under conditions of uncertainty and anxiety. The search for underground water is an excellent illustration of such conditions. In many areas of the rural United States, the maintenance of adequate supplies of water is a critical problem. In these areas the main source of water is underground. The cost of developing a productive well is generally quite high. If a site is chosen where water can only be reached at considerable depths or where no water at all is found, financial disaster can result. If, on the other hand, a site is chosen where good water can be obtained from relatively shallow depths, considerable savings result. Any methods or indicators that purport to reduce this uncertainty about where to locate a good site for a well are therefore more than welcome.

For these reasons, then, we first turned our attention to divining, and we found ourselves at once in the midst of a storm of controversy. Few subjects arouse such vigorous and emotional debate as the question of the validity of water witching. Undoubtedly there are still communities in which water witching is simply taken for granted. However, because the scientific opposition has made inroads into the rural community and because the practice itself has been called to the attention of the general public, many people have discovered that they are *for* witching or *against* it. The response of the county agricultural extension agents in our study, some of whom are diviners themselves, reflected this controversy. In our sample, 56 per cent of the agents expressed outright disbelief in the validity of witching, but as many as 20 per cent admitted that they believed in its efficacy, and the remaining 24 per cent indicated an open mind on this issue.

A few representative statements from the press will illustrate the varying degrees of feeling on the subject. From the pro-witching camp:

If we can do anything to rebuke the scientists and the ignoramuses who say that dowsing is nonsense, just let us know. They haven't a leg to stand on—unless you can call stupidity a leg [J. J. Grullemans in the *Boston Traveler*, June 3, 1954].

The volume [Kenneth Roberts, *The Seventh Sense*] is devoted to sense, all right, but actually to hammering some sense into the geological eggheads, literary critics, and the skeptical among the peasants who doubt that Henry Gross can dowse water, as Mr. Roberts says he can. It appears these ignorami have constituted a considerable and audible company [Bill Cunningham in the *Boston Herald*, July 16, 1953].

The opposition:

The only thing worse than a dowser, in the geologists' book, is a fellow earth scientist who dares harbor a lingering doubt that dowsing is completely ridiculous. Find water by walking over the ground with a forked stick in your hands? Absurd superstition! [Howard Meyerhoff in *Popular Science*, October, 1953].

Mr. Roberts has betrayed his readers by a tired tirade at "water geologists" and "minor scientists" who try to protect a gullible public from the consequences of this irresponsible resurrection and publicizing of a superstition that is as old as history and as worthy as witchcraft [L. Don Leet in *American Scientist*, October, 1953].

One writer who has not quite taken a side is frankly puzzled:

I don't pretend to know the facts. All I can say is that I am 95 per cent convinced that certain persons have some mysterious power that causes the divining rod to work for them. Through the generations there have been scoffers and skeptics, but if you are honest with yourself, how can you deny what you see? . . . Myth or fact? A delusion or a deliberate deception? [Haydn Pearson in the *Boston Sunday Herald*, April 22, 1956].

With our curiosity further aroused by this controversy, we set out to learn what we could about water witching. We went first to the published literature to find what is known about the origin and spread of the practice, hoping that this would give us some perspective on its persistence in the contemporary United States. In the literature, also, we found reports of investigations that shed considerable light on two basic questions: "Does the divining rod in fact find water?" and "What makes the rod move?"

Next, because of our particular interest in witching in America, we wanted a better understanding of its prevalence in the United States, of how much it is practiced and under what conditions—geographical, geological, meteorological, and cultural—it occurs. We were interested, also, in learning what kinds of people American diviners are—how they came to take up the rod, how they feel about it, and how they explain their activities to themselves and to others. Some of the countless articles about dowsers in newspapers and magazines suggested answers to certain of our questions. These, however, give an exaggerated, or at least incomplete, view of the importance of divining if considered alone. To answer our questions, therefore, we designed a study which would obtain comparable information from all parts of the country. We mailed a total of five hundred questionnaires to a stratified sample of county agricultural extension agents. These agents were sampled from 3,017 counties (the number of counties in the United States that have an agricultural extension service) containing 91 per cent of the total United States population. The counties were classified for sampling purposes according to whether they were predominantly rural or urban; they were further classified into one of ten ground-water regions of the United States (see Fig. 1 for a map of ground-water regions). The exact details of this study including how we pretested our questionnaire and how we handled such problems as non-respondents can be found in more detail in a paper by Hyman and Cohen (1957). In Appendix I we reproduce our covering letter and our chief instrument—the questionnaire.

Our initial request plus one follow-up letter resulted in a response from 72 per cent of our original sample. Our conclusions are based upon data from these responses, supplemented by information from a variety of other sources.[1] We had questionnaires from agents who took part in our pretest, from agents who formed a special sample of seventy-one counties used for studies by the U.S. Department of Agriculture, and, finally, from county agricultural agents whom we knew but who had not fallen into our sample. All told, our information from questionnaires covered more than five hundred counties.

The reactions of the county agents, of course, varied widely. A few agents refused to answer any of the questions on the grounds that they could not supply accurate answers. Others answered selectively, responding only to those questions for which they had sufficient information. Some answered all the questions but commented that some or all of their replies were mainly guesswork. The majority of our respondents, however, were conscientious about the task and apparently spent considerable time and effort in completing the questionnaire. Many sought the help of other informants, such as local farmers, well-drillers, "old-timers," the Soil Conservation Service, and newspaper reporters. One agent even appealed to his radio audience and the readers of his farm column to supply us with information.

---

[1] Responses from a small sample of the original non-respondents whom we made a special effort to reach revealed that they differed in no essential respect from the original respondents.

Many respondents could not refrain from making a few comments on the merits of our inquiry. An agent from Oregon stated his position on the subject in these words: "Questionnaires of this type are in general a waste of time. . . . You may feel fortunate to even get an answer." A man from Virginia put it this way: "A heck of a lot of foolish questions." This negative view concerning the worth of our study was most succinctly summed up in the comment of a Michigan man who simply replied, "Nuts!"

Fortunately for us, such expressions, while pungent, were in the minority. More of the agents included comments which seemed to be in accord with that of the agent from New York who said, "I have a keen interest in your study." A large number of the respondents explicitly asked us to send them a report of our completed study.

Besides information from questionnaires we gathered other kinds of data. We interviewed and observed diviners in action in New Mexico, Massachusetts, Nebraska, West Virginia, New Hampshire, and New Jersey. We talked with many more people who had witnessed the practice in other parts of the country. We carried on a voluminous correspondence with diviners or people who knew diviners all over the world. Many friends throughout the country kept us well supplied with newspaper clippings and magazine articles on water witching.

These data, taken together, provided us with a much clearer view of the patterns of water witching in the United States. The basic survey data, when combined with census, geological, and meteorological information and coded and punched on IBM cards, gave us answers concerning the extent of water witching and the conditions under which it is practiced in this country. The data further supplied us with information concerning who the diviner is, how he rationalizes his practice, and what beliefs and folk sayings about water witching are current.

We organize our book around six basic questions. The first question is, "What is water witching?" We answer this question in the next chapter by tracing its history and by describing that pattern as it currently exists in the United States.

The second question is one that everyone asks. "Does it work?" Chapters 3 and 4 will not only deal with this question but will also discuss the hidden "booby traps" in such an apparently simple query.

The third question is related to the previous one, but it requires separate treatment for its answer. Chapters 5 and 6 deal with the query, "What makes the rod move?" And in the course of answering this question we will encounter such improbable personalities as a mind-reading horse, a talking table, and a telepathic performer.

The first three questions are answered by a careful review and analysis of existing literature. Our answers are supplemented only occasionally by data from our own extensive survey. But in chapters 7 and 8 we deal with questions whose answers are supplied almost entirely from our own findings. The fourth question can be phrased: "Who is the water witch?" We try to supply a portrait of the American diviner in chapter 7 on "Who's Who in Witching."

The fifth question is really a composite. It is basically phrased as, "Under what conditions is witching practiced in the United States?" But this can be broken down into such questions as: "Where is witching practiced?" "How intensively is it practiced?" and "Under what conditions is the water witch hired?" The data from our study that are relevant to these questions form the subject matter of chapter 8.

Finally, chapter 9 deals with the last but most important question: "Why does water witching continue to be practiced in the United States?" It is this question that motivated our inquiry. The answers to the preceding five questions were necessary before we could speculate sensibly about this final, but crucial, question.

CHAPTER 2

The Family Tree

They tell us something strange and odd,
About a certain magic Rod,
That, bending down its Top, divines
When e'er the Soil has Golden Mines;
Where there are none, it stands erect,
Scorning to show the least Respect.

JONATHAN SWIFT, 1710

Water witching comes to us from a rich and colorful past, and the practice today becomes much more meaningful when we realize how it began, how it spread, and how it became modified. In this chapter we are interested in the ancestry of the divining rod. The history of the practice helps us to understand water witching in twentieth-century United States by providing the backdrop for the other questions we wish to ask about this ancient art.

WATER WITCHING AS A FORM OF DIVINATION

How old is the divining rod? Estimates of 7,000 years (Tromp, 1949) and of at least 3,200 years (Burridge, 1954) have been advanced, but the historical background given by Barrett and Besterman (1926) suggests that the actual age of the rod, as we now know it, is between 400 and 500 years. What accounts for these widely divergent estimates? Is each of these authors merely pulling numbers out of a hat? Probably not. The different guesses simply reflect different ways of viewing the divining rod.

At one level, we see that water witching is a form of divination by signs. When the stick does not bend, this is a sign that no water is present. A man who has confidence in the rod will not sink a well at a spot unless the rod gives him a favorable sign. In a similar fashion, the ancients consulted the oracles or the priests. They searched for omens in the flight of birds, the entrails of animals, or the fall of stones. If the signs indicated that they were not going to win a war, they kept their armies home. If the signs were favorable, however, they marched off to slaughter the enemy, confident that victory was theirs. The ancestry of water witching, conceived as a form of divination, is indeed old, for divination by signs is perhaps as old as man himself. But water witching is a special kind of divination in that it employs a divining rod, and these rods also have a long history in the field of divination. The much-quoted biblical reference to Moses striking the rock with his rod, thus producing water for his followers in the wilderness (Num. 20:9–11), has been regarded by enthusiasts of water witching as a significant reference to the divining rod; and we have been told by several American diviners that "Moses was the first water witch!" With a little imagination, one can also see the ancestors of the forked twig in the rods that the Scythians, Persians, Medes, Greeks, and Romans used for divination (Raymond, 1883). It is true that the Romans were responsible for the name *virgula divina*, "divining rod," but this instrument was used for taking auguries by casting bits of wood. Although the Greek words *rhabdos*, "rod," and *manteia*, "divination," are the roots for the term "rhabdomancy," there is no concrete evidence for water or mineral divining in ancient Greece.

Figures of Mediterranean idols bearing forked rods have been found, but it is more likely that these rods are symbols of power and authority (Besterman, 1938, p. 200). The most clinching evidence against these dubious early references is that the ancient naturalists like Pliny all give detailed directions for finding water but mention nothing akin to the divining rod of the Middle Ages (Hoover, in Agricola, p. 38 n.).

The alleged early ancestry of the divining rod adds color and romance to the history of water witching, but there are too many "missing links" to construct a family tree with roots that go back before the Middle Ages. If we stick to authenticated accounts about the use of the forked twig, our story can begin only four hundred years ago.

THE WRITTEN RECORD

In 1556 Georgius Agricola, who had served for some years as the town physician of a mining camp in Bohemia, published his great work, *De re metallica.* Agricola had spent his spare time visiting the mines and smelters and studying the techniques of the miners, and his book provides us with the first detailed description of the divining rod in the form of the forked twig still used in rural American communities:

There are many great contentions between miners concerning the forked twig, for some say that it is of the greatest use in discovering veins, and others deny it. Some of those who manipulate and use the twig, first cut a fork from a hazel bush with a knife, for this bush they consider more efficacious than any other for revealing the veins, especially if the hazel bush grows above a vein. . . . All alike grasp the forks of the twig with their hands, clenching their fists, it being necessary that the clenched fingers should be held toward the sky in order that the twig should be raised at that end where the two branches meet. They then wander hither and thither at random through mountainous regions. It is said that the moment they place their feet on a vein the twig immediately turns and twists, and so by its action discloses the vein; when they move their feet again and go away from that spot the twig becomes once more immobile.

The truth is, they assert, the movement of the twig is caused by the power of the veins, and sometimes this is so great that the branches of trees growing near a vein are deflected toward it. On the other hand, those who say the twig is of no use to good and serious men, also deny that the motion is due to the power of the veins, because the twigs will not move for everybody, but only for those who employ incantations and craft [Agricola, pp. 38–39].

Agricola's is the first account that depicts in unambiguous terms the rod as we know it today. (See also the illustration of the method, reproduced from his book, in Fig. 2.) Many scholars point to earlier, medieval references, antedating Agricola, but these leave much to the imagination, and we cannot be certain that they refer to anything like the present-day divining rod.

Sir William Barrett, the great authority who devoted much of his life to the study of water divining, found a sketchy 1430 reference in a manuscript left by a mine surveyor (Barrett and Besterman, 1926). And in 1518, Martin Luther proclaimed that the use of the rod violated the First Commandment.

By the end of the sixteenth century, the divining rod emerged from obscurity and became the topic of lively controversies. Enough publications were available by then to indicate that the practice was common in Germany for locating underground minerals. These records reveal the heated debates that were prevalent, even then, concerning the rod's merits. These spirited arguments stimulated innumerable scientific investigations and led, ultimately, to the publication of more than a thousand books, pamphlets, and articles in the past four hundred years. Agricola opened the debate on the technical side with his statement that "there are many great contentions between miners concerning the forked twig." In 1953 we read in the pages of Kenneth Roberts' *The Seventh Sense:* "Only in America do fearful minor scientists and their satellites swear till all's blue that water dowsing is a hoax and a superstition."

THE ROD VERSUS THE CHURCH

Despite Luther's proclamation against the rod in 1518, the divining practice apparently escaped ecclesiastical animosity for more than a hundred years. Many clergy, indeed, were prominent in promulgating the practice. But by the middle of the seventeenth century, this honeymoon of rod and church apparently came to an abrupt halt.

In 1658 the rod was the subject of an academic thesis at Wittenberg. This learned dissertation concluded that the movements of the rod were sometimes due to fraud and sometimes due to an implicit pact with the devil. Many similar dissertations followed—all tainting the rod with a satanic association (Barrett and Besterman, 1926). (This point of view is illustrated in an early engraving. See Fig. 7.)

Perhaps it was this sudden eruption of ecclesiastical opposition that led diviners to take steps to purify their art. They developed elaborate rituals to dissociate their practice from contamination by the devil and other heathen influences. For example, many diviners in Germany believed that the stick must be cut on St. John's Day and then duly Christianized by baptism. The diviner would place a forked stick in the bed with a newly baptized child, by whose Christian name it was afterward addressed. The following incantation used by a seventeenth-century diviner will serve as an illustration: "In the name of the Father and of the Son and of the Holy Ghost, I adjure thee, Augusta Carolina, that thou tell me, so pure and true as Mary the Virgin was, who bore our Lord Jesus Christ, how many fathoms is it from here to the ore?" (Raymond, 1883, p. 419). The rod was expected to reply by dipping a certain number of times, corresponding to the number of fathoms. Today the incantation has gone, but we can still observe the core of the practice. We note a diviner such as Henry Gross asking similar questions of his rod, and it, too, dips a certain number of times in answer.

As long as the rod was used to find minerals, the accusations of witchcraft did little to hinder its spread. It was only when the rod entered the moral and ethical realm that the church finally took a stand. The rod, so it was discovered, could track down criminals and ascertain their guilt.

In 1692 an incident in southern France greatly added to the notoriety of the divining rod. A wine-grower and his wife were murdered. The police were stymied in their efforts to apprehend the culprits. As a last resort, they turned to a peasant named Jacques Aymar for help. Aymar was already renowned for his divining ability, and there were tales that he could also track down criminals. In this situation, Aymar's rod led the police over a complex trail to a young hunchback. Under questioning the suspect broke down and confessed to the crime. He was executed. Aymar became a national celebrity and was invited to Paris.

The Aymar case extended the rod's applications into a new domain and eventually brought the practice into intense conflict with the ecclesiastical authorities. Finding ores was one thing. But tracking down criminals and proclaiming their guilt was an invasion of the church's domain. Something had to be done. In 1701 the Inquisition issued a decree against the further use of the divining rod in criminal prosecution. This ban effectively put down the rod's activities in the moral realm, but it did not hinder the rod's applications to other problems.

THE SEARCH FOR WATER

The rod began as an instrument for finding ore. As such it was of interest to a small group of people. But when the rod gained repute as a water-finder, its use spread rapidly among many people in several lands.

A reference to the earliest record of the rod's ability to locate water is in Helen H. Colvill's *Saint Teresa of Spain.* In 1568 Teresa was offered the site for a convent to which there was only one objection—there was no water supply.

But one day Antonio [a friar], standing in the church cloister with his friars, a twig in his hand, made the sign of the Cross with it; "or really," says Teresa, "I cannot be sure if it were even a cross; but at any rate he made some movement with the twig, and then he said, Dig just here." They dug, and lo! a plentiful fount of water gushed forth, excellent for drinking, copious for washing, and it never ran dry [Colvill, 1909, pp. 134–35].

The credit for actually popularizing the use of the rod for finding water, however, goes to the Baroness de Beausoleil. She and her husband spent a lot of time developing mines for the French government. For this purpose they often used the divining rod and became quite prominent as diviners. In her book *La restitution de Pluton,* published in 1640, the Baroness recommends the divining rod for discovering springs. It is of passing interest to note that the Baron and his wife were later imprisoned on charges of sorcery. The Baron died in the Bastille, and his wife, in Vincennes, about 1645.

THE SPREAD OF THE PRACTICE

From its probable birthplace in the mining districts of Germany, the divining rod in its present form spread rapidly. During the reign of Queen Elizabeth (1558–1603), when German miners were imported to England to lend an impetus to the mining industry in Cornwall, they brought the rod with them (Ellis, 1917). By the end of the seventeenth century it was found in every European country, and with European exploration and colonization the use of the rod was carried by European settlers to Africa, parts of Asia, North and South America, Australia, and New Zealand (Vogt and Golde, 1958).

The British, Dutch, and Germans all seem to be responsible for the adoption of the rod in South Africa, for it occurs in regions colonized by each. It is not found, so far as we know, among the native tribal peoples. In North Africa it is found in Spanish Morocco and, according to one informant, in Rabat, where the diviners and their clientele are all French colonials. The ubiquitous British colonials took the rod with them to Australia, New Zealand, and India, where there is, however, some suggestive evidence, especially in southern India, that water divining may have been practiced before the British arrived. Except for scattered reports of Europeans carrying on water divining, we have no evidence that the practice is found in the Middle East, in Southeast Asia, in the Far East, or anywhere (other than New Zealand) on the Pacific Islands in Oceania.

In the New World the rod is found among both English and French-Canadian populations of Canada, in every state of the United States, and probably all through Latin America, since we have definite evidence for Mexico, Cuba, Colombia, and Argentina, and there is little reason to believe it would be absent in other countries settled from Spain or Portugal where the practice is ancient and widespread.

Water witching apparently was completely absent in American Indian cultures before the Europeans arrived, bringing the pattern with them. We know of a few scattered cases of American Indians who are water diviners today, but in every case they seem to have learned it quite recently from their white neighbors. For example, in the 1930's a Navaho Indian learned how to witch wells from the leading water diviner in the small Mormon community of Ramah, New Mexico (Vogt, 1952). In 1955, one of our Harvard anthropologists discovered that the Omaha Indians in Thurston County, Nebraska, are practicing water witching, but they learned it from the Soil Conservation Service workers who were working in the area during the 1930's (Vogt and Golde, 1958).

On the basis of present evidence we conclude that the divining rod, as we now know it, is a European pattern stemming from the mining districts of Germany in the late fifteenth or early sixteenth century and spreading from there to the rest of Europe and thence to other regions as the Europeans spread their culture and established colonies in various parts of the world. The apparently complete absence of the practice among American Indians, African natives, the Pacific Islanders, the Australian aborigines, and the indigenous populations of China, Japan, and Southeast Asia—except for scattered cases of recent diffusion from European settlers—only adds to our conviction that we are dealing with a European culture pattern.

We have been unable to locate concrete evidence to date the introduction of the forked twig in America, but it probably crossed the Atlantic in the seventeenth century with the settlers from England (especially those from the mining districts of Cornwall) and from Germany (Katz and Paulson, 1948). Other groups, such as the French and Italians, may also have brought the practice with them, for we now find it among all the European immigrant groups who settled in rural areas, as well as among Negroes, who presumably borrowed the pattern from the white settlers in the Old South.

The published record on water witching is meager in this country prior to 1800. After 1775 we begin to find mention of the practice in newspaper columns in connection with witches and witchcraft (Katz and Paulson, 1948). And it is this association with witchcraft that may account for the American term "water witching." In other English-speaking countries the practice is called "dowsing" or "divining" but never "witching." The other theory about the term connects its origin with the witch hazel, which the early American settlers preferred for their divining rods. Whatever its origin, the term "water witching" is now by far the most common in the United States.

In 1821 the *American Journal of Science* carried the first learned treatise on water witching written in this country. Rev. Ralph Emerson (not to be confused with Ralph Waldo Emerson) took up the cause in a piece entitled "On the Divining Rod, with Reference to the Use Made of It in Exploring for Springs of Water." Emerson found the rods in use in New York and New Hampshire and adds that he was "totally sceptical of their efficacy, till convinced by my own senses" (Emerson, 1821).

But Emerson's testimonial is counteracted by the

negative evidence of another author, writing anony-
mously in the same journal for October, 1826, in an
article entitled simply "The Divining Rod." This author
tells us that the rod may be hazel, peach, or cherry, that
he has known of no woman diviners, and that "in New
England, where springs are most abundant and always
pure, the use of the art is less frequent, because less
necessary. In the states South and West where water is
not equally abundant, and fountains are not so certainly
pure, the art is better known and more highly valued."
He then reports an experiment he conducted with a
diviner of established reputation in Ohio. He blindfolded the diviner, and the diviner "could not then
again find a spot he had previously located." The author
concludes that the "pretensions of diviners are worthless."

These two articles were the first in a steady stream of
articles, books, magazine stories, and newspaper columns about water witching that has continued to the
present day. The United States Geological Survey has
played an active role in the controversy, especially with
the publication of Ellis' pamphlet (1917), which came
to completely negative conclusions concerning the efficacy of the rod. This and other learned articles did not
eliminate the practice from the American scene, however, for it seems, from our research, to be as vigorous
as ever.

WITCHING IN OUR TIME

Such is the background of what we know as water
witching. It is no survival from primitive days. It is not
a magical practice borrowed from non-literate societies.
It is an invention of a civilized culture, a product of
sixteenth-century Europe, and it has come to us in its

original form. Some of the accompanying ritual and incantation has been shed, but no sixteenth-century diviner would have the slightest difficulty in recognizing his art as it is practiced in the twentieth century.

In Germany, the birthplace of divining, learned studies of the rod's action and physical basis continue to appear. One of these, the *Handbuch der Wünschelrute* (1931), is a classic in the field. In France such men as Henri Mager (1931) and Henry de France (1948) keep pushing their brand of divining under the label of "radiesthesia." They try to relate the alleged ability of the rod to find water, ores, and buried treasure, diagnose disease, and perform other feats to the latest theories of radioactivity and electromagnetism. In Spain divining is still taken quite seriously as a method for locating water, as indicated by a 1953 publication of the Spanish Ministry of Agriculture. This publication, a technical manual on the various methods for locating subterranean water, includes one chapter on "Métodos Rábdicos" with descriptions on how to use the divining rod and the pendulum (Murcia Viudas, 1953).

The classic work of Barrett and Besterman (1926) in England amassed weighty evidence to prove that the rod's action is psychical rather than physical in origin, that the rod is merely an indicator of information coming into the subconscious by some unknown supernormal means. Meanwhile their countrymen, the physical scientists Maby and Franklin, published their investigations (1939), aimed at demonstrating, as the physical basis of divining, a dowsing reflex which responds to hertzian waves. A professor of geology in Egypt (Tromp, 1949), basing his conclusions upon researches done in Holland, has tried to show that the dowsing reaction is a natural, subconscious reaction of the human organism to changes in electromagnetic fields. And in the United States, on a less scholarly and more flamboyant level, Kenneth Roberts turned from his historical novels to water witching with his best-selling *Henry Gross and His Dowsing Rod* (1951). He reacted to the resulting controversy with two sequels, entitled *The Seventh Sense* (1953) and *Water Unlimited* (1957).

European diviners are better organized than their American counterparts. They form societies, sponsor journals, and hold international congresses. Some of the divining societies of Europe are: the British Society of Dowsers, L'Association des Amis de la Radiesthésie (France), Gesellschaft für Wissenschaftliche Pendelforschung (Germany), and Centre International d'Étude de la Radiesthésie (Belgium). There is also an International Association of Dowsers which held international congresses regularly until the outbreak of World War II. Such activity has apparently resumed, for we read in *Radio-Perception* (December, 1955) that an International Congress of Radiesthesia was to be held at Lake Locarno in Switzerland during four days in May, 1956. And in Paris today we find a Maison de la Radiesthésie—probably the only shop in the world that specializes in dowsing equipment.

THE TOOLS OF THE TRADE

The diviner's trademark, from Agricola's time through today, has been the forked twig. But even in the early days, variations from this standard rod existed (see Fig. 8, from a 1700 treatise). Sometimes a straight rod served instead of the forked branch. This might be bent and held in the form of an arc, or it might be balanced upon the forefinger of each hand.

Agricola mentions a variety of different woods from which the rod might be made—hazel, ash, and pitch pine. He also mentions rods of iron and steel. Forked rods of whalebone, springs, wire, and other materials have been advocated and used. Such diverse objects as walking sticks, surgical scissors, a stalk of grass, and even a German sausage have been put to work as divining rods.

Sometimes no instrument is employed at all. The Spanish *Zahoríes*, who sometimes use a forked twig, often discard the rod because they have the "power" actually to "see" the underground water. And recently fame has come to a South African boy, Pieter Van Jaarsveld, who can "see" diamonds, water, and other substances underground. He says that the water looks very much like moonshine!

The pendulum, a weight suspended from a string, was assimilated into the water divining pattern by the early 1800's. (A connection between it and the divining rod had been noted by a Jesuit, Father Schott, as early as 1662.) This device is now a leading alternative to the divining rod in Europe; like the rod, it is employed to search for well sites and to ascertain the depth of the water. Today, in this country as well as in Europe, we often find a diviner using the traditional forked twig and the pendulum, alternatively or in conjunction. In May, 1956, we watched a well-driller give us a water witching demonstration on his land in Acton, Massachusetts. He employed a pendulum of amber-colored beads to "locate the edges of the water vein" after he had found the vein with his divining rod.

We find a variety of materials in use as divining rods in contemporary American practice. In our random sampling of 500 counties, we obtained adequate information from a little more than 350 counties, or a return of 72 per cent. Of these counties, 258 reported having at least one diviner; in addition, many of these counties with diviners supplied us with information concerning the kinds of divining rods used. (Some of the variations are displayed in Fig. 9.)

Almost without exception, some form of the forked twig is employed in each county wherein water witching is practiced. Reports from early colonial days tell us that the witch hazel twig was the most popular form of the rod, but only two counties in our 258 report the use of hazel. By far the most popular single tree from which rods are obtained is the peach tree (mentioned by 36 per cent of our counties).[1] These are employed especially in the Southeast and the Middle West. The willow twig is the second most common (22 per cent), being especially favored in the northern Middle West.

Wire—including wire from bales of hay and barbed wire from the nearest fence—is used in various ways to make divining rods. About 13 per cent report its use, and it is rather popular in the Arid Basin country, where trees are often scarce. Other metal rods that are used include welding rods, iron bars, and crowbars (each reported by 3 per cent) as well as coat hangers, steel files, pairs of pliers, etc.

Less popular varieties of rods are cut from cherry trees (3 per cent), apple trees (slightly less than 3 per cent and mostly in New England), elm trees (less than 2 per cent), and persimmon trees in the deep South. A great variety of other trees are mentioned only once or twice in our sample, such as hickory, plum, pear, elder, birch, and maple. One informant asserts that, in an emergency, poison oak will do.

The ancient magic pendulum is used in about 4 per cent of the counties, and in a variety of ways: keys suspended from books (usually the Bible), watches attached to strings or chains, spools on strands of thread,

---

[1] Hereinafter the percentages given in this chapter refer to the 258 counties in our sample that report the certain presence of water diviners.

pennies on the ends of wires, and quicksilver or water in a bottle suspended from strings (see Fig. 15).

Other assorted implements are used in rural America in the never ending quest for underground water. Our respondents listed horsewhips, shovels, pitchforks, and "commercial gadgets" such as a pair of swiveling rods. (The swiveling rods are used by the water works department of a large New England city to trace leaks in water mains). We came across, from time to time, ingenious and fancy devices such as the aluminum dowsing rod in use in Texas. A small bottle is suspended from a hook between the forks. If the dowser is searching for water, he fills the jar with water; if he is after oil, then oil is put into the jar; or if it's uranium he's interested in, a small quantity of pitchblende in the bottle will lead him to fortune. An even better example of a carefully designed metal rod, holding cartridges of different substances that are being searched for, is the device used by Mr. Clarence V. Elliott shown in Figure 10.

THE WITCHING TECHNIQUE

The technique described by Agricola, the palms-up grip of the forked twig, is still the standard procedure, by all odds the most popular method in rural America. As we described it in the previous chapter, the standard grip is to grasp the two branches of the forked twig, one in each hand, palms up, with the neck (or bottom of the Y) pointing skyward at an angle of about 45 degrees. (For illustrations of this grip and the palms-down grip, see Figs. 11, 12, and 13.) Whichever grip is used, the forked twig (or wire) is placed under tension in such a way that the slightest movement of the wrists or forearms will cause the stick to rotate toward the ground. When this happens, a stake is driven into the ground to mark the spot for the well-driller.

In very rare cases in this country the stick is held straight out from the body or held pointing down; then when underground water is reached, the stick points up. But only one county reported this upward turning, and six additional counties in the South and Middle West reported that the stick can go "either up or down." We have heard of one or two "twirlers" in this country; these are diviners for whom the rod does a series of complete rotations between the hands. Such antics seem to be more common in Europe than in this country.

Actually, the technique is intimately tied up with the tool that is used. When a pendulum is employed, its gyrations as it is suspended from the diviner's fingers are the clues to the presence or absence of water. Where straight sticks or metal bars are used, they are held in such a way that they swing, revolve, or bob. In fact, anything that can be held so that it will move or change movement in a diviner's grip can be, and probably has been, used as a divining rod.

Most diviners do no more than attempt to locate the water vein. But for many parts of the country, the question is not "Will I find water?" but "How far will I have to dig to get an adequate supply?" Consequently, some diviners undertake to estimate the depth and the quantity of water at a given spot. The prevalent technique for estimating the depth in this country is by the "amount of pull" on the rod (reported by 23 per cent). The second most common method of estimating depth is by the "number of bobs" either of the divining rod or of a special stick cut for this purpose (reported by 16 per cent). Fritz Jacoby, for example, who is the outstanding water witch in the small bean-farming community of Fence Lake, New Mexico, holds a thin straight stick (five feet long) over the water vein. It begins "involuntarily" to nod up and down (see Fig. 16). Each nod indicates the depth in feet of the water. In Europe, where the same technique is used, each nod is considered to indicate a meter. The third technique (mentioned by 10 per cent) consists of measuring the distance on the ground from the point where the rod starts to dip to where it is pointing straight down. Rate of flow is less commonly estimated than is the depth, but, when it is, the diviner usually depends upon the "amount of pull" for his judgment (28 per cent). In two counties, the "number of bobs" is translated into so many gallons per minute.

All these variations can be found in Europe. Even the long-distance divining over a map, as Henry Gross practices it, is strictly a European import. Henry Gross was just an ordinary water witch until he came under the tutelage of Kenneth Roberts, who had made a study of European improvements. The ability to estimate the location, depth, rate of flow, and quality of water from a map—hundreds of miles from the spot—is something that seems to be restricted to a few high-powered practitioners like Gross. Even many outspoken advocates of water witching find this aspect of witching difficult to believe.

As far as we can tell, divining is called "water witching" only in the United States. Water divining and the rod go by many names. The diviner in Germany is called *Wassersucher* ("water-seeker") or *Rutengänger* ("rod-walker"); in France, *sourcier* ("spring-finder"); in Switzerland, *Brunneschmöker* ("water-taster"); and in England, "dowser." Some scientific-sounding names for divining which are popular in the European literature are "radiesthesia," "cryptesthesia," and "rhabdomancy." A few of the terms for the divining rod prevalent in Europe are *Wünschelrute*, "wishing rod," or

Schlagrute, "striking rod" (Germany); *baguette divina-toire* (France); *bacchetta divinatoria* (Italy); *varilla adivinadora* (Spain); and, in England, "dowsing rod" or "divining rod."

In the United States over 78 per cent of the counties reported "water witching" as the most common term. The English term "water dowsing" was second in popularity but was reported in only 7 per cent of the counties, and these are almost all in New England, New York, and Pennsylvania. This reflects, perhaps, the lingering influence of England upon New England. The term "water divining" was third in popularity (the preferred term in 6 per cent of the counties, mostly in the southeastern United States). The term "switching" is mentioned in slightly more than 1 per cent of the counties.

We came across twelve other names for the practice in our sample, but each of these came up only once or twice. These were "water smelling" (restricted to Pennsylvania Dutch territory), "channel surveying," "wishing for water," "water finding," "finding water with a stick," "hunting for water," "finding a stream," "locating water," "water-seeking," "doodlebugging" (which is the common term for oil divining), "water prophesying," and "peach twig toting."

SOME WITCHING FOLKLORE

As we might expect, a practice with such a long history as witching carries with it an elaborate folklore consisting of "explanations" of how it works and an equally impressive set of rationalizations to account for failures. While the Europeans have organizations and journals, write books with quasi-scientific theories, and show a strong predilection to "explain" their divining practice, the American diviner takes a more pragmatic attitude. He is interested in the practical consequences. He wants water, not theory. And so we find that many Americans are content to justify water witching with little more than the statement: "It works." Such a pronouncement serves as both a justification and a satisfactory explanation to our rural practitioners and their customers.

This distinction between the European approach and the American is, in reality, a matter of degree. If we look closely enough, we do find a body of beliefs, implicit and explicit, that go along with water witching in this country. Consider, for example, the diviner's notions of how underground water behaves. From the earliest times to the present these notions have resisted any change. The diviner persists in the belief that shallow underground water occurs in "veins," like the "veins in your body," as one American water witch told us. These "veins" may vary in magnitude from "the size of a pencil" to "underground rivers." The diviner's task is to locate one of these veins. The only real innovation to this notion of underground veins is the "discovery" by Henry Gross of "domes" of water which come up from deep underground reservoirs and feed water into veins that branch off the domes. While the conception of water "veins" bears some relationship to the cracks and crevices from which shallow underground water is obtained in crystalline rocks (see Appendix II) and also to the underground streams that are sometimes found in limestone country, the diviners apply the same notion to all areas of the United States. They search for "veins" even in regions underlain by gravels and sands or by flat sandstones. Needless to say, both the older notion of veins and the new conception of domes are at variance with known geological facts about the hydrologic cycle (compare Figs. 17 and 18). The diviners are merely learning and perpetuating an ancient definition of the ground-water situation that is part of our rural folklore.

If we ask an American diviner to "explain" why the rod moves, he is typically—as we have indicated—content simply to shrug his shoulders and say, "I don't know, it just does." If we press this diviner further, or seek out other diviners, we do get rationales. These range from supernatural interpretations (such as the notion that diviners derive their power from Moses) to quasi-scientific interpretations (such as the idea that the muscles of the diviner are affected by electromagnetic disturbances). The most frequent explanation by the diviner, according to our informants, is in terms of some kind of "attraction" between stick and water (17 per cent of our counties). A smaller number of diviners try to be explicit about the nature of this attraction. A hydrotropic theory, usually expressed as "the stick is thirsty for water," is reported to be prevalent in about 5 per cent of the counties. Other forces are "electricity" (7 per cent) and "magnetism" (3 per cent), and in one case a "chemical" force was given the credit.

Many of these beliefs seem to be an attempt to surround water witching with the sanctity and respect of science. This is illustrated by the following episode. Some years ago one of our Harvard colleagues was observing a diviner in action in upper New Hampshire. The diviner walked back and forth over a patch of land. Finally the rod dipped straight down. The diviner then took one additional long step and said, "Dig here, and you will get the water you need." Our colleague said to the diviner, "I understand what you are trying to do with this procedure, but why did you take that extra long step after the rod dipped?" To which the diviner replied, "Oh, I was just correctin' for the hypotenuse!"

We also find a few instances of attempts to explain the rod's action by "psychic" phenomena (1 per cent of the counties), and in 3 per cent of the counties the folklore has it that you "must have faith in it, or the rod won't work for you."

The folklore is also rich in explanations of how or why a certain person becomes a diviner. The most frequent saying has to do with the "power" being inherited —either "father to son," or "father to daughter, and mother to son," or "to one person in a family," or even "the seventh son of the seventh son." Water witching is an acquired talent in the sense that, in every case known to us, a man has become a water witch only after witnessing a performance by another diviner. We have never come across a diviner who spontaneously developed his art independent of outside influence. Yet the belief is widespread that "only certain people can do it" (26 per cent of the counties). Many believe that it is a special "gift" of some kind (divine or otherwise) —"If you have the gift you can do it" (5 per cent). Finally, there is still some belief that only men can be dowsers (3 per cent), though female diviners are by no means rare in this country (see chap. 7).

Another part of the folklore that crops up now and then in our American sample is the idea that a person who is not gifted as a diviner can temporarily gain the "power" if he is in physical contact with a gifted person. An informant from Kansas wrote us:

I am 30 years old, am a college graduate and now I am a farm manager and farmer. I have been water witching since I was 15 years old and have located numerous water wells in this vicinity. I use a forked stick from a live elm or peach tree. Most any tree will work though. I can hold the stick so tight that the bark will twist off when I pass over a vein of water. It won't work at all for my brother, but I can take hold of his ear lobes and walk along behind him and the witch will work for him but if I don't hold on it won't work.

No technique is infallible, and divining is no exception. Consequently, the folklore contains many rationalizations for failures. These frequently take the form of attributing the failure to faulty equipment (e.g., "I couldn't find a good stick that day") or to some other aspect of the situation that negates the findings of the dowser. He may say, "Hills throw me off," or, "I found I had a knife in my pocket which short-circuited the electric current," or, "The vein dried up before they got around to drilling the well," or, "They crushed the little water vein by drilling with a drill that was too big." He may suggest that his clients stopped digging too soon or that they refused to follow his instructions and put the well where it was convenient instead. Others argue that there are good dowsers and bad ones. One correspondent, not a dowser himself, writes:

Whether there is anything to dowsing or not has got to be decided by the actions of the *good* dowsers, not the average. I can make a forked stick turn down anywhere—anywhere I want it to—or anywhere you want it to!—as long as I know where you want it to turn down. But I can stand directly over a clay or iron pipe carrying water at the rate of 2200 gallons a minute and the forked stick won't budge! So you are right, the action of the "indicator" means different things to different people. And it can mean *nothing* to some of them. But I don't go by what dowsers say they can do. I go by what they "have done"—the record they have established. If they have been right 90% of their tries, I say they are good dowsers and know what they are doing. The rest haven't learned yet.

Similarly, Kenneth Roberts maintains that inexperienced diviners bring disgrace to the few good diviners

(Roberts, 1951). In a later book (1953), he suggests that many apparent failures by Henry Gross were really not failures but misreporting on the part of ungrateful beneficiaries of his witching skill. The implication is that these people are afraid to report the truth for fear of being branded as superstitious or gullible. Roberts laments: "I would be greatly edified if some of those for whom we worked in 1951 *could* be pressed for information by the F.B.I. Perhaps the F.B.I. might worm from them some of the answers that were withheld from us."

With ideas like these, many Americans make sense out of water witching; they "know" why it works and why, on occasion, it does not. To other Americans, unfamiliar with the practice, the question is not "Why does it work?" but "Does it work at all?" The answer to the latter question will occupy us in the next two chapters.

CHAPTER 3

Does It Work? Case Histories and Field Tests

We entertain a suspicion concerning any matter of fact, when the witnesses contradict each other; when they are but few, or of doubtful character; when they have an interest in what they affirm; when they deliver their testimony with hesitation, or on the contrary, with too violent asseverations. There are many other particulars of the same kind, which may diminish or destroy the force of any argument, derived from human testimony.

DAVID HUME, 1784

Does water witching work? We would like to give a simple answer to this question. However, difficulties appear at once, for this question has a wide range of interpretations. Before we go on, let us look at some of the different meanings assigned to the term "work."

For some people the rod "works" when it unaccountably moves in their hands. For people who are not acquainted with unconscious muscular behavior, such an experience in itself is strange and inexplicable. And even though no well is dug to confirm the accuracy of the rod's movement, they are convinced. So powerful is such an experience that even one trained geologist who is skeptical of dowsing still remains completely puzzled by his own experience with a rod some twenty-seven years ago. After writing an article that is essentially unfavorable to water witching, this scientist concludes,

36

"Although I haven't held a forked stick in my hands since 1926, I can't forget that that stick *did* bend down of its own accord in that upland 14 miles from Arecibo. I don't know why. I wish I did" (Meyerhoff, 1953).

For other people, the witching rod "works" when a well is sunk and water is found at the spot indicated by the diviner. The Bonds were convinced because they found water where Henry Gross's divining rod said they would find water. And this is what most people mean when they say the rod "works."

To still others, however, the fact that water is found as a result of a diviner's activities has no merit in itself. Even a series of successes is of no value. We can clarify this assertion with an example. We know a county in Alabama, near the Gulf of Mexico, where water witching is practiced. There the diviners have a perfect record, a hit in every try. In one sense, then, water witching "works" in this community. But, upon further inquiry, we find that the ground-water situation is such that good water can be found anywhere in the county and at the same depth. The batting average for everyone who sinks a well without the aid of a diviner in this community is also 100 per cent. Our informant writes us: "On my farm surface wells can be dug 20 feet deep and plenty of water for home use is available. I can't find a 'witcher' that believes enough in his business to dig a well on my farm and guarantee a *dry hole*." Even when the agent offered as much as two hundred dollars for a twenty-foot well that would be dry, he could not entice any of the county's fifteen diviners to accept the challenge.

The man with scientific training, then, cannot accept the simple fact that water was found after a diviner selected the site as evidence in favor of water witching. He demands more. He is prepared to say that witching "works" only if it can be demonstrated *under controlled conditions* that it is consistently more successful than (1) the performance that would be expected by "chance," and (2) the performance of the geologist using his knowledge of surface cues.

Before we go on to the evidence, we should mention that the claims made for the rod are various. The majority of diviners simply locate a suitable or desirable spot to sink a well. Even Henry Gross, before he came under the promotional protection of Kenneth Roberts, merely located the site where water could be found. But, as Roberts points out, if one is willing to go down as far as two hundred feet, he will find water almost anywhere in the northeastern United States; no diviner is worth his salt unless he can also indicate the depth at which the water will be found.

Accordingly, some diviners, in addition to saying where to drill, also claim to tell how deep the well will have to be. A smaller group go even beyond this and tell how much water there will be at the indicated depth. Others will say something about the quality or potability of the water. We have come across some diviners who do not claim to find water directly; their rods tell them only whether the water-bearing strata are of the kind that can yield water.

We should keep this diversity of claims in mind as we examine the evidence pro and con.

THE KINDS OF EVIDENCE FOR WATER WITCHING

We return to our basic question: Can the rod find water? Although there are facts and opinions galore, a scientist would find this a difficult question—a question for which a reasonable answer can be found only after careful and patient investigation.

Most people who express opinions on this issue are

actually in no position to answer the question. "Yet it is an unfortunate matter of fact," as Reichenbach (1951) reminds us, "that human beings are inclined to give answers even when they do not have the means to find correct answers." As Stouffer (1950) has pointed out, we live in a "society which rewards quick and confident answers and does not worry about how the answers are arrived at." He attributes this affinity for the quick answer to

the implicit assumption that anybody with a little common sense and a few facts can come up at once with the correct answer on any subject. Thus the newspaper editor or columnist, faced with a column of empty space to fill with readable English in an hour, can speak with finality and authority on any social topic, however complex. He might not attempt to diagnose what is wrong with his sick cat; he would call in a veterinarian. But he knows precisely what is wrong with any social institution and the remedies [p. 355].

In the arguments for and against water witching, however, there are many who are aware of the need for evidence. They succeed in amassing large numbers of "facts" to support their position. These "facts" are of two basic kinds. The first kind includes all evidence in which no objective standard is available against which we can evaluate the diviner's performance. Such evidence comes from personal experience, case histories and anecdotes, and field tests. It is this kind of evidence that provides the major support for those who argue for the reality of water witching. And it is this kind of evidence which will concern us in this chapter.

The second kind of "fact" includes all evidence in which an objective base line is available against which we can evaluate the diviner's performance. Such evidence comes from field experiments, laboratory experiments, and tests of consistency. It is this kind of evidence which is used by those who argue against the efficacy of water witching. We will consider this source of evidence in the next chapter.

The strongest argument for water witching comes from case histories of situations in which water witching was successful in solving a real problem. Such evidence comes in the form of eyewitness accounts and testimonials, secondhand accounts, accounts by the diviners themselves, or records kept by a governmental agency. Mrs. Bond's story, related in chapter 1, is typical of this kind of evidence. The three books by Kenneth Roberts on Henry Gross are full of such stories about how the diviner again and again comes to the rescue of people who need water.

The basic feature of these testimonials is their appeal to our faith in human integrity and credibility. "I was there. I saw it with my own eyes, and 'seeing is believing.'" The narrator is usually sincere and willing to swear to the truthfulness and accuracy of his report. The listener is hesitant to question the fidelity of the report for fear of insinuating that the speaker is untrustworthy. The speaker, for his part, becomes quite defensive if his report is not accepted at face value.

Yet, to the man of scientific training, such testimonials and reports cannot be accepted as evidence. This is not because he distrusts the layman. Rather, it is because the scientist, from bitter and often embarrassing experience, has learned that such testimonials are subject to inherent weaknesses and unconscious distortions. They violate almost every standard of sound scientific observation. The flexibility of the case-history approach is such that the believers can use it to make an airtight argument for their cause, and the skeptics, with equal success, can use the same procedure to prove that water witching is nonsense.

We know a well-driller in Massachusetts who divines all the wells that he drills. This diviner, in an interview, recounted one success after another in his water witching career; he had not one failure to report. The driller's assistant, however, was skeptical about the value of water witching. He explained it away as "just imagination." In a separate interview, he told one story after another of failures that followed upon a diviner's advice. We had no reason to doubt the honesty or sincerity of either of these men. One was a believer, and, if we accepted his testimony at face value, water witching was invariably successful. From the skeptic's accounts, however, we would gather that water witching was very unreliable, and successes with it were matters of luck. Both these men were illustrating the tendency to recall only those incidents that are in accord with what we believe or would like to believe.

HUMAN TESTIMONY AND FIDELITY OF REPORT

Observation is the basis of all knowledge in the empirical sciences. And all observation depends upon human perception. Why, then, do we distrust the "facts" that come to us by way of case histories and eyewitness accounts? Are they not also the product of human observation? What makes so-called scientific observation more reliable than everyday human observation? In the last analysis, do not both kinds of observation depend upon the same sensory mechanisms?

It is true that scientific observation is based upon sensory experience. But, as Hildebrand (1957) remarks, "One of the first principles of science is to be skeptical about sense impression. A careful scientist does not depend upon sensations of temperature, brightness, color, time, weight, and speed: he reads instruments." The reading of instrument dials is also a sense impression, but it is of a special kind. Two people may not agree about whether it is "hot," "warm," or "comfortable" in a particular room. But they can easily agree that a thermometer reads 73 degrees Fahrenheit. The scientist has found that the substitution of instruments for human judgment reduces disagreement about what is happening. And this is a feature of what we call "scientific" observation. It consists of specifying and arranging situations such that different observers can agree about what has happened.

Scientific facts are usually given in the form of a prescription: If you do such-and-such under such-and-such conditions, then you will observe such-and-such. The prescription includes the precautions, safeguards, and kinds of observations you will have to make in order to experience what others doing the same experiment will also experience. In other words, the scientist, in evaluating scientific evidence, need not worry about what *did* happen. He can always follow the prescription to see what will happen. The reason for demanding such a prescription is that we rarely, if ever, can go back and match the account with the actual event. Sometimes an incident is recalled faithfully with only a minor change of detail. But this minor change, quite frequently, may make an otherwise believable event appear to be an inexplicable marvel. Such a lapse of memory was evident in this incident as narrated by Carpenter (1887):

Sometimes the essential fact, under the influence of this proclivity, completely passes out of the mind of the narrator; as in the instance of a lady, cited by Miss Cobbe in her paper on the "Fallacies of Memory," who assured Miss C. that a table in her drawing-room had some years before correctly rapped out her age in the presence of several persons, *none of whom were near the table;* the fact being impressed on her mind by her annoyance at the disclosure, which was so great that she sold the table! Having assured Miss Cobbe that she could verify her statement by reference to notes made at the time, she subsequently corrected it, very honestly, by telling Miss C. that she found that there *were* hands on the table [p. 111].

Now, if we were confronted with this informant's original story, we would somehow have to account for the table's intelligent movements by natural means, or admit, with her, the reality of supernatural control. A scientist, if he believed her account, would want to reproduce the phenomenon in the laboratory so that he could study it. He would probably be quite unsuccessful in getting a table to rap out answers unaided by human agency. Further, he would have to deny her story as scientific evidence, because he is unable to observe what she saw, even when he repeats the conditions that she describes. In this particular account, of course, we know why the scientist cannot duplicate the woman's observation. She altered a very essential detail in describing what she had seen. If she had correctly reported that the table rapped out its answers *when several people were pressing their hands upon the table,* then it is likely that the scientist, if he were sufficiently patient, would eventually observe the table-rapping phenomenon. And, as we will see in chapter 5, with sufficiently more patience he would eventually be able to explain the phenomenon in terms of orthodox physics and physiology.

One reason why testimony is so unreliable is that at the time of original perception, there is too much to observe. A person can only attend to a finite number of things at one time. Thus, there is error in the original perception because of a limited span of attention. In addition, psychologists have isolated other factors that operate to produce inaccuracies in the recall of what happened. The subsequent report omits many pertinent details (leveling), emphasizes and exaggerates the status of other details (sharpening), and alters certain details to fit in with previous stereotypes, expectations, and prejudices (assimilation) (Allport and Postman, 1947). A typical classroom demonstration consists of having a stooge suddenly interrupt a lecture. After a brief exchange of words with the instructor, the stooge walks out of the classroom. When the class is then asked to describe this stooge, describe his clothing, or identify him when he is one of several suspects, they typically make many mistakes (Berrien, 1952).

An important factor in such recall is expectancy. There is a strong tendency to "fill in" or alter the report to coincide with what the observer would expect to see. Berrien reports that eight of his forty-three students asserted that the boy who interrupted his lectures wore a maroon-colored sweater. Actually he wore a gray-tan double-breasted coat. Berrien attributes this to the fact that the prevailing color of sweaters on the college campus at that time was maroon. In many studies of rumor (Allport and Postman, 1947) a subway scene is shown in which a white man, holding a straight razor, is shown standing opposite a Negro. When observers are subsequently asked to describe the scene, especially if they are southerners, they frequently report that the razor is in the Negro's hand. Here, their report has been affected by a stereotype.

The role of expectancy upon subsequent recall is well known to professional magicians. The maxim, "Never tell your audience what you are going to do in advance," is based upon the knowledge that if a spectator doesn't know what to look for in advance, he has little chance of detecting how the trick was accomplished. One of the authors, who used to be a professional magician, relates the following experience:

One day, when I was visiting two friends, I was asked to perform a card trick. A deck of cards was produced and offered to me, but I refused to touch them. "This time," I said as I relaxed in an armchair, "I'm going to perform in a lazy man's way. I'm not going to touch the cards at all." I requested a person to go to the opposite corner of the room with the deck of cards. He then selected a card, showed it to his companion, and replaced it in the deck. I then re-emphasized how I was going to accomplish my effect without going near the cards or handling them in any way. As I was explaining this, I casually strolled over to the cards, picked them up, while I emphasized that this is what I was not going to do. After a few minutes, while I was still talking, I returned to my armchair and settled back. I told my audience that I was going to ascertain the name of the chosen card, without going near the deck. I put my hand to my head, and, after some appropriate concentration, named a card which turned out to be wrong. I made another guess, and this, too, was wrong. I then apologetically announced that I failed and asked the person to name his card. "The three of diamonds," he replied. "I will have to redeem myself," I said, "for my failure. I know what! Even though my telepathic powers have failed me, I still might be able to demonstrate my powers of transporting objects just by willing." After some more byplay, I announced that the three of diamonds had transported itself from the deck and was now in the vase which was atop the mantelpiece. They were completely amazed when they discovered this was so, for they both swore that I had not left my armchair, much less handled the cards, during this performance. I asked them if they were sure that I had not handled the cards. And they both vigorously asserted that they had not the slightest doubt that I did not go near the cards.

If a third party were to hear this tale as related by the two observers (both of whom are now members of the faculties of well-known universities), he would be at a loss to explain how a card could transport itself half-way across a room with no human intervention. And since both these observers still swear that the magician did not go near the cards, he would have to assume—if he were willing to accept such testimony as evidence—that something contrary to natural law had taken place. But, if the third party were a scientist, he would not accept such testimony as fact. Rather, he would want to duplicate the original situation as closely as possible and see if the same thing happened. He would contact the magician and ask him to repeat his trick. But if the magician wanted to preserve his secret, he would refuse, on some pretext, to repeat, for the magician would realize that under the new conditions, the observers know what to look for. (This is the reason for another maxim of professional magicians: "Never repeat the same trick on the same occasion.") On the first occasion the observers did not know that the effect was going to involve the disappearance of the chosen card from the deck, and so the casual handling of the cards by the magician did not register with them. But this time they know that the card is supposed to leave the deck. Hence, they will closely observe any approach by the magician to the deck of cards. He cannot get away with his "miracle" this time, because his audience has been alerted and knows what to look for.

Another feature of case histories is the tendency to embellish or "fill in" details to conform to expectations, desires, or subsequent re-evaluation of the original event. Such a "filling-in" occurs when people confuse what they were thinking about with what they were seeing or sensing at the time of the observation. An excellent example is provided by the "fishing" technique of tea leaf readers. The reader, as she turns the emptied teacup and interprets the configuration of leaves, will make one statement after another touching upon such topics as love, health, business, trips, conflict, success, children, etc. She phrases her statements in general terms and frequently finishes each one with a rising inflection or question. This forces the client to search through her memory to find *specific* details to match the general statements of the reader. Thus, the reader will say, "I see two tall, dark, slim men who have come into your life. Do you recognize them?" The client will say, to herself or out loud, "Two tall, dark, slim men? Who could they be? Oh, yes, those twins, John and Jim Harris, whom I met at Sally Johnson's party!" Later when she recounts what happened, she will very likely confuse the reader's general statement with the specific thoughts she had at the time. She will vehemently declare that the reader told her about John and Jim Harris and Sally Johnson's party.

One of the authors took a young lady to visit a tea leaf reader in Boston. The lady was skeptical and declared in advance that she did not believe in fortune-telling. While the reading was taking place, the psychologist sat in the background and took notes. After the reading, the young lady was "positively dumbfounded" at the reader's ability to name facts and events that had actually taken place in her past history. The psychologist then pointed to his notes which indicated that she had done 75 per cent of the talking and that the tea leaf reader had merely sat back and let her answer questions. At this, the lady became quite indignant. She asserted that she had not spoken one word and that the tea leaf reader had done all the talking!

Still another kind of "filling-in" occurs when the original perception was made under conditions that make for ambiguity. Such is especially the case in spiritualistic seances where the lights are dimmed or completely out. Then a flashing light, or a luminescent cloth, under the right suggestion takes on the form of an actual person. Many experiments in the psychological laboratory have demonstrated, again and again, how the subjects see more than is there under ambiguous viewing conditions. A striking example occurs with what is called the autokinetic effect. A subject is brought into a dark room. All that is visible is a pinpoint of light. Under such conditions, with no frame of reference, many subjects report that the light moves and describes erratic patterns. Two psychologists have added a variation to this experiment. They tell the subjects that the light is the end of a pencil that is writing words and that they are to try to make out what words are being written. Most subjects readily report seeing the words and say what they are, even though the pinpoint of light actually is stationary throughout the experiment (Rechtshaffen and Mednick, 1955).

When we consider the fallibility of human testimony under ordinary conditions of observation, we can see why the scientist cannot accept such testimony as valid evidence. But when we realize, further, that much of this testimony comes from people with strong motivations to have the world conform to their desires, we can expect even greater distortions in the resulting report. We have an abundance of evidence, both observational and experimental, to illustrate the strong blocking and selective effects that emotions can have in the reporting of "what happened."

One of us attended a spiritualistic meeting where the featured guest was a renowned message reader. The spectators would write their questions and problems on slips of paper. These were folded and collected in a large glass bowl. The medium, while blindfolded, would then divine the contents of the folded slips and give appropriate answers. On this particular occasion, the psychologist's report was as follows:

The people in the audience were obviously devout believers in the Spiritualistic doctrine. Many had lost loved ones and were hoping to make a "contact" by way of the medium. The medium was surprisingly crude and careless. He reached into the bowl and came out with a fistful of slips. He then put one hand to his forehead and adjusted his blindfold upward so that his eyes could see downward at an angle of 45 degrees. With the other hand, partially but not completely shielded by the lectern, he clumsily opened up the messages one at a time and with difficulty read their contents. He then called out names and pretended to divine the messages' contents directly through the intervention of a spirit from the other world. During this crude display, I observed the rest of the audience. They, for the most part, kept their eyes on the ceiling, the side walls, or the floor. I did not see one person, other than myself, look directly at the medium. Afterwards I questioned several of the spectators as to what had happened. Each very vehemently asserted that the medium had remained completely blindfolded, had not gone near the bowl of slips, and that if he had done so, it would easily have been detected with so many eyes upon him. It was obvious that these spectators' need to believe was so strong they could not allow themselves the suspicion that something could be amiss.

Here the strong effect of a need to believe upon perception was quite obvious. The discrepancy between "reality" and the perceptions of the believers would easily be detected by any dispassionate observer. All too often, however, the effect of our motives upon what we "see" is more subtle and not so readily apparent to the outsider. This is especially true when such "psychological motives" enter into observations made in the scientific laboratory. The history of science records many blunders that resulted from placing too much faith in the trustworthiness of a human being as a recording instrument (cf. Jastrow, 1935). A striking example is that of the "*n*-rays" (Seabrook, 1941; Coover, 1917; Jastrow, 1935).

In 1902, six years after Roentgen had discovered the X-ray, Professor M. Blondlot, an eminent physicist of Nancy and a member of the Academy of Science, announced his discovery of the *n*-ray (named after the city of Nancy). The discovery was quickly confirmed in other laboratories by such scientists as Gutton, Mascart, Meyer, Becquerel, Rothe, and others. In the year 1904 alone, *Science Abstracts* listed seventy-seven scientific publications involving the *n*-ray. The next year, however, the number declined to eight, and after 1909 there were no more publications involving the *n*-ray.

Blondlot determined the presence of the *n*-ray by the decrease of the resistance of a spark gap, by the increased glow of a platinum wire, and by the increased luminosity of a phosphorescent surface. Since the *n*-ray gave no photographic effect, all these determinations had to be made by eye. Applications of *n*-rays were made in many fields. Corson applied *n*-rays to chemistry, Lambert and Meyer studied their effects upon biological phenomena, Meyer upon plants, and Charpentier found that compression of a nerve was accompanied by emission of *n*-rays. The famous brain specialist, Broca, studied the relation between *n*-rays and the brain.

Despite this accumulation of scientific data involving *n*-rays, a sour note was struck when several other physicists tried to duplicate the *n*-ray effects and got negative results. Physicists in Italy, Germany, and the United

States could not find *n*-rays. The discussion nearly created an international incident when it turned out that *n*-rays could not be found outside of France.

In the United States, at Johns Hopkins University, the noted physicist R. W. Wood read about Blondlot's *n*-rays and vainly tried to duplicate them in his own laboratory. When he was on a visit to England, Wood's colleagues persuaded him to visit Blondlot's laboratory in person to obtain a firsthand impression of the phenomenon. Wood's own account begins as follows:

So I visited Nancy before rejoining my family in Paris, meeting Blondlot by appointment at his laboratory in the early evening. He spoke no English, and I elected German as our means of communication, as I wanted him to feel free to speak confidentially to his assistant, who was apparently a sort of high-class laboratory janitor [of course Wood could speak and understand French].

He first showed me a card on which some circles had been painted in luminous paint. He turned down the gas light and called my attention to their increased luminosity when the *n*-ray was turned on. I said I saw no change. He said that was because my eyes were not sensitive enough, so that proved nothing. I asked him if I could move an opaque lead screen in and out of the path of the rays while he called out the fluctuations on the screen. He was almost 100 per cent wrong and called out fluctuations when I made no movement at all, and that proved a lot, but I held my tongue [Seabrook, 1941, p. 237].

Wood then tried other tests which clearly demonstrated that Blondlot's rays existed only in his imagination. Blondlot claimed to be able to see the face of a dimly lighted clock through a metal file with the aid of *n*-rays. Wood asked permission to hold the metal file in front of Blondlot's eyes. Blondlot agreed. Unknown to Blondlot, Wood secretly substituted a wooden ruler for the metal file; in the darkened laboratory, Blondlot did not notice this switch. Instead, he continued to "see" the clock through the ruler even though the wood was one of the few substances that allegedly was impervious to *n*-rays. Blondlot's major demonstration was saved for last. The French scientist sat before a spectroscope with aluminum lenses and prisms. By moving a graduated dial, an eyepiece consisting of a luminous thread could be moved across the spectrum. When the thread reached that part of the spectrum where the invisible lines of the *n*-ray spectrum were supposed to be, it was supposed to brighten. Blondlot repeated his settings a number of times, always getting the same measurements. Wood continues his account at this point:

He read off the numbers on the graduated scale for a number of lines, by the light of a small, darkroom, red lantern. This experiment had convinced a number of skeptical visitors, as he could repeat his measurements in their presence, always getting the same numbers. He claimed that a movement of the thread of 0.1 mm. was sufficient to change the luminosity, and when I said that seemed impossible, as the slit of the spectroscope was 2 mm. wide, he said that was one of the inexplicable properties of the *n*-rays. I asked him to repeat his measurements, and reached over in the dark and lifted the aluminum prism from the spectroscope. He turned the wheel again, reading off the same numbers as before [Seabrook, 1941, p. 238].

When Wood published his findings that the *n*-ray was merely the result of faulty human observation combined with suggestion, the *n*-ray immediately disappeared from physics. But not without tragic repercussions to Blondlot. Just prior to the exposure, the French Academy had awarded Blondlot the Lalande prize of 20,000 francs and its gold medal "for the discovery of the *n*-rays." After Wood's account appeared

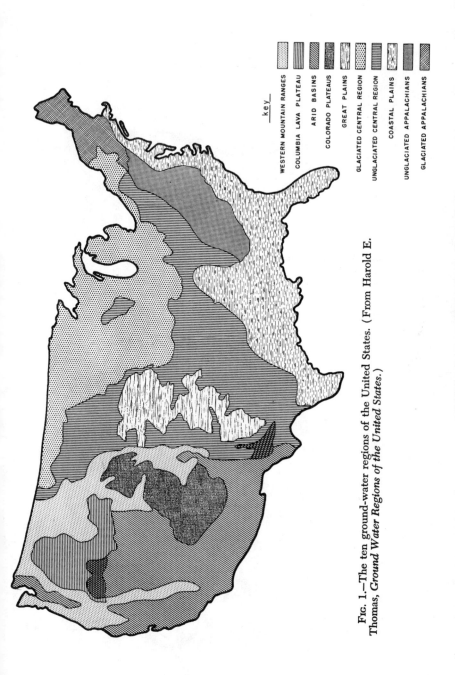

FIG. 1.—The ten ground-water regions of the United States. (From Harold E. Thomas, *Ground Water Regions of the United States*.)

key

WESTERN MOUNTAIN RANGES

COLUMBIA LAVA PLATEAU

ARID BASINS

COLORADO PLATEAUS

GREAT PLAINS

GLACIATED CENTRAL REGION

UNGLACIATED CENTRAL REGION

COASTAL PLAINS

UNGLACIATED APPALACHIANS

GLACIATED APPALACHIANS

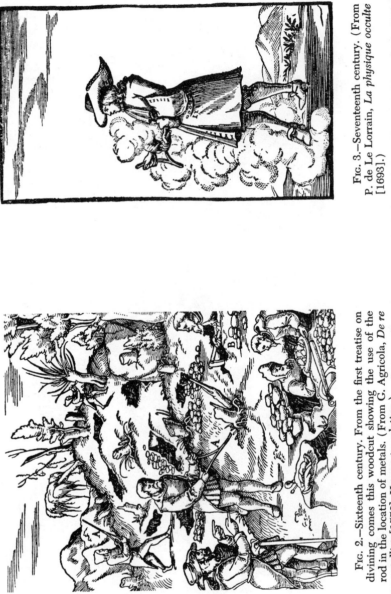

Fig. 2.–Sixteenth century. From the first treatise on divining comes this woodcut showing the use of the rod in the location of metals. (From G. Agricola, *De re metallica* [1556], Hoover translation.)

Fig. 3.–Seventeenth century. (From P. de Le Lorrain, *La physique occulte* [1693].)

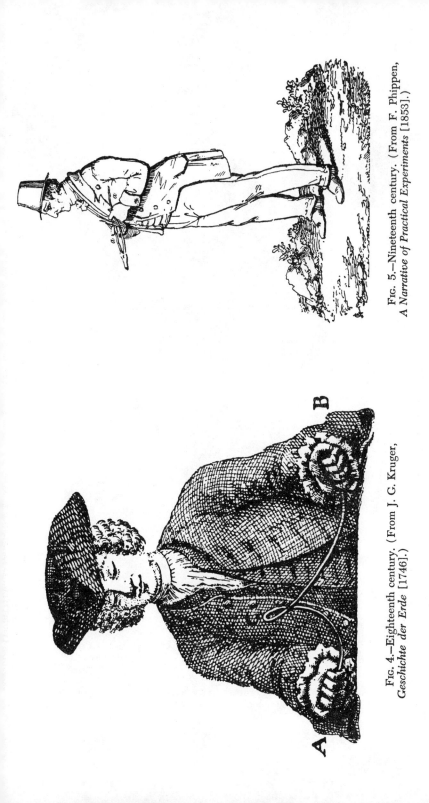

Fig. 5.–Nineteenth century. (From F. Phippen,
A Narrative of Practical Experiments [1853].)

Fig. 4.–Eighteenth century. (From J. G. Kruger,
Geschichte der Erde [1746].)

FIG. 6.—Twentieth century. Jerry Smith of Corona, California, dowses for water. (Photograph by Gaston Burridge.)

Fig. 7.—Water witching has been controversial since its beginnings. This eighteenth-century woodcut shows the attitude of the church toward the dowser. The priest in the foreground, removing the dowser's mask, finds the Devil himself behind it. (From T. Albinus, *Das entlarvete Idolum* [1704].)

Fig. 8.—A seventeenth-century diviner displays a collection of dowsing rods then in use, including an open book, a piece of sausage, a candle snuffer, a knife and fork crossed, two pipes, held with the stem of one in the bowl of the other, a pair of scissors, and (*on the table*) a bucket handle, a nutcracker, and a saw. (From J. G. Zeidler, *Pantomysterium* [1700].)

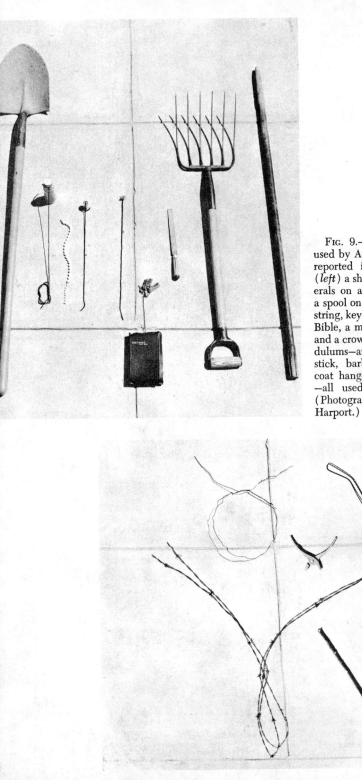

Fig. 9.—Among the articles used by American diviners (as reported in our survey) are (*left*) a shovel, a bottle of minerals on a string, glass beads, a spool on a string, a coin on a string, keys suspended from the Bible, a metal file, a pitchfork, and a crowbar—all used as pendulums—and (*below*) a forked stick, barbed wire, pliers, a coat hanger, and bailing wire —all used as dowsing rods. (Photographs by David De Harport.)

FIG. 10.—Clarence V. Elliott, of Los Angeles, demonstrates
dowsing equipment of his own design. The forked metal rod
has a detachable top in which can be fitted samples of the substance sought; the containers are carried, ready to hand, in a
cartridge belt.

FIG. 11.—The standard palms-up grip. (Photograph by David DeHarport.)

FIG. 12.—The alternative palms-down grip. (Photograph by David DeHarport.)

Fig. 13.—This series of three photographs shows how the rod dips using the standard palms-up grip. (Photographs by David DeHarport.)

Fig. 14.—The principle of long-distance dowsing over a hand-drawn map of a New England lot is illustrated in this photograph. (Photograph by David DeHarport.)

Fig. 15.—The principle of the pendulum is illustrated by keys suspended from the Bible. The water vein is supposedly located by "involuntary" circular or back-and-forth movement of the keys. (Photograph by David DeHarport.)

Fig. 16.—One of the familiar techniques for measuring the depth to water is by counting the number of times a stick, held over the "water vein," bobs up and down. The number of bobs is supposedly the depth in feet to the water. (Photograph by David DeHarport.)

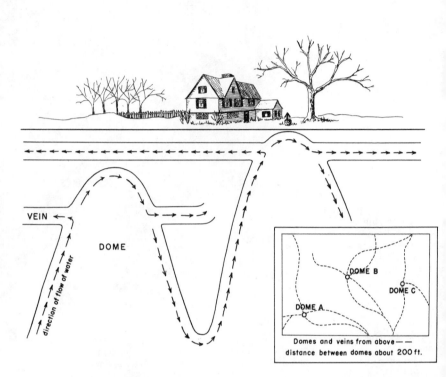

VEIN ←

DOME

direction of flow of water

DOME B

DOME C

DOME A

Domes and veins from above——
distance between domes about 200 ft.

FIG. 17.—The occurrence of ground water as seen by a well-known water diviner: Underground water originates in *domes,* which are "single spouts of water rising from deep underground" and which always occur on high land, "far above the so-called water table" (Roberts, 1951). The depth of a dome beneath the surface varies. From these domes emerge *veins* of *flowing* water (as distinct from saturated earth)—from two to as many as fifty from a single dome—which spread out in all directions. The veins from a particular dome tend to be at the same level, the water seeking a geologic fault or a layer of gravel, but the depth of veins in general varies; some flow at three feet and some at thirty. Veins join and split and change direction, and they vary in size and rate of flow. A vein may be crushed by pressure from above; when this happens, the water turns off and makes a new channel in another direction. It may be pushed out of its course by the concussion of a drill; in this case, the diversion of water is only temporary, as the flow resumes its original course with the first heavy rains. Finally, the vein may simply run out at a great distance from the dome, its flow remaining constant for many hundred feet and then gradually diminishing to a trickle and at last to seepage, forming a damp deposit where there is actually no flowing water at all.

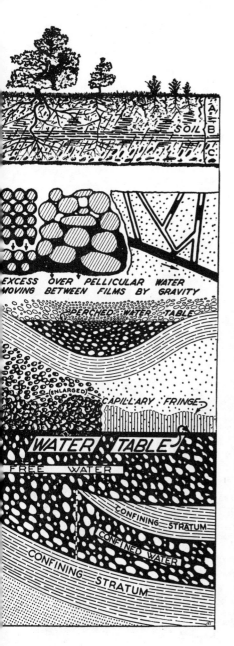

FIG. 18.—The geologist's view of the occurrence and distribution of subsurface water: Surface water (rainfall) seeps downward through the earth by the force of gravity. It passes first through the soil, where some of it is removed by plants and returned (by a process called *transpiration*) through them to the atmosphere; at this level, too, some of the water is *evaporated*. These two processes operate also in the layers immediately below the soil, where additional water is trapped on rock surfaces (*pellicular water*). The water that escapes all these obstructions (*gravity water*) continues downward through the permeable layers of rock until it reaches a barrier in the form of a layer of impermeable material (*confining stratum*). At this point it collects in the layers immediately above and saturates them completely. While water may accumulate in "pockets" of sediments overlying local occurrences of impermeable rock (*perched water*), the *water table,* or the top of the zone of material saturated with ground water, occurs as a continuous layer and is usually a "subdued replica" of the surface topography. Water in this layer is called *free water* or, when it occurs between two confining strata, *confined water.* It moves by seepage through the rock in the direction of the slope of the water table. (By permission, from C. F. Tolman, *Ground Water* [New York: McGraw-Hill Book Co., 1937].)

Fɪɢ. 19.—The type of well-drilling equipment in common use in rural America. (Photograph by Evon Z. Vogt.)

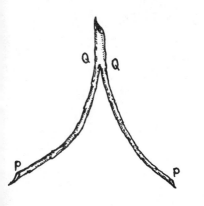

Fig. 20.—The movement of the rod is illustrated in physical terms in the diagram at the left. (From P. A. Ongley, "New Zealand Diviners," *New Zealand Journal of Science and Technology,* **30** [1948], 50–51; for further details the reader is referred to this excellent paper; it is also suggested that the reader cut a forked stick and try for himself the various possible movements of the rod.) When the forked stick is held in the usual manner, there are in each limb two types of tension: that type due to the force (H) with which the diviner's hand holds the limb, and that due to the stresses (T) in the rod. For the rod to move, T must become greater than H. This may be the result of any or several of four types of usually unconscious and often unnoticeable muscular movements by the diviner's hands. (1) The diviner may ease his grip slightly, i.e., H decreases. (2) The diviner may rotate his hands slightly about the wrists. Since palms upward is an unnatural position in which to hold the hands, rotation is quite likely to occur. As has been shown with an artificial pair of hands holding the rod, such a movement, however slight, gives a pronounced kick of the rod because of additional bending of the rod near the hands. The resulting tension adds to that already existent in the limbs. (3) If the hands are moved closer together, the curvature of the limbs near P (*in the diagram*), and the forces there, increase. (4) If the hands are moved farther apart, the curvature of the limbs near Q, and the forces there, also increase.

Fig. 21.—This series of three photographs shows clearly how two divining rods can be made to rotate in opposite directions merely by rotating the wrists outward. (Photographs by David DeHarport.)

Fig. 22.—The principle of "table turning" as practiced in the nineteenth century is illustrated in this photo. (Photograph by David DeHarport.)

Fig. 23.—A variation of the Ouija board is illustrated in this photograph. The pointer dips and spells out answers to questions by touching appropriate letters. (Photograph by David DeHarport.)

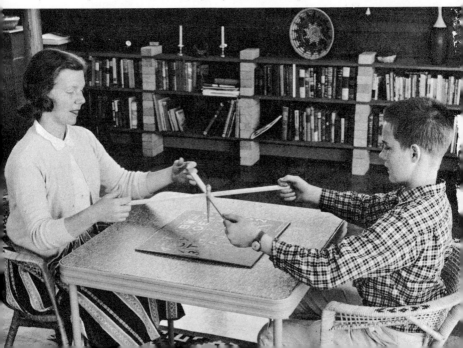

in *Nature*, the Academy—recognizing that Blondlot's mistake was an honest blunder—went through with the award but changed the announced reason to the other contributions of the French scientist. But this was not sufficient to soften the blow. Blondlot eventually went mad and then died as a result of his disgrace.

We have a striking illustration in the literature of the divining rod of how one's convictions can alter the way he "objectively" reports the "facts." We have referred to the tale of Jacques Aymar, the French peasant and diviner who became a national celebrity for discovering a murderer with his rod. His story is well documented with legal and other records and is recounted in most historical works on the divining rod. We have three good secondhand accounts by men who are acknowledged as outstanding scholars in their fields. We would expect that the facts in the Aymar case would be reported in an objective, impartial manner so that a reader could come to some proper conclusion. Let us look at the account given by Barrett and Besterman (1926), who are universally acknowledged as the outstanding scholars in the field of the divining rod and who defend the view that the diviner has supernormal powers. They tell how the baffled authorities finally decided to engage the services of Aymar to help them track down the murderers. But here they omit a very important detail in the story. Barrett and Besterman fail to tell us that Aymar was already in Lyons and waiting to be called upon. Raymond (1883), in making his case that what Aymar did was not so remarkable, makes this piece of information a key point in the argument.

Barrett and Besterman and Raymond all emphasize that the hunchback found by Aymar confessed to his crime without being tortured. They concur in implying that the man was probably guilty of the crime for which he was broken at the wheel. Yet, Andrew Lang (1908), in recounting the same story, gives us the impression that the hunchback may not have been actually guilty. "The story gave rise to a prolonged controversy, and the case remains a judicial puzzle, but little elucidated by the confession of the hunchback, who may have been insane, or morbid, or vexed by constant questioning till he was weary of life. He was only nineteen years of age."

Aymar, of course, made a sensation in France. He was brought to Paris and put through various tests by the Prince de Conde. All our accounts agree that the results of these tests were negative. But now let us see how they are treated by Barrett and Besterman, who obviously are convinced that Aymar had supernatural powers. These authors dismiss the experiments with a few sentences. "Of these experiments we unfortunately lack details; it seems that they were of the absurd nature that is always to be expected when such delicate experiments are carried out by persons who approach them not only in complete ignorance of the subject but in a fashionably satirical spirit." These details that Barrett and Besterman tell us are lacking are fully expounded in Raymond's account, which is not so intent upon presenting Aymar in his best light. According to Raymond, the tests of Aymar by Conde were "shrewd and rigorous," and "they exposed the emptiness of his [Aymar's] pretensions." Raymond describes the experiments with sufficient detail so that they appear neither absurd nor unfair. Each experiment tested a specific claim made by Aymar, and each one revealed that Aymar could not live up to his claims.

And it is Raymond, the unbeliever, who describes the various scandals and blackmail swindles that Aymar got into with his rod. In one case he was hired to use his rod to detect whether a young lady had been faithful to her lover. He then demanded money from the lady if she wanted him to turn in a good report with his rod. These and other impostures soon drove Aymar from popularity and Paris. Such details, however, are left out of the account given us by his defenders. When outstanding scholars can report the same incident in such a way as to support two opposing viewpoints, it is little wonder that scientists are unwilling to accept as evidence the case histories that come from people of all walks of life. The stories always seem to accord with the viewpoint of the beholder.

OBJECTIVE RECORDS OF WELL-SINKINGS

There are many reasons, then, why case histories do not qualify as evidence. The very minimum that would

TABLE 1

RESULTS OF WELL-SINKINGS AT DIVINED AND NON-
DIVINED SITES IN FENCE LAKE, NEW MEXICO
(After Vogt, 1952)

Classification	Divined	Not Divined
Successful wells	24	25
Dry holes	5	7

be required is that an objective record be kept of all well-sinkings in a community and of the results obtained. Such a record would at least meet the objection that people naturally tend to report the good cases in support of their arguments. We can find only two occurrences of such records. One is from Fence Lake, New Mexico (Table 1). There is no significant difference between the percentage of successes among the divined wells (83 per cent) and the non-divined wells (78 per cent). The number of cases presented in Table 2 is much larger, but it tells us the same story. Indeed, the percentage of absolute failures among divined wells is almost twice the percentage recorded for non-divined wells in this series. We should say that these comparisons may not be as fair as they seem. We don't know enough about the conditions under which the diviner was called in as compared with those when he was not. It may be that the diviner is used only in places where

TABLE 2

RESULTS OF WELL-SINKINGS AT ALL DIVINED AND NON-DIVINED SITES IN CENTRAL NEW SOUTH WALES, AUSTRALIA, DURING THE PERIOD 1918–43
(From Ward, 1946)

CLASSIFICATION OF BOREHOLES	DIVINED		NOT DIVINED	
	Number Drilled	Per Cent	Number Drilled	Per Cent
Bores in which supplies of serviceable water, estimated at 100 gallons per hour or over, were obtained......................	1,284	70.4	1,474	83.8
Bores in which supplies of serviceable water, estimated at less than 100 gallons per hour, were obtained......................	184	10.1	93	5.3
Bores in which supplies of unserviceable water were obtained..................	87	4.7	60	3.5
Bores which were absolute failures, no water of any kind being obtained	268	14.7	131	7.4

the water problem is exceptionally difficult. The two tables illustrate that even when objective records are kept, the case-history approach is incapable of providing unequivocal evidence for or against the efficacy of water witching.

EVIDENCE FROM FIELD TESTS

Even defenders of water witching realize the deficiencies of case histories. And so they point to evidence that they feel is more experimental in nature. Such scholars as Barrett and Besterman (1926) and Henri Mager (1931) rest their cases upon a series of situations that they call "experiments." These "experiments" are what we will designate "field tests." In these field tests, the diviner is observed as he operates under natural conditions. The observations differ from those of case histories in that the diviner is performing for the specific purpose of having his abilities tested. And since this is a test, the observations and records are usually free of the defects that beset accounts of case histories.

But, despite the claims of some people, these field tests cannot be put in the same class with what a scientist calls an "experiment," for the field test, like the case history, suffers from a very serious drawback. Neither the field test nor the case history provides us with an adequate base line against which we can assess the diviner's ability. No matter how unusual or remarkable the feats of a diviner may appear in these tests, they cannot be assessed scientifically unless we know what someone other than the diviner might have accomplished under the same conditions. Without this control, as we shall see, the evidence provided from field tests will always be inconclusive. The results that convince the believer can always be "explained away" by the skeptic on other grounds.

Let's look at an actual example. Barrett and Besterman (1926) present us with what they call "three notable experiments in dowsing." Each of these they selected as having special weight in demonstrating the reality of the water witching phenomenon. We will present one of these "experiments" to illustrate how the argument goes.

After examining all the available evidence for witching, Sir William Barrett decided that what was needed was a field test conducted under his personal supervision. Elaborate precautions were taken in preparing for the test. Barrett made sure to select a geological site that would be unfamiliar to the diviner. He then brought the well-known British diviner, William Stone, to the site, which was a mountainous area south of Dublin, Ireland.

Stone's rod pointed out two spots that would yield water and another one that would produce a dry well. Three weeks later another diviner independently traversed the same field and substantially repeated Stone's selections. Barrett then drilled at these spots and found water in the two spots, as predicted, and no water in the third spot, as predicted.

Two geologists each told Barrett that they considered such a performance, by a man not trained as a geologist, to be quite remarkable. Armed with these opinions, Barrett was quick to decide that "the possibility of the dowsers' success being explicable by geological observation" was thereby ruled out. And he sums this test up as follows: "We have thus an experiment which conclusively proves the reality of dowsing."

Here we see the necessary weakness of all field tests. Barrett's whole argument rests on the unwarranted assumption that the diviners used no geological clues. He uses the opinion of two geologists as his guide. A scientific experiment would never let the matter rest on "opinion"; it would have made sure, by experimental controls, that the possibility of such cues was ruled out. Because such controls were lacking in this test, the results are inconclusive.

To show how this substitution of opinion for scientific control creates ambiguity, let us see how another geologist, Gregory (1928), views the results of this same test. "Sir William Barrett was emphatic that Stone paid little attention to the surface features," Gregory comments, "but the line he chose was that which I think any person experienced in finding water would have selected from obvious surface indications."

The field test approximates the ideal of scientific observation in that the diviner performs in front of observers who are watching with an intent to make an objective record. The diviner goes through his paces under these conditions, makes his designations, and then a well is sunk and the agreement between the diviner's predictions and the actual yield is noted. The report of what happened is usually trustworthy and free from obvious defects.

The departure from the scientific ideal occurs, however, when it comes to deciding how successful was the diviner's performance. At this point, a subjective, intuitive judgment is substituted for an objective standard. In place of an objective indication of what might have occurred by chance or what might have occurred had an expert selected the site, we are asked to regard the performance as "amazing," "convincing," "no better than chance," "a failure," etc., on the basis of one person's say-so.

Unfortunately, what is amazing to one person is ordinary to another. And as long as we rely on subjective assessments, we will always be faced with the inconclusiveness of the Barrett field tests. According to Barrett's opinion, the diviner's performance was amazing and obviously due to supernatural powers. But, according to another expert, the performance is what we could expect from any person who has any knowledge about finding underground water from surface cues. Whose judgment do we accept? In a well-designed experiment, we would not have to argue about such matters. We would have found a person with a background comparable to Stone's, but one who was not a diviner, and had him designate sites that would produce water or dry holes. Then we could have compared his performance with Stone's.

This tendency to rely upon subjective standards leads to erroneous and often embarrassing conclusions from results that superficially appear to have been obtained under experimental conditions. Not long ago a psychologist published a paper in which he described an experiment he conducted with a character-reader. The character-reader gave a group of women students a personality analysis consisting of from fifteen to twenty statements. Each student then indicated whether the statements in her sketch were true or false. It turned out that 96 per cent of the statements were correct, and, on this basis, the psychologist concluded that the character-reader could accurately diagnose personality.

One of this psychologist's implicit assumptions must have been that 96 per cent was better than chance; and he probably made the error of assuming that 50 per cent correct was the chance base line against which to compare this success rate. In the published article, the psychologist included two of the character sketches. One of us took these sketches and handed them to the secretaries in his building. Each secretary was asked to check which of these statements was true of herself. The number of statements so checked ranged from 90 to 100 per cent. In other words, this psychologist was led astray by his subjective base line; when we provide him with an objective base line—How many of these statements would be accepted as true by any woman? —we find that the performance of his character-reader is no longer amazing.

Recently, psychologists have been conducting many experiments in subjective probability. Among other things, they have discovered that the human observer is a poor judge of whether something is due to chance. In one experiment (Hake and Hyman, 1953), the subjects were required to anticipate which of two symbols would next appear in a long series of random symbols. The subjects did not see the series as random; by their behavior they showed that they were perceiving much more structure than there actually was. This was in part because the subjects tended to recall unusual sequences, just because they were unusual. Thus, they tended to characterize the whole series by a few unusual events (the man-bites-dog phenomenon). In another experiment (Hyman and Jenkins, 1956), we found it impossible to convince subjects that a random series was actually random. Each subject had a theory about the structure of the series, and each one saw it as lawful and regular.

Experiments such as these merely illustrate what scientists have known all along: the human being is a poor assessor of the operation of chance. He has a tendency to see order where none exists, to see departures from chance where only chance is operating, to see miracles where only laws of probability are operating. It is for this reason that the field test only partially approximates the necessary conditions for adequate proof. As long as the base line is a subjective one, there will always be equivocal interpretations. All of what we have said simply points out that without experimental controls the "facts" can be made to tell more than one story.

CHAPTER 4

Does It Work?
Controlled Experiments

There is no higher or lower knowledge, but one only, flowing out of experimentation.

LEONARDO DA VINCI

A young couple was recently watching a television play when the picture suddenly disappeared. Impatiently the wife walked up to the television set and gave it a smart blow with the palm of her hand. In a moment the picture returned, and she settled back in her chair to watch with satisfaction the conclusion of the play.

This story illustrates what we will call the "practical" approach to a problem, as distinguished from the "scientific." If the wife were to see the end of the play she had to do something right away. Her action was partly an expression of frustration and partly a desperate measure to "do something." We are not sure whether the physical jarring of the television set had anything to do with the return of the picture. The disappearance of the picture might have resulted from a temporary interference, and the restoration of the picture might have been related to the housewife's action only by coincidence. But, at that moment, the relevance of the blow to the television picture was not the important issue. What was important was the immediate goal of seeing the conclusion of the play. This goal was satisfied when the picture returned.

When we raise the question why the picture returned, we have a different goal in mind. We want to achieve some intellectual satisfaction concerning the processes underlying what happened. This search for an answer to a problem in terms of general principles or "laws" is what we will call the scientific approach.

Beginning with the same problem—the disappearance of the television picture and its subsequent return—the scientist, ever concerned with the general rather than the specific, would search for order by relating this couple's immediate problem to the general problem of the conditions under which pictures fail and the conditions under which they return. He might undertake a lengthy series of investigations to isolate and classify the various factors that lead to picture failure; he then might break these factors down into those which are temporary or reversible as against those which are relatively permanent (such as a burned-out tube). With this backlog of information, he might then consider what effects are obtained from hitting the set and whether any of these effects could, in themselves, lead to the restoration of a picture.

The essential difference between these two approaches is this: in the practical approach we are concerned with the *result;* in the scientific approach we are concerned with the *relationship* between our actions and the subsequent result. The housewife was more interested in the fact that the picture did return (the result) than in which of her actions, if any, brought about this result (the relationship). In a similar manner, the farmer who seeks water is more interested in the fact that he did or did not get it than in whether the diviner's actions had anything to do with the result. The scientist focuses his attention upon such questions as "Did the woman's (or the diviner's) action have anything to do with the result?"

In contrasting these two approaches, we do not wish to imply that one is necessarily "better" than the other. Nor do we want to convey the impression that they are opposite or alternative to each other. Each approach complements the other. It is because we have to act immediately in most of the problems confronting us in our daily lives that we develop a need for general principles to help guide us in specific situations. And it is because scientists are finding laws relating our actions to consequences that, in our practical approach, we are better able to act correctly as well as quickly.

In our daily affairs we could not use the scientific approach even if we wanted to. We have to be practical because we have to act immediately. The scientific approach necessarily involves a long-range attack. The search for generality entails patient investigation of many situations and problems, and this takes time. In this age of specialization, the scientific approach has become identified with specialists, and these specialists —chemists, physicists, biologists, physiologists, astronomers, geologists, psychologists, etc.—have evolved their own jargon, specialized tools, and technical guides. Consequently, we tend to set aside the scientist and his approach—the so-called scientific method—as something apart and different from the ordinary activity of our daily lives. This apparent division between the scientific approach and our daily affairs has been further emphasized by a spate of treatises and books on *the* scientific method, *the* nature of science, and *the* philosophy of science. It is little wonder that such formal analyses have created an attitude toward science that views it as something mysterious, threatening, inhuman, conscienceless, esoteric, and foreign to our daily conduct.

But, if the layman had opportunity to view the scientist at work, he would be surprised to find that the scientific approach is neither strange nor mysterious. Indeed, he would see that it makes a lot of sense; in many situations, this scientific approach is just the way the layman would handle a problem if he had the time and the facilities. "For science is not a special activity," as Bronowski tells us (1953). "It is a type of all human activity." This essential continuity between the common sense of everyday life and the methods of science is aptly summed up by the chemist Hildebrand (1957):

Scientific method is often defined as if it were a set procedure, to be learned, like a recipe, as if anyone could become a scientist simply by learning the method. . . . That there is no such thing as *the* scientific method, one might easily discover by asking several scientists to define it. . . . Indeed, no two scientists work and think in just the same ways. . . . We proceed by common sense and ingenuity. There are no rules, only the principles of integrity and objectivity, with a complete rejection of all authority except that of fact. The main motivation of scientists is curiosity, an urge to see and understand, to discover order in the vast complexity of nature. . . .

To be successful in unlocking the doors concealing nature's secrets, a person must have ingenuity. If he does not have the key for the lock, he must not hesitate to try to pick it, to climb in a window, or even to kick in a panel. If he succeeds, it is more by ingenuity and determination than by method [pp. 8–9, 26].

Although science is essentially a human activity and each scientist puts his questions to nature in his own idiosyncratic manner, the scientific approach is held together by some general principles and guiding rules. The scientist, by his training and knowledge of the history of his field, has been able to profit from errors and blunders of his predecessors. He has learned how to avoid the pitfalls and mistakes of previous generations. We saw, for example, in the last chapter, how, from bitter experience, the scientist has learned to distrust evidence from case histories and anecdotes. Such data are overly subject to human bias and frailties; the scientist has learned to place more confidence in data obtained under conditions that minimize the human element. C. S. Peirce (1955) emphasized this necessity for evidence upon which there can be universal agreement: "To satisfy our doubts, therefore, it is necessary that a method should be found by which our beliefs may be determined by nothing human, but by some external permanency—by something upon which our thinking has no effect. . . . The method must be such that the ultimate conclusion of every man shall be the same. Such is the method of science."

It is this aspect of science that makes the kind of evidence presented in the preceding chapter unacceptable. A testimonial is not evidence because we cannot, in most cases, reproduce the essential conditions and produce an effect upon which all observers can agree. A scientific law, on the other hand, is not a statement about what happened at such and such a time in the past. Rather, it is a prescription telling us that, if we conduct an experiment under specified conditions, we will observe a particular result. Scientific evidence never asks us to depend upon someone's word about what happened; it says, "If you want to see what happened, then follow this formula." If a scientist doesn't believe a finding of a colleague, he merely has to duplicate the experiment. Only if different experimenters—regardless of their biases—can agree about what will happen when we perform certain operations do we accept the findings as belonging to the category of "scientific evidence."

Perhaps the best way of conveying to the reader what we mean by the "scientific approach" is to describe an ideal, but hypothetical, test of a diviner.

A HYPOTHETICAL EXPERIMENT

Let us imagine that a famous diviner has offered his services for experimental purposes. And, further, money being no object in this imaginary enterprise, we have the land and facilities for sinking innumerable test wells. We devise the following test: We turn our diviner loose and instruct him to designate one hundred sites at which we should find water at a depth of thirty feet or less. After he has done so, we sink a test well at each designated site and count as a "success" each well that yields water from a depth of thirty feet or less. (We are simplifying our problem greatly by ignoring the problems of determining whether the site is yielding adequate water and how long it will do so, etc.).

Suppose our tally is: "successful," 75; "unsuccessful," 25. What are we to make of the fact that our diviner was successful 75 per cent of the time? We have already learned that without an objective base line we do not have a conclusive experiment. To some people the 75 per cent success rate will be a vindication of the diviner's claims. To others, the 25 per cent failure rate will strengthen their conviction of the unreliability of water witching. To the scientist, however, the 75 per cent figure is meaningless until we are provided with a base line against which we can compare it.

One way of providing a control comparison is to instruct our diviner to designate an additional one hundred sites at which we will *not* find water at thirty feet or less. This is one way of seeing whether his rod can actually distinguish between water-bearing and non-water-bearing locations. Suppose we had done this and obtained the results shown in Table 3. With such results

TABLE 3

	RESULTS OF TEST WELLS	
DIVINER'S PREDICTION	Water	No Water
Water....................	75	25
No water.................	75	25

we can give "meaning" to the figure of 75 per cent. The control comparison tells us that 75 per cent of the well sites where the diviner's rod did not move also yield water. Indeed, regardless of what the diviner says, 75 per cent of the well sites yield water within thirty feet of the surface. In this case, the scientist would say, with justification, that the action of the divining rod has no relationship to the presence of water. The diviner did no better than chance.

At this point, the scientist's interest in the diviner's claims would cease. Under controlled conditions, he was unable to demonstrate that his rod could detect the presence of underground water. But what would the scientist say, if, instead, the results had come out as in Table 4? These results would lead us to conclude that

TABLE 4

	RESULTS OF TEST WELLS	
DIVINER'S PREDICTION	Water	No Water
Water....................	75	25
No water.................	25	75

the diviner can discriminate between the presence and the absence of water. Our results show that the diviner's success rate of 75 per cent is quite high relative to the control comparison (only 25 per cent of the wells yielded water where he said they would not). Indeed, the statistician would tell us that the probability of the diviner being this "lucky" in this experiment just by chance is less than one in a billion.

At this point in our experiment, the information may have practical importance. Existing records may indicate that wells in this community typically yield water within thirty feet only about 50 per cent of the time. The diviner's tested ability to discriminate makes him a good bet. Presumably, by employing him, the farmer would increase his "odds" of hitting water at a reasonable depth.

But we do not stop here. Having found a connection between the rod's behavior and underground water, we now want to "explain" this result. Our first step might be to examine the conditions under which the diviner's rod seems to work as contrasted with those under which it fails. One step might be to go over all the well sites with a geologist. We would ask him to classify each site according to whether there are obvious surface cues or whether there are few surface cues. Let us imagine that he classifies one hundred as ones with "good surface cues" and one hundred as ones with "poor surface cues." Tables 5 and 6 represent the results of this

TABLE 5

Diviner's Prediction with "Good Surface Cues"	Results of Test Wells	
	Water	No Water
Water....................	45	5
No water................	5	45

TABLE 6

Diviner's Prediction with "Poor Surface Cues"	Results of Test Wells	
	Water	No Water
Water....................	30	20
No water................	20	30

breakdown applied to our imaginary data. Table 5 suggests that the diviner's ability to discriminate between sites with water and those without when "good surface cues" are available is excellent. When his rod says there will be water, it is mistaken only 10 per cent of the time. But, as Table 6 indicates, his ability to detect water is markedly impaired when good surface cues are not available. With reduced cues, his designations are now only 60 per cent correct.

So far our inquiry suggests that the diviner's ability to find water depends upon surface cues. But, to be fair, we should carry our study at least one step further, because we have not entirely eliminated surface cues in the field situation and our assumption can only be tentative. And, on the other side of the coin, the diviner might point to the data and argue that, even with small surface cues, there still is a tendency for him to be right more often than not.

And so, in the laboratory, we might construct a large platform and divide its surface into several small squares. Under each square we place a container that has water or that is empty—the choice for each square being determined by a randomization device such as the toss of a coin or consulting a table of random numbers. The diviner is to use his rod over each square and report to us whether there is water under it. In this laboratory experiment we have arranged things so that the diviner should be approximately 50 per cent correct just by chance. This is our objective base line. If the diviner, in fact, gets much more than 50 per cent correct, then we have to search for some explanation other than his use of ordinary surface cues. If he gets only 50 per cent correct, we would attribute his performance to chance. And we would tentatively conclude that the diviner can discriminate water only when there are reliable surface cues to its presence.

Such is one example of how the scientific approach might be applied to the problem of whether the divining rod "works." As you can see, the final answer is never achieved. By successive approximations we examine various possibilities, and the outcome of each experiment leads to a more refined answer or "explanation" of what is behind the phenomenon that we are studying. This hypothetical experiment is one way in which an investigator might proceed. Different investigators, depending upon their ingenuity and preferences, might tackle the question with a wide variety of techniques. But the feature of the "scientific approach" is that ultimately each will arrive at the same answer. In the remainder of this chapter we will describe some alternate approaches that have actually been employed in the investigation of water witching, all of them illustrating this "scientific approach."

EVIDENCE FROM FIELD EXPERIMENTS

The field experiment is similar to the field test in that the diviner is observed in action in his natural working habitat for the purpose of evaluating his ability. It differs from the field test, however, in that the experiment is conducted in such a way that a meaningful base line is provided against which we can compare the diviner's performance. The base line may simply be the number of successes made by independent judges who find spots without the aid of a rod.

An excellent example of an experiment with such base lines is the one performed under the auspices of the American Society for Psychical Research (Dale *et al.*, 1951). The investigators ran the experiment in such a way that two base lines were provided. They were able to make one comparison of the diviner's performance against a chance base line; they made another comparison of the performance against the indications of two ground-water experts who were not diviners.

The experiment took place in Maine during the first week in August, 1949, when the "relative drought insures the absence of surface water." The field was carefully chosen, so that such cues as surface water, wells, and other indicators of the presence or absence of water were absent. Each diviner witched the field in his own manner and selected the "best" spot for sinking a well. He was asked to estimate the depth as well as the amount of water found at this spot. He then went through this procedure a second time but with a blindfold placed over his eyes. All told, the experimenters ran a total of twenty-seven diviners (twenty-two men, four women, and one adolescent girl), one at a time, through this same process.

As a control, two "experts," a geologist and a water engineer, made estimates of the depth and rate of flow of the underground water at sixteen different points which had previously been staked out on the field. These experts made their estimates by "relying upon normal utilization of facts about underground water."

Test wells were then sunk at each of the spots assessed by the diviners and the experts; the depth and the amount of water were measured for each well. The results showed that the experts did a good job of estimating the over-all depth of the water as well as the depth at specific points. Neither expert did a good job in guessing the amount of water to be found at specific points, although the engineer made a close guess on the over-all estimate of the rate of flow. The diviners, on the other hand, were complete failures in terms of estimating the depth or the amount of water to be found at their selected spots. There was no correspondence between their estimates and the geological facts. This was true not only for the group as a whole but also for each diviner as an individual. As the authors put it, "Not one of our diviners could for a moment be mistaken for an 'expert.' . . . We saw nothing to challenge the prevailing view that we are dealing with unconscious muscular activity, or what Frederic Myers called 'motor automatism'!" This experiment is the only one that we know about where an adequate number of test wells were sunk so that a legitimate statistical evaluation could be made.

An experiment by Ongley (1948) was unusual in two respects. He used a large number of diviners, a total of seventy-five, and each diviner was tested only on those substances that he claimed his rod could detect. Some diviners, for example, claimed that their rods could detect only flowing water; others maintained that their rods reacted to any moisture. For each claim, Ongley tried to devise a fair test. Each test was so arranged that the results could be compared with a suitable chance base line. Out of the seventy-five diviners, only fifty-eight made claims concerning an ability to find water. Not a single one of these water witchers made a record significantly better than chance in a series of experiments which consisted of the following:

1. Asking a dowser to locate an underground stream and return to it with his eyes closed

2. Having the dowser locate an underground stream and then later identify which pegs were on the same stream and which were not—the experimenter having placed half of a number of pegs over the underground stream previously designated by the dowser and the other half of the pegs off the stream

3. Asking two or more dowsers to check one another on the location of underground water

4. Asking the dowser to say whether a hidden bottle was full of water or empty

5. Asking two or more dowsers to determine the depth of the water below the surface of the ground

The remaining diviners were tested, according to their claims, on the detection of minerals, medical diagnosis of patients, tracking of people, discovering the owners of lost objects, and detecting the presence of electrical fields. The results in these series of tests were also no better than would be expected by chance. Some of the failures were especially noteworthy. A healthy patient was said to be afflicted with no less than twenty-five different ailments by seven health diviners, and a person with a wooden leg was diagnosed as having a bad case of varicose veins by a blindfolded diviner. After surveying the large body of negative findings, Ongley comments, "It seems divining reactions are due not to any earthly radiations but to suggestion."

EXPERIMENTS IN THE LABORATORY

Laboratory experiments differ from field experiments in that they are conducted within a laboratory setting. This means that greater control over extraneous variables can be obtained than when the experiment is conducted in a natural setting. Under the controlled conditions of the laboratory it is much easier to provide an objective base line for comparison. And because the experimenter has considerable leeway in manipulating the environment, he can have greater confidence that no factors other than those under investigation have influenced the results. Laboratory experiments on water witching typically involve single diviners. Experiments are performed in which the diviner is given a chance to prove that certain of his claims are in fact true.

Let us look first at the cigar-box test of Williamson (1938). Williamson is a consulting geologist who specializes in finding oil. Over the past twenty years he has had a standing offer to diviners who claim to find oil. If a diviner, or doodlebugger (as he is known in the oil industry), can convince Williamson that his rod consistently responds to the presence of oil, then the geologist and his associates will back him in oil-prospecting with financial help and other resources. To each person who accepts the challenge, Williamson presents the following test: Ten cigar boxes are placed before the diviner. Each cigar box is filled with sand. In one of the boxes a bottle of oil is buried in the sand. If the rod can respond to oil that is several hundred, or even thousands, of feet in the ground, Williamson argues, then it should easily detect oil that is only a few inches away. The diviner has to guess which box contains the oil. After each guess, the boxes are reshuffled, and the diviner makes another guess. The complete experiment consists of ten such trials.

As Williamson states, if the boxes are sufficiently shuffled on each trial, the chances of the diviner's guessing the correct box just by luck are one in ten. In the complete experiment of ten trials, we should expect, on the average, that a person who is just guessing should get about one right. The highest score made by the fifty different diviners who underwent this test was three correct. Although this is not a sufficiently high batting average for practical purposes, Williamson is willing to concede that the high man's performance was better than chance. Actually, the probability of a man's getting three or more correct in this experiment is about eight in one hundred. This is not so low a probability, according to current standards, that it clearly supports the diviner's skill, but if we had been testing only this one diviner we might have considered his performance of sufficient interest to be worth further investigation.

It is at this point that students of statistics, some engineers, and many laymen make a serious mistake. They fail to realize that if one gives a rare event sufficient opportunity to occur, it will eventually happen. In considering Williamson's experiment we must take into account the fact that he conducted it fifty times. If each diviner was just guessing, we would expect, on the average, that as many as four out of fifty diviners would get three or more correct. Indeed, we wouldn't be surprised—on a chance basis—if one diviner guessed correctly four or more times. Because only one of the subjects had as many as three correct answers, the total performance of Williamson's diviners is not as good as we would expect it to be by chance.

If Williamson continues to conduct his experiment, he will eventually encounter a diviner who will be lucky enough to guess correctly on five or more trials. In itself this is a very unlikely occurrence, but in a sufficiently large number of trials it is bound to happen sometime (on the average, once every thousand tries). If the investigator reported only this surprising event and neglected to point out that it was selected out of a few thousand trials, then it would look very impressive, indeed. Levinson (1950) gives an excellent illustration of this subtle point:

If you make a throw with two ordinary dice, the odds are 35 to 1 against your throwing the double six, and 1,679,615 to 1 against your making this throw four consecutive times. Suppose, though, that ten million people throw two dice simultaneously, four times in succession. Then it will be exceedingly likely that a few will throw four straight double sixes. Each individual who does so, however, finds it very astonishing that chance should have selected *him* as a favorite [p. 25].

We dwell upon this business of selecting a "rare

event" from a large number of cases with good reason. Just because the event is rare, it stands out; people tend to recall it and emphasize it (Hake and Hyman, 1953). Since the larger number of "not-so-rare" events are commonplace and do not stand out, they are neglected. Our memories are such that we overemphasize the rare events and underemphasize the occurrence of the common.

We believe it is this tendency, which is a very strong one, to be impressed with the rare events and to ignore the common ones, that accounts for the fact that some geologists and water engineers give too much credit to the exploits of the diviner. On the basis of the cases that have come to their attention, many geologists (Riddick, 1952; Meyerhoff, 1953; Gregory, 1929) feel that there are too many successes to be entirely attributable to chance. They therefore claim that many diviners must be good amateur ground-water geologists. Although this may be plausible in a few specific situations, we do not feel that there is much scientific justification of even this possibility.

The Williamson experiment is not an ideal laboratory experiment. The shuffling of the boxes is not done by a mechanical randomization process, and psychologists have proved over and over again that human beings cannot produce a random series in their heads, no matter how hard they try. Even if the results had been more favorable to diviners, we would not be sure whether this was because of the diviner's rod or because his guessing habits were similar to that of the experimenter's notion of "random."

More typical of laboratory experiments is the one reported by Foster (1923). This was similar to most laboratory experiments in that it was a test of only one diviner. This man, a pastor in a neighboring church, came to the psychology laboratory at the University of Minnesota and asked to be tested. He had built up a reputation over a period of forty-five years by using his rod to locate water, oil, natural gas, iron, gold, and silver. He presented documents and testimonials from engineers and other witnesses who attested to his successes in Wisconsin, Minnesota, West Virginia, and Texas.

The psychologist subjected the diviner to a series of experiments, each of which was an attempt to test a specific claim of the diviner under controlled conditions. As in a number of other such laboratory experiments, the results were negative.

That is, the results were negative except for one test, and it is this test that we want to examine in further detail as a clue to what happens in the divining process. The pastor claimed that his rod could estimate the depth at which a box of metal objects was located. The box was placed at different levels on a ladder which was one floor below the pastor. The pastor's rod had little trouble in differentiating the step of the ladder on which the box was as long as the pastor knew which step it was on. When the experiment was run without the pastor's being informed, then the rod's performance went down to a chance level. Finally, the experimenter reran the test, this time providing an audience of six spectators. These spectators were placed on a landing so that they could simultaneously see the experimenter's placing of the box on the ladder and the pastor with his rod one floor above. Under these conditions, the pastor's performance was significantly better than chance.

Why did an audience improve the pastor's performance? The answer was easy. The spectators knew which step the box was on. When it was placed on a high step, they had to stoop somewhat to see it. When it was on a low step, they didn't have to stoop at all. The pastor was able to take advantage of these involuntary cues of the onlookers and thereby improve his score. The important point is that the pastor was not aware that he was reacting to such subtle cues. Indeed, throughout the experiment, whether his rod was responding correctly or not, he was sure it was reacting with infallible precision. When the experiment was over, he was absolutely astounded at the results. Indeed, he couldn't believe that they were his actual record. It was also clear, in another part of the experiment, that the pastor was able to use involuntary cues from an observer when he went outdoors to trace the location of an underground pipe.

TESTS OF CONSISTENCY

Barrett and Besterman (1926) outline a number of cases wherein a diviner's performance was compared with that of another diviner, or wherein the diviner was blindfolded to see whether he would consistently locate the same spot. All these "tests" suffer from the fact that they are little more than anecdotes and fulfil almost no scientific criteria. Barrett considers them strong evidence for the reliability of water witching, but a careful study of such cases leaves the evidence in doubt. Ongley's experiment, which we have previously discussed, also contained such consistency checks. His data, unlike those reported by Barrett and Besterman, give us a known chance base line for comparison, and when such a comparison is made, the consistency between diviners or in repeated tests for one diviner is no better than chance.

We should be careful not to consider consistency per se as direct evidence for the reality of water witching. Two or more diviners may agree perfectly about the best place to sink a well. But this does not prove that they are reacting to underground water. They may be reacting to the same surface cues, even though these cues are false. John Gould describes just such a case of consistency (*Christian Science Monitor,* December 8, 1955). A farmer in Lisbon Falls, Maine, called in a dowser to locate a well site. After witching the farm, the diviner placed a stake at the spot where he suggested a well should be dug. When news got around, another diviner (who enjoyed a local reputation of being quite successful) dropped by to check on the work of the first diviner. The farmer pulled up the first stake, remembering its location, and turned the second diviner loose. After carefully witching the area, the second diviner placed a stake in exactly the same spot as had the first diviner. The farmer thereupon began to dig. "He went down about 30 feet, and the dirt kept getting drier the farther he went. The only moisture in the hole was the perspiration from Randall's brow. It was a lovely hole, with nice straight sides, but it didn't have any water in it."

One caution should be observed in interpreting the results of blindfold tests. One of us has attempted to be blindfolded according to the pictures of blindfolded diviners he has seen in these tests. In each case, he has been able to see, not only straight down, but also straight ahead for an angle of 45 degrees. In fact, it is extremely difficult to blindfold a person by ordinary means so that his vision directly downward is completely obscured.

SUMMARY

The experiments we have presented in this chapter form only a small portion of the case against water witching. We have felt justified, in this chapter and in the previous one, in presenting only some of the data, selected to illustrate the various levels of evidence, around which the controversy rages. The reason we have emphasized representativeness rather than completeness is that both the proponents and opponents agree on the story to be derived from this mass of evidence. Believer and skeptic alike readily admit that the more closely the investigation approximates the conditions of a laboratory experiment, the worse the diviner performs. Case histories and field tests provide the major support for the reality of water witching. Almost without exception, the experiments that fit into our categories of field experiment and laboratory experiment yield negative results concerning the prowess of the diviner. Up to this point, there is little discord.

The difference of opinion between skeptic and believer is in the interpretation of these facts. Each side draws a different moral from the same story. To the skeptic, the inability of the diviner to produce in the laboratory situation suggests that water witching has no basis in fact. It has failed to justify its existence according to scientific standards. To the believer, however, the unsatisfactory results are clearly due to the inadequacies of the scientific approach. The diviner produces "when it counts"—in his home environment, unhindered by the artificialities of scientific control. If science fails to see its value, then so much the worse for science.

It is commonplace to say that the scientist dismisses water witching out of prejudice. While it is probably true that many scientists would be prejudiced against such a proposition as water witching, the argument we are presenting is not one based on prejudice. If we substituted some innocuous name such as "gluxting" for water witching, or substituted some other more plausible phenomenon, and then backed it up with the same amount and kind of evidence that now exists for witching, we have no doubt that the unanimous scientific verdict would be "not proven." In other words, we don't have to resort to prejudice to dismiss water witching as invalid. The evidence for it, when assembled and examined, is not merely insufficient; according to current scientific standards (the same ones we would apply to "acceptable" and plausible hypotheses), it is appallingly negative. We know of few other hypotheses that have been put forth so persistently over such a long span of years with such consistently negative experimental findings as the hypothesis that water witching "works."

But history and current experience warn us that the firm believer is not easily discouraged. If experiment refuses to support his claims, he resorts to other weapons. It is instructive to examine the believer's reactions to the scientist's inability to justify water witching's validity. A crude classification of these, with our comments, follows:

The "one good case" argument.—Matthews (1952) explicitly puts the argument this way: Diviners are aware of the multitude of negative experiments, but such failures, even though numerous, cannot cancel out the evidence of acknowledged successes achieved under non-test conditions.

There is merit to this argument. Even one good case, based on solid evidence, would be an argument in favor of divining. But, as we have seen, all the "good cases" come from anecdotes and field tests. We have already stated why the scientist cannot seriously consider such evidence. A scientifically "good case" would consist of an unselected series of comparisons with controls in which the diviner (or diviners) was consistently superior to the alternative water-finding procedure. To our knowledge, no such "good case" exists for water witching.

The "test of time" argument.—Burridge (1954) argues that "any practice that has come down through at least 3200 years must have much more basis than 'muscle twitching'!" And Tromp (1949) more than doubles the time span as he echoes the same theme: "Nonetheless, undeterred by public ridicule, persistent generations of dowsers have upheld their belief for at least 7,000 years, almost as long as civilization itself has existed. This should suggest even to the most critical scientist that there may be some possibility of truth in the stories of diviners."

If we were to accept this point of view, we would have to admit that there is even a stronger possibility of truth in such ancient practices as astrology, palmistry, and other forms of divination. These practices have survived right up to the present day from an even earlier beginning than water witching. Yet we feel no more inclined to admit their validity than we do that of water witching.

The "core of truth" argument.—This argument is a variant of the preceding one. Positive evidence, goes this argument, from a single case may be of dubious value because of the unscientific nature of the data. But when the evidence piles up from case after case, whatever the untrustworthiness of each single one, then there must be a common "core of truth" to all this evidence. When so many people attest to its value, regardless of the scientific merits of the evidence, there must be something to it.

In reply we can only remind the reader of an old Chinese saying: "If a thousand people say a foolish thing, it is still a foolish thing."

The "testimonial" argument.—Surely when such an

outstanding man as the Nobel Prize winner Charles Richet indorses water witching, there must be something to it. And what about all the other important men who have supported the cause?

This fallacy of arguing for the truth of a position by pointing to the prestige of some men who support it is known to logicians as *argumentum ad vericundium*. We can turn it around by pointing to the even larger array of important men who have denounced water witching as unscientific nonsense. If we were to pit prestige against prestige, water witching would lose in a landslide.

The "It would be a good thing for mankind" argument.—By opposing water witching, some have argued, scientists are hindering the welfare of mankind. Roberts (1953), for example, says, "When in *Henry Gross and His Dowsing Rod,* they [those scientists who reject water witching] were brought face to face with the evidence of a clearly defined Seventh Sense, and shown to be so closed-minded that they would sacrifice the welfare of the human race rather than admit they might just possibly be wrong, they grew almost incoherent in their furious contradictions."

We believe that all scientists would welcome any technique, be it water witching or whatever, that would benefit mankind. But the essence of the scientific approach is to get at the truth, whether it be pleasant or unpleasant. Almost every major scientific boner—and there have been many of them—can be traced to a zealous desire to see the world as we would like it to be rather than as it actually is.

The "good versus the bad diviners" argument.—Water witching has gained a bad reputation, so this version goes, because too many amateurs and incompetent diviners have got into the act. Roberts claims that he has met only eight diviners whom he would regard as competent. The rest are seepage diviners; their rods respond to any water even if it is not flowing. It is the seepage diviners who are responsible for the failures; the good diviners never make a mistake.

Again we must admit that there could be some truth in this argument. Maybe, by some odd coincidence, the scientists have always managed to get hold of the bad diviners. The good ones have consistently managed to escape their scrutiny. In defense, we can merely point out that it is only after a diviner has achieved considerable renown that he ever gets into a laboratory. Foster's (1923) diviner had testimonials from engineers and prominent men for his work over a period of forty-five years. And it is strange that we discover that the diviner belongs to the "incompetent" category only after he has undergone scientific test. Before then, he resembles all his "competent" colleagues in his reputation for successes.

The "unfairness of the artificiality of laboratory conditions" argument.—The diviner looks bad in the laboratory because the conditions are artificial. They are not like the conditions under which he normally operates.

This is always a hindsight defense. The diviner and his defenders never object to the artificiality before or during the experiments. Foster (1923), Dale *et al.* (1951), Ongley (1948), Lovibond (1952), and others report that the diviners in their experiments were completely confident that their rods were behaving in the ordinary way. At the time they made their designations, they were absolutely sure they were correct. Only after they learned the results did they and their defenders suggest that the test had been unfair.

The "unfavorable atmosphere" argument.—This, too, is often a hindsight alibi. It is a variation of the preceding rationalization. Tromp tells us that "it is often the subconscious wish of many research workers to obtain a negative result." And water witching is so sensitive and shy that it shuns the limelight or analysis under scientific eyes. In this respect, water witching is like many other elusive phenomena, such as spiritualistic manifestations and flying saucers. A scientist, with the wrong attitude, merely has to look in their direction, and these marvelous phenomena suddenly vanish.

The essence of all scientific investigation is doubt and questioning. Surely we cannot ask a scientist to give his seal of approval to a phenomenon which is said to exist only in the absence of doubt and questioning.

The "Accept us on our own terms" argument.—This argument is the sequel to the preceding one. The proponents readily concede that water witching will not survive orthodox scientific scrutiny. So they prevail upon us to put aside our scientific tools and accept the reality of water witching on the same basis that they do, i.e., on non-scientific grounds.

In other words we are supposed to waive the rules for water witching. Evidence or not, so they say, let's believe it anyway.

The "They persecuted Galileo" argument.—Many defenders of water witching take the martyr role. They compare their ridicule at the hands of science to the persecution that Galileo suffered because of his unorthodox views.

Galileo was persecuted by the clergy (and not by his fellow scientists) for his unorthodox views. But it is true that history records cases of men who met ridicule and opposition for views that later turned out to be correct. And it is also true that history records many, many more stories about views that met with opposition and were false. We can agree that many people suffered ridicule for novel ideas that later turned out to be correct. But we cannot see how such an admission can be turned into an argument in favor of water witching. Water witching is either valid or invalid regardless of what happened to Galileo.

As we make our way through the believer's wall of defenses, we realize that "truth" has a different significance for him than it does for the scientist. To the scientist, truth is approximate and tentative. What is true today may have to be revised tomorrow when new observations and evidence are available. To err is not only human for the scientist; it is the way he gains new information by which he can revise his map of "reality." But, for the believer, "truth" is already given; it is static. He "sees the light"; his only task is to convert the skeptic. Negative evidence does not lead him to revise his picture of "reality"; it only leads him to distrust and detest the scientist. For the adherent there are only two kinds of evidence. "Good evidence" is that which reinforces his belief; "bad evidence" is that which is at odds with his conviction that water witching "works."

Many laboratory experiments testify to the effect of strong emotional commitments upon our ability to reach logical conclusions. Thistlethwaite (1950) gave a test of reasoning ability to a total of 559 college students from seven universities in the North, South, and West. The instructions to each student read:

The following test contains a series of items designed to test reasoning ability. Some of the items will be very easy. Some will be more difficult. In each case a statement is given, followed by a conclusion which begins, "Therefore . . . ." You are to determine whether the conclusion follows from the given statement or statements.

The complete test consisted of seventy-two arguments; thirty-six were designed to be of neutral content and thirty-six of emotive content. The arguments contained content referring to Jews, Negroes, patriotism, and women. For every emotional argument there was a corresponding neutral argument, identical in formal pattern and alike in sentence length and comprehensibility. An example of such a matched pair would be this pair of statements:

Given: If the Iroquois Indian is of the same stock as the South Sea Islander, then the Iroquois migrated to this country from Asia.
The Iroquois Indian is not of the same stock as the South Sea Islander.
T. F.   Therefore: The Iroquois Indian did not migrate to this country from Asia.

Given: If the Negroid race is biologically similar to the White race, then the Negroid group represents an advanced and mature race.
The Negroid race is not biologically similar to the White race.
T. F.   Therefore: The Negroid group does not represent an advanced and mature race.

Thistlethwaite assumed that a person would respond to the first statement on the basis of the logic of the argument. If he correctly analyzes this particular argument, he will circle "False." In responding to the second argument, a person will do so on the basis of the logic of the argument and, *in addition,* on the basis of his attitude toward Negroes. If he responds logically, he will circle "F" as he did for the same formal argument about Iroquois Indians. If he has responded correctly to the first item but circles "T" for the second item, we assume that he has a negative attitude toward Negroes and that this has led to a distortion in his reasoning.

When this test was administered to students at New

York University and the College of the City of New York, their average score on Negro items was approximately the same as it was on the matched neutral items. This indicates that they showed very little, if any, distortion in responding to the items. But when the same test was given to students in the South (Duke University, University of Arkansas, Vanderbilt) the students made more errors on the Negro items than on matched neutral items. This revealed, as expected, that their negative attitude toward Negroes distorted their ability to reason logically.

Results such as these help us understand the kinds of illogicalities we encounter among skeptics and believers in evaluating the same evidence for water witching. Imagine how a vehement skeptic might react to the following argument:

Given: If water witching is a superstition, it will be denounced by governmental officials.
Water witching is denounced by governmental officials.
T. F. Therefore: Water witching is a superstition.

Although the conclusion doesn't follow from the premises, we can predict that those who believe water witching is false will tend to circle "T." An illustration of such distortion of logic is provided by the publication of objective records comparing witched wells with non-witched wells. We reported one set of findings (Table 2, p. 56) showing that 14.7 per cent of the divined wells in central New South Wales were "absolute failures" as compared with only 7.4 per cent absolute failures for non-divined wells. Many critics point to this data as evidence of the inferiority of water witching. But, as we pointed out, the conclusion does not follow from the evidence. Before we could logically justify such a conclusion we would have to know how correct the diviner's judgment would have been on the non-divined sites, as well as how the alternative modes of choosing a well site would have succeeded on the divined sites.

On the other side of the coin, imagine how a firm believer might respond to the following argument:

Given: If water witching is valid, it will have survived over a long period of time.
Water witching has survived over a long period of time.
T. F.   Therefore: Water witching is valid.

Again we can see the possibility that the believer's attitude will lead him to circle "T."

The unfortunate aspect of such distortions is that the people who make them are often perfectly capable of logical thinking outside the small content area in which they have strong emotional commitments. Thus, if we gave to both the skeptic and the believer the following argument—identical in logical form to the previous two—they would have little trouble in coming to a correct conclusion:

Given: If the team doesn't play to win it will lose.
The team lost.
T. F.   Therefore: The team didn't play to win.

Here the reaction will involve little emotional content and the subject will very likely realize that the conclusion does not necessarily follow from the premises.

In this passionate clinging to a conviction, we see an analogy with the psychiatric patient portrayed in a recent anecdote. The patient, who believes that he is dead, is brought before the psychiatrist. The psychiatrist employs his best logic and psychological persuasiveness to convince the patient that he is still alive. But to no avail. Suddenly the psychiatrist has a flash of in-sight.

PSYCHIATRIST: Tell me, do dead men bleed?

PATIENT (*after carefully considering the question*): No, dead men do not bleed.

PSYCHIATRIST (*takes a pin and pricks the patient's finger, whereupon blood gushes forth*): Well, now what have you to say for yourself?

PATIENT (*contemplating the bleeding digit*): Well, by golly! I guess dead men do bleed after all!

CHAPTER 5

From Talking Horses
to Talking Twigs

*All the phenomena when attentively examined,
will be found to consist in the occupation of the
mind by the ideas which have been suggested to
it, and in the influence which these ideas exert
upon the actions of the body.*

WILLIAM B. CARPENTER, 1852

We begin with a talking horse. The horse will carry us
over a trail marked by such esoteric signposts as mind
reading, the magic pendulum, the Ouija board, the turning table, automatic writing, and hypnotic phenomena.
These signposts mark the way to our goal—an understanding of what makes the rod move. To get to the
talking twig by way of talking horses and animated toys
may seem roundabout. But a look at these phenomena
will simplify our task. When we understand why the
horse talks and why the Ouija board spells, we will understand why the divining rod moves.

CLEVER HANS OF BERLIN

In the year 1904, there appeared in Berlin a Russian
trotting horse known as Clever Hans. Here was a horse,
so it seemed, that could have settled the age-old question of animal consciousness. For Hans was renowned
for his ability to solve arithmetical problems, to spell
and define words, to identify musical notes and inter-

vals, and to behave in other ways that indicated he had powers of abstract reasoning.

The public sang his praises in songs, articles, and books. His picture appeared on postcards and liquor labels. Children's toys were made in his image. Men of renown investigated him and found him to be truly endowed with human intelligence. He was intensively studied by a committee consisting of a circus manager, several educators, a zoölogist, a veterinarian, a physiologist, and the famous psychologist Carl Stumpf. The committee reported that it was baffled; it maintained that no trickery or known cues were involved. Educators declared that Hans had achieved the developmental stage of a fourteen-year-old child.

The horse's trainer, Von Osten, a man of about seventy years of age, stood proudly at the horse's right. A former arithmetic teacher, he had spent three years teaching Hans the three R's. His approach was not that of the circus performer but that of the patient schoolmaster. Instead of the whip he used occasional rewards of carrots which he kept stuffed into his pockets. He declined to profit commercially from Hans's fame, refusing several lucrative offers to exploit the talents of his pupil. The achievements of his student were rewarding enough. Even the group that gathered in the courtyard to watch Hans go through his paces came free of charge.

Hans could answer almost any question put to him in German. He could count up to one hundred, and he could do all the basic arithmetical operations including those involving compound fractions and decimals. He could spell words, identify persons and objects by name, designate the pitch of musical notes, and even express a like or dislike for certain kinds of music. Hans, of course, could not talk in a vocal sense. He responded to questions by tapping with his hoof, shaking his head, or walking over and pointing to letters on a board or objects on a rack.

Other animals, to be sure, had been advertised as capable of such feats. But these other animals had been trained to respond to cues and signs from their masters. If Hans's performance was in the same category with the acts of trained circus animals, it was not obvious to the investigators—including ringmasters—who carefully put Hans through his paces.

Furthermore, it developed that Hans could often perform even when his master was not present. In September, 1904, after examining Hans thoroughly, a commission of thirteen outstanding scientists and animal experts could only report:

In spite of the most attentive observation nothing in the way of movements or other forms of expression which might have served as a sign, could be discovered. . . . As a result of these observations the undersigned are of the opinion that unintentional signs of the kind which are at present familiar, are likewise excluded. They are unanimously agreed that this much is certain: This is a case which appears in principle to differ from any hitherto discovered, and has nothing in common with training, in the usual sense of that word, and therefore it is worthy of a serious and incisive investigation [Pfungst, 1911, pp. 253–54].

It remained for the psychologist Oskar Pfungst to carry out this "serious and incisive investigation."

THE INVESTIGATION OF HANS BY PFUNGST

The results of Pfungst's systematic inquiry are recorded in his book *Clever Hans* (Pfungst, 1911). This amazing document not only presents us with an illustration of scientific investigation at its best but unfolds its findings in the manner of the best contemporary detective thrillers.

Mr. Pfungst first took pains to make friends with Hans. Then, when Mr. Von Osten was not present, he put questions to Hans. To the scientist's amazement, the horse answered correctly each problem put to him. Mr. Pfungst knew that he was not coaching or signaling the horse. Yet, with no one else present, the horse was going through his paces with perfect precision.

Some other eminent men had gone through the same experience with Hans. Faced with this unexplainable situation, they honestly admitted their bewilderment. And these eminent men publicly indorsed the claim that Hans was capable of abstract reasoning. Mr. Pfungst was also honest enough to admit his bafflement. But it is at this point that his scientific training distinguished him from the other eminent onlookers. Instead of jumping from his inability to explain the horse's behavior to the conclusion that Hans was quasi-human, Pfungst investigated further.

He designed a series of experiments in which the horse was questioned in the usual fashion. But half of the questions were ones to which the questioner knew the answer and half were ones to which the questioner did not know the answer. The results were clear-cut. Hans could answer questions only when his questioner knew the answer. Hans, then, was only as intelligent as his questioner. When his questioner was ignorant, so was Hans. Obviously, then, Hans was getting his cues from the questioner. But what were these cues and how was Hans receiving them? After eliminating auditory and tactual cues, Pfungst used blinders to block the horse's view of the questioner. Here Hans balked. He insisted on turning his head and orienting himself so that he could see his interrogator. As long as Hans could not see his questioner, he could not answer his question.

So far, two facts had been established. Hans could answer questions only when the questioner knew the answer, and he had to see the questioner to give him the answer. But here the investigation met a snag. It appeared that the horse was responding to visual cues, and Pfungst, to whom the horse responded perfectly, was unable to detect any behavior or postures in himself that could serve as a sign.

Again, Pfungst revealed the ideal of scientific spirit. He did not give up. He kept looking and finally discovered the answer where all others had failed. The horse was responding to a postural cue from the questioner, a cue so small and subtle that it was almost impossible to detect.

When the questioner asked his question, he focused attention upon the horse's hoof, which began tapping the answer. In many questioners, this close attention produced a tenseness that was translated into an almost imperceptible slouching of the head—just a trace of the more overt gesture of bending over and watching the hoof. This was a sufficient cue for Hans to begin tapping. When Hans had tapped a sufficient number of times in response to the question, the questioner, confident that the horse was not going to tap any more, would almost imperceptibly raise his head and straighten up. This was Hans's cue to stop tapping.

Pfungst had been unable to discover this cue by studying himself. It was only after long observation of other questioners that he discovered it. Even then, he found it difficult to voluntarily control these cues in himself. But once he had discovered the secret, Pfungst was able to teach himself and others to give the cues that would control Hans's behavior.

PFUNGST OUTDOES HANS

But Pfungst did not stop his investigations at this point. Instead, he carried his investigations into the laboratory. He wanted to know if naïve questioners would unintentionally give the same cues that the successful questioners had given to Hans.

For these experiments, Pfungst played the part of Hans. His right hand became the right foreleg of Hans, and it tapped in the same language so familiar to the horse. A questioner would stand before Pfungst. He would merely *think* of a question that could be answered in terms of a number of taps of the hand. Pfungst would look for the cue, the almost imperceptible slouch, to begin tapping. He would tap, all the while observing the questioner; when he thought he observed a slight relaxation in the questioner, he would cease tapping.

In all, Pfungst went through these paces with twenty-five different persons who ranged in age from five upward. None of these subjects was aware of the purpose of the experiment, and none discovered what particular phenomena Pfungst was looking for. The results were startling. All but two of the subjects gave the same involuntary head movements that Pfungst had discovered in the questioners of Hans. And Pfungst was able to use these involuntary movements to successfully "read" the minds of his questioners. He was able to devise other kinds of experiments to correspond with Hans's complete repertoire. In each case the subjects gave involuntary cues; and in each case, when being told, they denied any knowledge of these involuntary movements.

And still Pfungst wasn't satisfied. He carried on with further experiments. He found that he could train a subject to give him cues of various kinds even while the subject did not know he was being trained to give such cues. He then built special apparatus to record objectively such movements along with reaction times and breathing rates.

The results of all these experiments were undeniably clear. When subjects asked a question and then concentrated on the movements of the experimenter, they invariably made involuntary movements which cued the experimenter when to start and stop. And the experimenter had little trouble in utilizing these cues to read the minds of the questioners in a manner similar to Hans.

THE TRAINING OF HANS

One question remained to be answered. How did Hans learn to respond to these cues? Did his owner, Mr. Von Osten, deliberately train him to react to these cues? Or did he accidentally pick them up by the simple process of noting that he was rewarded with a carrot if he stopped at certain signs?

Pfungst reviews all the evidence that bears upon this question. All the facts lead to the conclusion that Mr. Von Osten was as much the dupe of his involuntary actions as were all the later investigators. Pfungst reviews the training of Hans in detail. Even though Von Osten believed that he was training the horse to learn in much the same way as a schoolboy learns, the actual procedures were also those that would lead to rewarding the horse for simply starting and stopping on certain cues. (In fact, Von Osten's training procedure was very much like that called "operant conditioning" by modern psychologists.)

Von Osten spent three years patiently training his horse. Others who came after him, knowing the real secret of Hans's success, succeeded in teaching other horses Hans's complete repertoire in a matter of weeks.

THE TALKING HORSE SURVIVES

Clever Hans was merely the first of a whole series of talking and mind-reading horses. In Germany, a man by the name of Krall established a laboratory to study the psychology of such horses, and, in our own time, the horse Lady Wonder has not only made headlines on several occasions but was investigated by J. B. Rhine and the psychologist William McDougall in 1928 (Rhine, 1929).

Lady Wonder, owned by Mrs. Claudia Fonda of Richmond, Virginia, "could make predictions, solve simple arithmetical problems, answer questions aptly and intelligently, and do all this without verbal command. All that was needed was that the question be written down and shown to Mrs. Fonda" (Rhine, 1929). In 1927, Lady Wonder attracted national interest by correctly predicting that Dempsey would beat Sharkey. And in 1952, she made headlines again when the police of Quincy, Massachusetts, credited her with finding the body of Danny Matson, a four-year-old child missing for two years. A police official questioned Lady Wonder and she spelled out "Pittsfield Water Wheel." After a search of water wheels in the Quincy area proved fruitless, a policeman suggested that "Field and Wilde Water Pit" might be what the horse meant. The child's body was found there. In 1957, at the age of thirty-three Lady Wonder died quietly. (For more information on Lady Wonder and other animal wonders see Christopher, 1955.)

Dr. J. B. Rhine and his wife first investigated Lady Wonder on six different days during the period of December 3, 1927, to January 15, 1928. All the tests were conducted at Mrs. Fonda's residence in a special demonstration tent. The horse faced a table upon which were placed, as needed, cubical letter blocks or number plates with one digit on each. Mrs. Fonda stood by Lady's head, on the left side, and all other onlookers were stationed across the table from the horse. With no restrictions upon Mrs. Fonda, Lady Wonder performed with elegant precision. Lady Wonder could walk up to the table and correctly choose one of ten letters or numbers whenever Mrs. Fonda knew the location of the chosen symbol. Rhine quickly discovered that knowledge of the chosen symbol by someone present was necessary for successful performance. Therefore, Lady did not have superior intelligence but was responding to cues of some kind.

We can see that Rhine's investigation, up to this point, showed what Pfungst discovered in the case of Clever Hans. Rhine now set about to discover the nature of the cues. He had Mrs. Fonda stand motionless, turn her head away, and even wear a blindfold. Lady still performed better than chance. Rhine then tried to separate Mrs. Fonda from the horse. But the three-year-old filly stopped working in the absence of her trainer. Some experiments were tried where Mrs. Fonda held a three-foot screen in front of herself (her feet and coat were visible) and which showed some measure of success, although the trials were all too few. Rhine concludes that such precautions "served to eliminate certain possibilities of signalling," but, as long as Mrs. Fonda was in sight of her filly and was holding a screen that she could move, such precautions were far from adequate protection from signaling.

Finally, the experimenters attempted a series of trials in which Mrs. Fonda was kept ignorant of the chosen number. She was kept near the horse "to control" her. Although these experiments were executed with great difficulty because Lady Wonder was acting up and often out of control, Rhine concluded that she was still better than chance in this series. Therefore he and his wife concluded: "There is left then, only the telepathic explanation, the transference of mental influence by an unknown process. Nothing was discovered that failed to accord with it, and no other hypothesis proposed seems tenable in view of the results."

Perhaps, to Rhine, already committed to a belief in mental telepathy, such an explanation seemed only natural. Only a firm conviction in the naturalness of extrasensory communication can account for Rhine's surprising conclusion on such inadequate evidence. Pfungst spent considerably more time and effort, using much better controls and methodological procedures, before he isolated the cues to which the horse responded. Yet, under conditions where the trainer was *always* present and at least partly visible, Rhine and his wife jumped to the conclusion that only extrasensory communication could be involved.

Rhine's approach to the wonder horse had too many drawbacks to be called "experimental." His randomization of the correct symbol was not according to accepted standards; he didn't allow for the possibility of more than one kind of signal to the horse, it being his opinion that auditory and visual cues were eliminated; and he never really "eliminated" Mrs. Fonda from the experiments. In a later paper, Rhine admits that, while he didn't tell Mrs. Fonda what the chosen number was in the last series, he did write it down upon a pad of paper. In a separate visit, a professional magician discovered that Mrs. Fonda was an accomplished pencil reader; that is, she could read what someone was writing by merely watching the movements of the pencil's top. (For alternative explanations of how Mrs. Fonda and

Lady may have duped Rhine see Gardner, 1957.) At any rate, Lady Wonder never performed better than chance again for any scientist, not even in later tests by Rhine himself. Many observers agreed that Lady Wonder, like Hans, was responding to visual signals from her trainer.

MIND READING

Hans and Lady Wonder were both accomplished muscle readers. In this respect, they were merely following in the tradition of their equine ancestors. As Beard (1877) points out, "Every horse that is good for anything is a muscle reader; he reads the mind of his driver through the pressure on the bit, and by detecting tension and relaxation knows when to go ahead, when to stop, and when and which way to turn, though not a word of command is uttered."

In the 1870's some human beings found that they could emulate the horse. For centuries, the horse has been reacting to the tension and relaxation of his master. Now man found that he, too, could stop and start and turn in response to unspoken commands of another man, and he crowed loud and widely about this talent that was quietly taken for granted in horses. He called his talent "mind reading" and gave public exhibitions before awed spectators.

One of the famous exhibitors of this skill was John Randall Brown (later followed by Washington Irving Bishop and Stuart Cumberland). He would leave the lecture hall; a committee accompanied him to make sure that he did not know what took place in his absence. The spectators would hide an object somewhere in the hall. Brown would return. He would choose a spectator to be a transmitter. This spectator was to concentrate his thoughts on the hiding place. Brown would place this subject's hand on his forehead and, holding this contact, would rush about the hall in various directions—the man being dragged along with him. In short order, if the transmitter was a good subject, Brown would find the hidden article.

Such a performance created much controversy in those days. Learned men and committees debated whether this was real mind reading. A few had the audacity to suggest that the transmitter was giving muscular cues. Both the "mind reader" and the transmitters vehemently denied such charges. A physician by the name of Beard had the presence of mind to substitute experiment for debate. His experiments were not elaborate. But they were sufficient to demonstrate that this so-called mind reading was simply muscle reading. The mind reader could only perform tests in which the cue was of the old "Am I hot or cold?" variety. And the transmitter merely gave him these cues by almost imperceptible contractions and relaxations. This physician came to a conclusion that careful investigators of strange behavior have come to over and over again (Beard, 1877): "The question whether it is possible for one to be a good muscle reader and pretty uniformly successful, and yet not know just how the trick is done, must be answered in the affirmative." Pfungst learned to emulate Hans by deliberately looking for cues. But many people can apparently react to such cues without being aware that they are doing so. In the last chapter we saw how the water diviner's score went up when he was in the presence of an audience who knew the actual depth of his target. And Beard gives many examples of "mind readers" who were unaware of the cues to which they were responding.

This kind of muscle reading was known as "contact mind reading" for obvious reasons. The early perform-

ers had to have direct physical contact with their transmitters. But, as we have seen, both Hans and Pfungst
were able to react to their subjects' involuntary cues
without direct contact. They were able to detect vis-
ually the relaxation and tensing of their questioners.

During the 1920's, a Moravian by the name of Eugene
de Rubini made a sensation in this country with his
telepathic demonstrations. His feats were very much
like those of the contact mind readers of the late nineteenth century. But where the earlier telepathists found
hidden objects by holding the hand of a "transmitter,"
Rubini performed his feats without physical contact.
An example of his prowess is given by this description
of a demonstration he gave before a committee from
the Society of American Magicians in 1929:

> As an opening test, Mr. Rubini gave a blank card and an
> envelope to Mr. Al Altman, of the Society of American
> Magicians, and the same to two ladies present. He requested
> that each person should write on the card the name of some-
> body in the room and then seal it in the envelope, and that
> under their mental direction he would find the person and
> deliver the card to him, which should be done without con-
> tact with any of those concerned in the test. . . . The place
> in which the tests were being carried on was a large living
> room and library combined, in which were seated about
> forty-three persons.
>
> Mr. Rubini began walking along the aisle in the room
> about four feet in front of Mr. Altman, who made no physi-
> cal signs that would guide him, and in a few minutes Mr.
> Rubini stopped in front of Mr. Guest and, after opening the
> envelope, handed him Mr. Altman's card (which Mr. Alt-
> man had addressed to Mr. Guest) [Rinn, 1950, p. 531].

Rubini performed many similar feats to the bafflement of the magicians present. Joseph Rinn sent a description of Rubini's performance to George Newman,

who was noted also for this ability to do contact and non-contact mind reading. Newman wrote back his explanation, which was similar to Pfungst's explanation of the performances of Clever Hans. "No matter how much control the transmitter may exercise or believe he exercises," observed Newman, "there can be no doubt that he *unconsciously* or *involuntarily* gives some sort of indication, which in turn is unconsciously detected by the percipient, who is therefore unable to explain *how* he knew what was in the transmitter's mind" (Rinn, 1950).

Although Rubini continued to mystify American audiences through the 1930's, his abilities had been tested and explained by psychologists at the University of California in 1921 (Stratton, 1921). In these tests Rubini was quite willing to work with ear plugs but refused to wear a blindfold. Finally, he compromised with the experimenters and wore a pair of blinders that permitted him to see straight ahead but not out of the sides of his eyes. Under these conditions, the transmitter, who always walked behind him and to his side, could not be seen in his peripheral vision. Rubini's success rate immediately dropped to a chance level. "From this it is clear that while Rubini can with sight and without the help of touch attain about one and a half times as many successes as chance would give, yet when all visual cues from his guide's behavior are excluded, the successes at once drop to the number expected by pure chance." Rubini, then, was merely another Clever Hans who reacted to involuntary cues given by his guides. Apparently neither the transmitter nor Rubini was conscious of these cues.

THE MAGIC PENDULUM

Perhaps you have tried the Ouija board or have held

a divining rod. Or maybe you have played with the pendulum or "sex detector" or sat around a tapping table. If these instruments have "worked" for you, then you have some personal involvement in the phenomena that we are describing. You know how convincing and eerie this experience can be.

If you are not personally familiar with this kind of experience, then you may profit from the following experiment. Take a small weight such as a key, a ring, or even a watch. Suspend this weight from a string or a chain. A length of a foot to two feet is just about right. Now hold the string or chain at its loose end by the tips of the right fingers. Stand erect so that the weight hangs suspended from your outstretched arm. With your free hand impart a swinging motion to the weight so that it swings back and forth like a pendulum. Now forget about your arm. Concentrate your eyes upon the swinging weight. Merely imagine or think of the weight as gyrating in a clockwise circle. In almost every case, the pendulum will start to gyrate in such a circle without any conscious effort on your part. With a little practice, you will be able to concentrate on the pendulum and have it reverse its gyrations, or go swinging back and forth, etc. If the experiment has worked for you, you have experienced the same phenomenon that has, for centuries, in various guises, baffled wise men and convinced them that supernatural forces were operating.

We find our first detailed account of the pendulum in a work by the Latin historian Ammianus Marcellinus, who died in A.D. 390. A band of conspirators had been apprehended for planning the assassination of the Emperor of the East. One conspirator, in his confession, described the manner in which the group ascertained the name of the emperor's successor. A priest held a fine thread upon which was suspended a ring. The ring was held over a disk, around the edge of which were printed the letters of the alphabet. The ring, oscillating in the priest's hands, pointed out successively the letters *T, H, E,* and *O.* This told the conspirators that the emperor's successor would be named Theodorus (Chevreul, 1854). Thus, in this first account of the pendulum, we also find the first story of the Ouija board.

Other Roman accounts tell of another variation of the magic pendulum (Jastrow, 1935). The pendulum was held so that it was suspended in a glass. The alphabet was recited, and the ball would ring out against the glass at the right letters. That was some 1,500 years ago in ancient Rome. Today, in southern Illinois, you can see a man holding his pendulum so that it is suspended in a glass. The pendulum rings out against the glass as it did in the days of ancient Rome; but now it no longer spells out the successor to emperors; instead, it tells the diviner how far he will have to dig for water.

The pendulum was, and still is, applied to the solution of an unbelievable number of problems. In the late eighteenth and early nineteenth centuries, several scientific men discovered the magic pendulum. They wrote learned works on its behavior and its ability to react differently to magnetic poles and chemical substances. These academicians even developed elaborate treatises on the forces impinging upon this pendulum (Raymond, 1883). One of the men, Professor Ritter, included the divining rod in his studies and concluded that the rod was merely a double pendulum.

At the height of this "Pendulum Revolution" in science, in 1812, the chemist Michel Eugène Chevreul began to experiment with the pendulum (Chevreul, 1833, 1854). Chevreul read the famous theories, especially the book by Professor Gerboin of Strassburg. He knew how the pendulum was supposed to behave, according to the theory, over various substances. So Chevreul held his pendulum over a dish of mercury. And, to his utter amazement, the pendulum gyrated just as the book said it should.

Again we come to that quality that distinguishes the true scientist from his lesser colleagues. When Chevreul's predecessors, such as Fortis, Gerboin, Ritter, and Amoretti, found the pendulum behaving for them, they immediately developed elaborate and fanciful rationales for its antics. But Chevreul, like Pfungst, took a second look. He experimented further. He wanted to know under what conditions the phenomenon appeared and under what conditions it disappeared. He placed a glass barrier between the mercury and his pendulum. To his surprise the oscillations of the pendulum stopped. And this was as it should be if a physical force was involved.

Chevreul carried on. He rested his arm on a support. The oscillations diminished, but did not stop. He was still suspicious. He had an assistant blindfold him. The assistant interposed the plate between the pendulum and mercury and took it away without Chevreul knowing when. And the pendulum suddenly lost its mysterious behavior! "So long as I believed the movement possible, it took place; but after discovering the cause, I could not reproduce it." At the time Chevreul wrote (1833) there was no separate discipline of experimental psychology. His was the first contribution to the literature and the first demonstration of the effect of expectant attention upon involuntary movements.

Chevreul continued his interest in involuntary movements. In 1854 he published a book that linked the pendulum, the divining rod, and the currently popular table turning under the same psychological law. Chevreul concluded, in relation to the divining rod, that "the movement is the consequence of an act of the mind."

VARIATIONS UPON A THEME

The principle of the magic pendulum has formed the basis for countless numbers of gadgets, many of which were quite complicated, allegedly capable of detecting and reacting to a host of substances and secret rays. Some of these variations were deliberately constructed to meet the objections that the freely hanging pendulum was influenced by involuntary movements of the hand. Such a gadget, for example, was Rutter's magnetometer (Carpenter, 1874).

Rutter's apparatus consisted of a ball suspended by a string from a metal frame. Because the frame was quite sturdy and because the ball was not suspended from a person's hand, Rutter convinced many onlookers that the ball's movements could not be explained away on the same basis as were those of the ordinary pendulum. In a typical demonstration, Rutter would hold his finger against the frame of the apparatus for a short time; with his other hand he touched other individuals or objects, and the ball discriminated among them with changes in intensity and direction of movement.

These experiments appeared to many persons of great general intelligence, to indicate some new and mysterious agency not hitherto recognized in our philosophy; for even among those who might be disposed to attribute the oscillations of a button suspended from the *finger,* to the involuntary movements of the hand itself, some were very slow to believe that the simple *contact* of the finger with a frame of *solid metal* could produce the like vibrations through such a medium [Carpenter, 1874, p. 286].

Interestingly enough, the secret of the magnetometer was discovered by a follower of Rutter himself. This man, a homeopathic physician of Brighton, England, named Dr. H. Madden, used the magnetometer to test the value of his various remedies. The magazine *Lancet* carried the following account of what ensued in 1851:

Globules in hand, therefore, he consulted its oscillations, and, found that they corresponded exactly with his idea of what they *ought* to be; a medicine of one class producing *longitudinal* movements, which were at once exchanged for *transverse* when a medicine of opposite virtues was substituted for it. In this way Dr. Madden was systematically going through the whole Homeopathic Pharmacopoeia; when circumstances led him to investigate the subject *de novo*, with a precaution which had never occurred to him as requisite in the first instance, but of which the importance is obvious to every one who holds the real clue to the mystery;—namely, that he *should not know* what were the substances on which he was experimenting, the globules being placed in his hand by another party, who should give him no indication whatever of their nature. From the moment that he began to work upon this plan, the whole aspect of affairs was altered. *The results ceased altogether to present any constancy.* Oscillations at one time transverse, at other times longitudinal, were produced by the very same globules; whilst remedies of the most opposite kinds frequently gave no sign of difference. And thus, in a very short time, Dr. Madden was led to the conviction, which he avowed with a candour that was very creditable to him, that the whole system which he had built up had no better foundation than *his own anticipation of what the results should be* [quoted in Carpenter, 1874, pp. 286–87].

The effect that our anticipations can have upon our sense of reality has formed the basis of many strange discoveries and many peudoscientific contrivances. We have already observed the role of expectation in creating the controversial *n*-rays, and today versions of Rutter's magnetometer still form a rallying point for those who war against the stuffiness of orthodox science. These machines go under such names as Psionic Machine,

Hieronymus Machine (Patent No. 2,482,773), etc. (see Gardner, 1957, pp. 346–48).

TABLE TURNING

In 1848, two sisters found that they could produce a loud rapping noise, with their big toes, on a floor or other sounding board. By some quirk in the thinking process of man, these rappings were interpreted as messages from the spirit world. Among the converts was Sir Arthur Conan Doyle. Like his famous detective, Sherlock Holmes, Sir Arthur could form quick conclusions—and back them up with uncompromising conviction—from the most superficial basis. With his help, therefore, the "spirit rappings" that accompanied the Fox sisters set going the modern spiritualistic movement. The movement swept not only the American continent but all of western Europe. The spirits, as the movement grew, found many ingenious ways to announce their presence. They levitated tables, blew horns, spoke, wrote on slates, left thumbprints upon wax, threw vases across rooms, and otherwise behaved like mischievous children.

In the middle nineteenth century, a favorite mode of expression among the spirits was table turning (see Fig. 22). According to Carpenter, the practice of sitting around a table to commune with the "other world" reached epidemic proportions in England by 1850 (Carpenter, 1874, pp. 292–93). He describes a typical session of the day as follows:

A number of individuals seat themselves round a table, on which they place their hands, with the *idea* impressed on their minds that the table will move in a rotary direction; the direction of the movement, to the right or to the left, being generally arranged at the commencement of the experiment. The party sits, often for a considerable time, in a state of expectation, with the whole attention fixed upon the table, and looking eagerly for the first sign of the anticipated motion. Generally one or two slight changes in its place herald the approaching revolution; these tend still more to excite the eager attention of the performers, and then the actual "turning" begins. If the parties retain their seats, the revolution only continues as far as the length of their arms will allow; but not unfrequently they all arise, feeling themselves obliged (as they assert) to *follow* the table; and from a walk, their pace may be accelerated to a run, until the table actually spins round so fast that they can no longer keep up with it. All this is done, not merely without the least consciousness on the part of the performers that they are exercising any force of their own, but for the most part under the full conviction that they are not.

By 1852 France's great chemist Michel Eugène Chevreul and England's great physicist Michael Faraday became so concerned over the table-turning hysteria that each independently took time out from his researches to investigate the phenomenon. In a letter to the *Athenaeum* Faraday (1853) wrote:

I have been greatly startled by the revelation which this purely physical subject has made of the condition of the public mind. . . . I think the system of education that could leave the mental condition of the public body in the state in which this subject has found it must have been greatly deficient in some very important principle.

Faraday's approach was characteristic of the scientist. "The proof which I sought for, and the method followed in the inquiry, were precisely of the same nature as those which I should adopt in any other physical investigation." He obtained subjects who were "very honorable" and who were also "successful table-movers." First he made sure that the table turning would occur for these subjects under his laboratory conditions. It did.

Then he carefully experimented with various substances such as sandpaper, millboard, glue, glass, moist clay, tinfoil, cardboard, vulcanized rubber, wood, and others to make sure that they did not interfere with the table turning. They did not. He could detect no trace of electrical or magnetic effects associated with the phenomenon. He further discovered that the movement would take place even if only one subject was seated at the table rather than several. From careful observation he was unable to discover any special force to account for the table's movements. "No form of experiment or mode of observation that I could devise gave me the slightest indication of any peculiar force. No attractions, or repulsions, . . . nor anything which could be referred to other than the mere mechanical pressure exerted inadvertently by the turner." Faraday then set out to analyze the nature of this mechanical force.

His first experiment was ingeniously simple. He took five pieces of smooth, slippery cardboard and put one on top of the other with little pellets of a soft cement between them. The lowermost of these cardboards was attached to a piece of sandpaper whose rough surface was against the table top. The edges of the cardboard sheets overlapped slightly, and on the under surface, a pencil line was drawn over the laps so as to indicate the initial position. The uppermost cardboard was larger than the rest, so that a subject saw only one large piece of cardboard covering the table top. The table turner placed his hands upon the uppermost card and waited for the table to move to the left. The cement between the stack of cards was sufficiently strong to offer considerable resistance to mechanical motion and also to hold cards in any new position that they might assume. Yet, it was weak enough to give way to a continued force.

When at last the tables, cards, and hands all moved to the left together, and so a true result was obtained, I took up the pack. On examination, it was easy to see by displacement of the parts of the line, that the hand had moved farther than the table, and that the latter had lagged behind; —that the hand, in fact, had pushed the upper card to the left and that the under cards and the table had followed and been dragged by it.

Faraday then built a more elaborate apparatus, one that would provide a visual indicator for the subject to comprehend immediately whether the table or he was initiating the movement. Four glass rollers were placed between two flat boards which rested upon the table. A lever arrangement was attached so that if the upper board began moving to the left before the lower one, a vertical reed would lean to the right; if, on the other hand, the table moved first and the subject's hands followed—as the subject claimed—then the lever would lean to the left. When the indicator was not visible to the subject, the table moved to the left as usual showing that this form of the apparatus was no hindrance to the appearance of the phenomenon.

It was soon seen, with the party that could will the motion in either direction (from whom the index was purposely hidden), that the hands were gradually creeping up in the direction before agreed upon, though the party certainly thought they were pressing downwards only. When shown that it was so, they were truly surprised; but when they lifted up their hands and immediately saw the index return to its normal position, they were convinced.

To a person for whom the table is turning, the pendulum is swinging, the horse is responding, or the rod is moving, the most peculiar problem is that these effects are taking place without any awareness of muscular involvement on his part. Indeed, the most characteristic feature of the phenomena we are describing in this chapter is the subject's vehement insistence that he is not the agency through which they are occurring. The rod moves, but the subject has no feedback from his muscles to indicate to him that he is moving the rod. And when the table turns, the subject has no feedback from his hands and muscles to tell him that he is the agency through which the table is put in motion.

It was Faraday who saw the necessity of giving the subjects this necessary feedback. His visual indicator was so placed that any initiation of movement by the subject's hands would immediately be registered before his eyes. When the index was in view of the table turner, the table ceased to turn.

But the most valuable effect of this test-apparatus is the corrective power it possesses over the mind of the table-turner. As soon as the index is placed before the most earnest, and they perceive—as in my presence they have always done—that it tells truly whether they are pressing downwards only or obliquely; then all effects of table-turning cease, even though the parties persevere, earnestly desiring motion, till they become weary and worn out. No prompting or checking of the hands is needed—*the power is gone;* and this only because the parties are made conscious of what they are really doing mechanically, and so are unable unwittingly to deceive themselves.

Faraday notes that most of us do not realize how difficult it is to press directly downward upon a fixed obstacle such as a table, "or even to *know only* whether they are doing so or not." This is especially the case, when, after prolonged pressure, the feedback from the hands is negligible or misleading. These carefully obtained experimental results admit of only one conclusion:

It is with me a clear point that the table moves when the

parties, though they strongly wish it, do not intend, and do not believe that they move it by ordinary mechanical power. They say, the table draws their hands; that it moves first, and they have to follow it,—that sometimes it even moves from under their hands. . . . Though I believe the parties do not intend to move the table, but obtain the result by a *quasi* involuntary action,—still I had no doubt of the influence of expectation upon their minds, and through that upon the success or failure of their efforts.

Faraday, finally, brings his masterly report to a conclusion with this apology: "I must bring this long description to a close. I am a little ashamed of it, for I think, in the present age, and in this part of the world, it ought not to have been required."

THE TALKING TABLE

Faraday's report was not welcomed by the cult of table turners. Perhaps Faraday did prove that the subjects in his experiment moved the table, but this was beside the point. "The table moves of its own accord," the firm believers maintained, "when we sit around it." How did they know this? "Because we know that we don't move it; so it must be moved by another agency." But the table turners were not interested in defending their cause against the skepticism of science. A new possibility had opened up. Instead of the table merely turning, people were discovering something more astounding, that it actually could talk. In the very year that Faraday published his letter, table turning had given way to the talking table.

A typical talking-table seance might appear something like this: A small group of people would sit around a table; ideally this would be a three-legged table, but any table would do. Each person rested his or her finger tips upon the table top. A prayer or incantation might be recited, followed by a delay in which each person is filled with anxious expectancy. After a while, one of the sitters would ask: "Are you there, good spirit?" And suddenly the table would sway once, and then twice, and each swaying motion would be accompanied by a clearly audible rap. The two raps indicated in the jargon of table communication, "Yes." Each sitter, in turn, would ask a question of the table. And the table would tap out in code an appropriate answer.

Three books quickly appeared in England by clergymen who were concerned about the satanic influence behind the table's antics. Rev. N. S. Godfrey "proved" that the devil was behind the table's movements by personally interviewing a table:

I spoke up to the table, and said, "If you move by electricity, stop." It stopped instantly! I commanded it to go on again, and said, while it was moving, "If an evil spirit causes you to move, stop." It moved round without stopping! I again said, "If there be any evil agency in this, stop." It went on as before. I was now prepared with an experiment of far more solemn character. I whispered to the schoolmaster to bring a small Bible, and to lay it on the table when I should tell him. I then caused the table to revolve rapidly, and gave the signal. *The Bible was gently laid on the table, and it instantly stopped* [quoted in Carpenter, 1874, pp. 298–99].

Because of the way the table responded to these "test" questions, Godfrey concluded that the devil himself was the agency. He was confirmed in this finding by the results of similar experiments conducted by Revs. E. Gillson, M.A., and R. W. Dibdin, M.A.

The next innovation was to use the table in conjunction with an alphabet card. The medium would sit at a table facing a subject. The subject would move a pointer across the semicircular arrangement of letters. Only the subject's head and shoulders were visible to the medium; the pointer and the alphabet board were hidden from view. Messages would be spelled out, laboriously and slowly, by the simple expedient of the table's rapping as the pointer landed on certain letters. Several skeptics quickly realized that the medium got her cues from the facial expressions of the subjects. A Mr. G. H. Lewes (Carpenter, 1874) noticed that he could get the famous medium Mrs. Hayden to rap the table whenever he hesitated slightly at certain letters. After having her give several absurd answers to questions, he finally asked the table: "Is Mrs. Hayden an imposter?" More intent on picking up facial cues, Mrs. Hayden unwittingly allowed her table to spell out *Y-E-S!*

OUIJA AND THE REST OF THE FAMILY

We can go on endlessly with accounts of movements and cults arising from the simple truth that "when we think, we move." In 1855 a professor of chemistry at the University of Pennsylvania decided to investigate the spiritualistic movement. He built a special table with a dial attached to it. When the medium rested her hands upon the table top, a pointer would indicate various letters of the alphabet. When these letters spelled out a message for Professor Hare, he became an ardent supporter of the cause. He braved the ridicule of his colleagues to propagate the truth that emanated from his Ouija table (Jastrow, 1935).

The modern Ouija board became a fad in the United States as the result of the experience of a St. Louis matron (see Fig. 23). In 1913, Mrs. Curran was playing with her Ouija board when it suddenly spelled: "Many months ago I lived. Again I come—Patience Worth, my name." Further messages revealed that Patience Worth was a British lass who had lived in the seventeenth century. Through the medium of Mrs. Curran's Ouija board, Patience had come back to haunt the twentieth century with her poetry and literature. Several books and novels were published under the name of Patience Worth just prior to the First World War.

The Ouija board is not the most efficient way to compose novels. And Mrs. Curran quickly abandoned this approach for the more efficient technique of automatic writing. An early form of automatic writing involved the planchette, a little three-legged table. The medium would place her hands on this little table and it would move and point to letters on a board. Someone replaced the pointer with a pencil, and now the movements of the table were converted directly into writing. Soon it was discovered that if one just held a pencil and concentrated on something other than the pencil, it would begin to write—as if controlled by another mind or intelligence. It was in this latter manner that Patience Worth, through the medium of Mrs. Curran's good right hand, dashed off the majority of her books and poems.

The story of Patience Worth is but one of many in which involuntary movements have been translated into proofs and demonstrations of spirit manifestations and reincarnation by people who have strong will to believe. But to the psychologist, the talking horses, the Ouija boards, the mind readers, the pendulum gyrations, and the divining rod are but illustrations of one phenomenon. And to this phenomenon he gives the name "ideomotor action."

In a sense we have already given a definition of what we mean by ideomotor action. We have pointed out several examples of involuntary motor behavior and have said, in effect, that ideomotor action is what all these examples have in common. Such a definition will probably not satisfy many readers. They will justly ask,

"How do you know other than by analogy, that these illustrations really have a common denominator?" This is a reasonable question. And to answer it, we will have to look more closely at the behavior of the rod and also bring to our aid laboratory experiments on suggestibility and hypnosis. This will be our task in the next chapter.

CHAPTER 6

Why Does the Rod Move?

Not only does the divining rod move in the hands of the gifted diviner, but it turns with such force that the bark frequently comes off in his hands. The subjective feeling, according to diviners' own accounts, is that the rod is being pulled by an external force against the restraining grip of the diviner. The diviner typically will assert that he was trying to prevent the rod from moving at the moment of its action.

The experience of having the rod turn in one's hands, seemingly of its own volition, has a powerful and often irreversible impact upon the rod-wielder. Such an experience has converted many skeptics into firm advocates of the position that some unknown force or agency moves the rod. Certainly, they maintain, the diviner does not move the rod. The conviction that he does not activate the rod is, in most cases, sufficient to make a person a firm believer in the efficacy of water witching. Rarely in the history of water witching has a diviner recuperated from this initial experience to the extent of making a more rational inquiry into the rod's antics. The following account illustrates what happened when one diviner took a second look at the rod's behavior:

Having duly provided himself with a hazel-fork, he set out upon a survey of the neighborhood in which he hap-

pened to be staying on a visit; this district was one known
to be traversed by Mineral Veins, with the direction of some
of which he was acquainted. With his "divining rod" in his
hand, and with his attention closely fixed upon his instrument of research, he walked forth upon his experimental
tour; and it was not long before, to his great satisfaction, he
observed the point of the fork to be in motion, at the very
spot where he knew that he was crossing a metallic lode.
For many less cautious investigators, this would have been
enough; but it served only to satisfy this gentleman that he
was a favourable subject for the trial, and to stimulate him
to further inquiry. Proceeding in his walk, and still holding
his fork *secundum artem,* he frequently noticed its point in
motion, and made a record of the localities in which this
occurred. He repeated these trials on several consecutive
days, until he had pretty thoroughly examined the neighborhood, going over some parts of it several times. When he
came to compare and analyze the results, he found that
there was by no means a satisfactory accordance amongst
them; for there were many spots over which the rod had
moved on one occasion, at which it had been obstinately
stationary on others, and *vice versa;* so that the constancy of
physical agency seemed altogether wanting. Further, he
found that whilst some of the spots over which the rod had
moved, were those *known* to be traversed by Mineral Veins,
there were many others in which its indications had been
no less positive, but in which those familiar with the Mining
Geology of the neighborhood were well assured that no
veins existed. On the other hand, the rod had remained
motionless at many points where it *ought* to have moved,
if its direction had been affected by any kind of terrestrial
emanation.—These facts led the experimenter to a strong
suspicion that the cause existed in *himself* alone; and by
carrying out his experiments still further, he ascertained
that he could not hold the fork in his hand for many minutes
consecutively, concentrating his attention fixedly upon it,
without an alteration in the direction of its point, in consequence of an involuntary though almost imperceptible move-

ment of his hands; so that in the greater number of instances in which the rod exhibited motion, the phenomenon was clearly attributable to this cause; and it was a matter of pure accident whether the movement took place over a Mineral Vein, or over a blank spot. But further, he ascertained on a comparison of his results, that the movement took place more frequently where he knew or suspected the existence of mineral veins, than in other situations; and thus he came, without any knowledge of the theory of *expectant attention,* to the practical conclusion that the motions of the Rod were produced by his own Muscles, and that their actions were in great degree regulated automatically by the Ideas which possessed his mind [Carpenter, 1874, pp. 290–91].

Such an experiment does not completely solve the mystery. It still leaves the question of why the rod moves unanswered. But, as a result of the experiment, the question has a different focus; we no longer look to the supernatural or to the known and unknown physical forces for our answer. Instead, we look for our answer in the realms of physiology and psychology. In the more than four hundred years of divining's recorded history, it is surprising how seldom we encounter such a straightforward attempt to investigate the nature of the rod's movements. For the most part, the controversies about the rod were more concerned with whether it was reacting to a physical or other kind of force; rarely did interest focus upon an explanation of what caused the rod's movements if they were not attributable to the presence of underground veins or water.

Agricola argued that since the rod would not work for everyone, and since it reacted by revolving rather than being pulled toward a vein as it should if it were attracted, the motion of the divining rod must depend upon manipulation by the operator. It was a Jesuit,

Father Kircher, who first attempted to verify this assertion experimentally (1645). His experiment seems almost ridiculously simple today, but in 1641 it was a
big advance toward making sense out of the divining
mystery. Kircher balanced a divining rod so that it was
suspended horizontally on a vertical support. He found
that when so suspended no movement of the rod ever
took place, even when it was supposed to take place.
Obviously a human hand was necessary to make the
rod move. Kircher is credited with being the first man
to attribute the rod's movements to unconscious muscular movements (Barrett and Besterman, 1926).

While it is rare to find anyone, believer or skeptic,
who still seriously maintains that there is a direct attraction between the rod and underground water, there are
those who hold out for a direct physical cause. As late
as 1931, we find the famous French exponent of water
witching, Henri Mager (1931) stoutly defending the
view that the rod's action is purely physical. He cites
what he claims to be experimental evidence that the
rod's movements are governed by the laws of electro-
dynamics rather than by unconscious muscular action.
Even such stalwart defenders of the divining rod as
Barrett and Besterman, however, find it difficult to take
Mager seriously.

In the same tradition, Henry de France (1948) up-
holds Mager's thesis but admits the possibility of auto-
suggestion as a factor in the movement of the pendulum
and the rod. De France details the necessary "adjustments" and the "non-conductors" needed to guarantee
that the rod's movements are due only to the influence
of an external object. Not only will the rod and pendulum react directly to water and minerals but, according
to De France, it will react to quality and amount of
food substances (alimentary radiesthesia), to diseases

(medical radiesthesia), to "injurious rays," etc. Although Mager and De France stoutly maintain that the rod is reacting to physical emanations, they both believe in what they call "teleradiesthesia"—the ability to do water witching from a map. This extrasensory aspect of divining, which they admit is rarer than the physical aspect, holds great promise for the future, according to De France. "We may well ask whether we are not dealing with one of the most extraordinary discoveries of all time—on a par with the atomic bomb!"

In another class are the experiments of such physical scientists as Maby and Franklin (1939) and Solco W. Tromp (1949). These invesigators attempt to make a plausible case for water witching in terms of a physical theory that is compatible with orthodox science. Tromp's book is an amazing document. It attempts to review almost every experiment that involves the action of external electromagnetic fields upon cellular processes, nerve conduction, and motor behavior of living organisms. All this is done to show that the presence of other organisms or fields can set up unconscious impulses and physicochemical changes in a living being. This alone, argues Tromp, is sufficient to make out an a priori case for water witching.

Of more relevance to us, however, is a sequence of experiments by Tromp attempting to establish that a subject can respond to changes in electromagnetic fields. Though they lack many additional controls to make them conclusive, Tromp's demonstrations that the subject can react to dowsing zones are quite impressive. But if we were to accept them, Tromp's claims would spell doom for dowsing as it is practiced in this country and almost everywhere else. For Tromp lists a staggering number of phenomena, such as varying contact with the rod, the nature of the rod, periodic variations of the

earth-magnetic field, varying sun radiation, local vege-
tation, movement of the body, presence of other living
organisms, varying sensitivity of the central nervous
system, etc., that can produce a typical dowsing reaction. If Tromp is correct, the divining rod is so sensitive
to almost any environmental influence that it is a wonder the diviner ever is successful, even by chance alone.

Tromp is aware of such an argument; if the rod is so
sensitive, it is worthless. However, he feels that with
necessary precautions this need not be so. For a dowsing
survey to be valid, he advises, several trials have to be
made, the best available geological measuring devices
need to be available, and an expert survey must be
made by trained geologists. The survey should be repeated on different days. The end result of these precautions and instructions is a map such as would be
prepared by an expert geologist, and this map would
demand an expert geologist for proper interpretation.

We have never known such time-consuming, metic-
ulous precautions to be approximated even by the most
cautious diviner. Indeed, if diviners worked according
to Tromp's prescription, they would eliminate their
strongest appeal—the extreme simplicity of their method. Not only does the Tromp method require expert
geological advice, instead of replacing it, but the end
result is a contour map which leaves the well-driller to
decide the exact spot. It is because the diviner can walk
around for a matter of hours or even minutes and then
say, "Dig *here*," that, we believe, he appeals to his rural
clients. Without such uncomplicated straightforward-
ness, we would expect water witching to die a quick
death. In any case, we do not find that Tromp's experiments provide sufficient evidence to deny the thesis
that the rod moves because the diviner makes it move.

Most sophisticated defenders of water witching are

willing to concede that the rod moves because of almost imperceptible, unconscious motor activity on the diviner's part. The argument is that the rod's movements serve merely to amplify a "dowsing reaction." Maby and Franklin (1939) and Tromp (1949) view the ultimate cause as physical forces such as rays or fields that act directly upon the muscles of the forearm to produce the "dowsing reflex," and this muscular reflex, in turn, manifests itself in the rod's movement.

Barrett and Besterman (1926), on the other hand, with equal conviction try to demonstrate why all such physical theories as those of Tromp and of Maby and Franklin must be wrong. The explanation of the phenomenon they give is that the "dowser . . . is a person endowed with a subconscious supernormal cognitive faculty, which, its nature being unknown, we call, after Professor Richet, cryptesthesia. By means of this cryptesthesia, knowledge of whatever object is searched for enters the dowser's subconscious and is revealed by means of an unconscious muscular reaction."

We agree in part with the explanation of Barrett and Besterman. We agree that the ultimate cause is psychological rather than physical. We also agree that the unconscious muscular reaction results from a suggestion from the subconsciousness of the diviner. And we agree that this suggestion is based on cues and information stored in this subconscious. But we disagree about how the subconscious gets its information. We see no need, on the available evidence, to assume that there is any supernormal faculty by which the subconscious gets its cues.

The assertion that the rod's behavior can be understood as the resultant of suggestion and unconscious muscular activity needs further amplification. This will take us into a brief discussion of the concept of ideomotor action (the notion that ideas manifest themselves in muscular contractions) and the principle of suggestion. But before we describe how these notions can account for the rod's behavior, we should briefly describe the immediate cause of the movement—the mechanical force applied to the rod by the diviner's grip.

THE MECHANICS OF THE DIVINING ROD

The exact mechanics of the movement depends upon the kind of divining instrument that is used—the pendulum, the straight rod, the forked twig. It also depends upon the kind of grip that is used. Because the forked twig, held in the standard palms-up grip, is the overwhelming preference of American diviners, we will detail only the mechanics of that method. If you grasp the forked twig in the standard grip—palms upward, rod pointing forward at an angle of 45 degrees, hands compressed together (see Figs. 11 and 13)—you will cause the rod to move by any of four slight changes of grip. The movement occurs, in each case, when forces and stresses in the rod become greater than the force by which the diviner grips the rod (see Fig. 20). Typically the diviner holds the rod under considerable compression, i.e., he pushes the two forks toward one another to create the tautness in the rod. In this case, if he just eases his grip slightly, the rod will move. It moves because the tension in the rod is now greater than the force of the grip. A second way to move the rod is to rotate your wrists slightly toward each other. Even a slight imperceptible rotation is sufficient to give quite a kick to the rod's rotation (if you rotate your wrists outward, the rod will tend to rotate upward). The remaining two ways to produce the rod's movements are to pull the hands slightly apart or to push them slightly together. Either of these movements creates greater tension in the rod than in the force of the grip. When the balance is so upset, the rod acts like a coiled spring and may straighten out with such force that the bark may literally come off in the hands of the diviner.

Each of these movements, or a combination of them, are almost always made imperceptibly and unconsciously. The subjective impression is always that the stick twists in opposition to your grasp. In a sense, this is true. The tighter your grasp, the less chance the rod will have to move. But, as is inevitable, a slight relaxation or strengthening of the force of your grip will send the rod flying against your grip. In every case, the movement is always the resultant of mechanical forces applied or removed by muscular action of the diviner.

The late Kenneth Roberts vigorously and frequently rejected explanations such as the foregoing mechanical analysis to account for the rod's movements. "What makes the rod work? We don't know. For three hundred years, opinionated but ill-informed scientists have insisted that it works because of unconscious muscular action on the part of the dowser. That isn't so, and we have proved that it isn't" (Roberts, 1957, p. 59). The major proof is provided by what happens when Henry Gross holds two forked twigs simultaneously over flowing water. The upper twig is tilted slightly backward, and the under one is tilted slightly forward. In this position, the upper rod rotates upward while the lower rod rotates downward—in directions opposite to each other. "If this is muscular action, his muscles are moving in opposite directions at the same time. This can't happen any more than a person can run forward and backward at the same time."

But it is the rods and not Henry's muscles that are moving in opposite directions. Whether the rod rotates forward or backward is a matter of balance (with some diviners it goes in either direction). From our previous mechanical analysis, we would expect Henry's rods to behave just as Roberts says they do merely from a change in the balance of forces between Henry's grip and the tension in the two rods. As we demonstrate in Figure 21, one merely has to turn his wrists slightly inward, while holding the two rods as does Henry Gross, to cause them to rotate in opposite directions.

THE PSYCHOPHYSICS OF THE DIVINING ROD

The actual change in the compression and force of the grip involves physiological and psychological considerations. The mechanism we propose is ideomotor action, and its trigger is a suggestion. In applying these concepts to water witching, we should keep these aspects of the divining situation in mind:

1. The diviner learns his trade through diffusion or *imitation*. In every case where we have data about how a diviner discovered his talent, he first saw someone else using the divining rod. Quite frequently, after this *visual experience*, he was given a *verbal suggestion* from the diviner in the form of assurance that the rod would work for him also. ("Here, son, you try it. It'll work for you. See if it won't.")

2. The witching process involves *intense concentration* and the focusing of attention upon the task at hand. The eyes are typically riveted upon the point of the rod.

3. During this process the diviner is usually described as being in a *trancelike state* and oblivious of all distracting stimuli. Often the witching of the well is accompanied by physical exhaustion.

4. The muscles and the body of the diviner are under considerable *tension*. The rod is compressed with great force and this compression is maintained over a considerable period of time.

5. Not only is the witching activity physically exhausting, but it is frequently described in terms of an *intense emotional experience.*

6. In this state the diviner is *receptive to cues* of which he is not consciously aware. We have already mentioned Foster's experiment in which the diviner unconsciously used involuntary cues from the observers. Lovibond (1952) reports an experiment in which each of two diviners was allowed to designate a good spot for sinking a well. Each was then blindfolded and presumably brought back to a known starting point. But by varying the starting point, the experimenter was able to predict just where the diviner would end up. And this end point had nothing to do with underground water but only with where the diviner thought he was in relation to his original starting point. These and other experiments demonstrate that the diviner will unconsciously seize upon whatever cues are available when he is searching for underground water.

7. The divining ability improves with *practice.* In many first attempts to wield a rod, no movement takes place, but a "tingling sensation" is felt when the neophyte water witch passes over the site where the water is alleged to be. But with increasing experience, the tingling becomes transformed into an overt movement.

8. The diviner has no feedback from his arms to tell him that his muscles are initiating the action; he is *unaware* of any involvement on the part of his muscles until after the rod has begun its move, and he feels that his hands are trying to prevent the action.

9. Not only is the diviner unaware of any muscular involvement on his part but he seems to have a *defensive need* to assert (even when no one questions him) his innocence in regard to the rod's behavior.

These are the features we want to recall when we

identify the rod's behavior as another example of ideo-motor action.

THE CONCEPT OF IDEOMOTOR ACTION

According to William James, it was William B. Carpenter who first used the term "ideo-motor action." Carpenter (1852) used the term to tie together manifestations of behavior that were independent of conscious volition. Carpenter classified all behavior into two large classes, volitional movement and automatic, or reflex, movements. Stimuli could lead directly to a reflex by way of the spinal column such as in the classic knee-jerk. The same stimuli could also give rise to "sensations"; these in turn produced "ideas" which then developed into "emotions" which stimulated the "intellectual process," and by way of the "will" a volitional act would result. However, Carpenter observed, "*Ideas* may become the sources of muscular movement, independently either of volitions or of emotions." This is especially true when the ideas are suggested to the subject or are the result of expectant attention such as is the case in hypnosis, table turning, and water witching.

Voluntary movements are the result of a deliberate act. Thus, a person might pick up a divining rod, hold it in the classic grip, and deliberately turn his wrists to make the rod spring downward. Another person might also hold the rod in the classic grip but make no voluntary effort to move it. The idea that the rod will move, however, has already been suggested to him; he does not will the rod to move, but he is possessed with the expectation that the rod will move. In these circumstances, Carpenter believed that the *idea* was sufficient to produce the necessary motor behavior to activate the rod. "Here the movements express the ideas that may possess the mind at the time. . . . Thus, the *ideo-motor* principle of action finds its appropriate place in the physiological scale, which would, indeed, be incomplete without it."

Carpenter elaborated this principle in greater detail in his later writing (1874). The notion of ideomotor action was necessary to explain behavior not covered by voluntary action. "We may range under the same category all those actions performed by us in *our ordinary course of life,* which are rather the automatic expressions of the ideas that may be dominant in our minds at the same time, than prompted by distinct volitional efforts." Our use of language is one illustration of the ideomotor principle. In writing or speaking, we are so intent upon the choice of the correct word or expression that we are completely unconscious of the movements by which we produce the writing or sound. This is made clear most frequently when we misspell or mispronounce a word by anticipating a syllable or word that will come later. Many other habits, such as tying our shoes, brushing our teeth, getting dressed or undressed, illustrate the ideomotor principle.

William James continued Carpenter's interpretation of the concept of ideomotor action and, in addition, made it the basic process in volitional behavior. "Wherever a movement *unhesitatingly and immediately* follows upon the idea of it, we have ideomotor action. We are then aware of nothing between the conception and the execution. All sorts of neuro-muscular processes come between, of course, but we know absolutely nothing of them. We think the act, and it is done; and that is all that introspection tells us of the matter" (1948, p. 423). James viewed the ideomotor principle not as a curiosity but as "simply the normal process stripped of disguise."

Examples of ideomotor action in our daily activities are plentiful.

Whilst talking I become conscious of a pin on the floor, or of some dust on my sleeve. Without interrupting the conversation I brush away the dust or pick up the pin. I make no express resolve, but the mere perception of the object and the fleeting notion of the act seem of themselves to bring the latter about. Similarly, I sit at table after dinner and find myself from time to time taking nuts or raisins out of the dish and eating them. My dinner properly is over, and in the heat of the conversation I am hardly aware of what I do; but the perception of the fruit, and the fleeting notion that I may eat it, seem fatally to bring the act about [James, 1948, p. 423].

James carefully notes that the ideomotor principle acts only when no opposing or inhibiting ideas are simultaneously present in the mind. "In all this the determining condition of the unhesitating and resistless sequence of the act seems to be *the absence of any conflicting notion in the mind.*" It is because we have so many ideas that do not result in action that the doctrine of ideomotor action, according to James, "is not a self-evident truth. . . . But it will be seen that in every such case, without exception, that it is because other ideas simultaneously present rob them of their impulsive power." Thus, the natural course of every idea, if we are to believe James, is to manifest itself in overt action. Only when conflicting ideas are also present will the idea not result in action. But even in these cases, the movement is not entirely thwarted; "It will *incipiently* take place." James quotes the nineteenth-century psychologist Lotze to illustrate this point:

The spectator accompanies the throwing of a billiard-ball or the thrust of the swordsman, with slight movements of his arm; the untaught narrator tells his story with many gesticulations; the reader while absorbed in the perusal of a battle-scene feels a slight tension run through his muscular system, keeping time as it were with the actions he is reading of. These results become the more marked the more we are absorbed in thinking of movements which suggest them; they grow fainter exactly in proportion as a complex consciousness, under the dominion of a crowd of other representations, withstands the passing over of mental contemplation into outward action [James, 1948, p. 425].

From such considerations, James concluded: "We may then lay it down for certain that *every representation of a movement awakens in some degree the actual movement which is its object; and awakens it in a maximum degree whenever it is not kept from so doing by an antagonistic representation present simultaneously to the mind*" (p. 426).

Although James made his famous pronouncement back in 1890, it was not until the 1930's that physiologists and psychologists developed recording instruments sensitive enough to detect implicit responses. By that time a controversy was raging about whether all thinking involved implicit muscle reactions (that is, muscular action that was too slight to result in perceptible behavior). John B. Watson touched off the debate with his assertion that all thinking depended upon muscle responses too small to be seen by the naked eye but sufficiently strong to send back impulses into the nervous system (Watson, 1924). More specifically, Watson maintained that thinking was merely subvocal speech. At the very least, before such a theory could be tenable, the existence of such implicit responses had to be demonstrated. The classic experiments were carried out by Jacobson (1932, 1938), who was able to employ electrophysiological techniques to record minute muscular responses.

Jacobson trained his subjects to relax while lying in a darkened room. Electrodes were attached to various parts of the body to record and amplify minute muscular responses. The subject was told, for example, to think of bending his right arm. Action currents from the muscles of his right arm would increase under these conditions. When the subject was told to relax, these action currents died out, indicating that the implicit muscular response was no longer taking place. On control tests, the subject was told to think of bending his left arm or foot or to think of extending his left arm. Under the latter conditions, the action currents did not occur in the muscles of the right arm. When the subject was asked to think of striking two blows with a hammer, two separate bursts of activity were recorded in the action potentials of the arm muscles. When the subject thought of looking up at the Eiffel Tower, activity in the neck muscles could be detected. In a similar manner, action potentials from the lips, tongue, and throat were recorded during most of the subject's thinking. Records of implicit muscular activity in the appropriate muscles were obtained when the subject thought of such activities as throwing a ball, turning an ice-cream freezer, climbing a rope, and the like.

These experiments showed that implicit movements of the speech apparatus and of other appropriate parts of the body accompany thinking. However, Watson's critics pointed out what they thought was a serious deficiency in his thesis that thinking was nothing but subvocal speech; they asked how is it that non-speaking deaf persons could think? Max (1937) therefore extended the electrophysiological recording technique to nineteen deaf persons who "talked" with their hands. Electrodes were placed on their hands during sleep, and the action currents were carefully watched. These currents decreased when the subject went to sleep, but occasionally bursts of activity would come onto the record. When such bursts occurred, the experimenters awakened the subjects and in thirty out of thirty-three instances discovered that the subject had just been dreaming. As a control they were awakened sixty-two times during periods of no action current activity, and in fifty-three of these instances no dreams were reported. When these subjects were compared to normal subjects while they were doing mental arithmetic, 84 per cent of the deaf subjects and 31 per cent of the normal subjects showed action currents in the hand.

Since these experiments, many more have been done with much better recording apparatus. They more than support the thesis that implicit muscular responses accompany thinking. (They do not prove, of course, that *all* thinking is necessarily accompanied by such muscular activity.) A subject merely has to watch another person throw a ball, clench his fist, or otherwise use his right arm, and although this spectator is completely unaware of any activity on his part, the sensitive recording apparatus reveals that the subject is following the perceived behavior with implicit muscular activity in his own arm muscles.

A very important feature of many of these implicit muscular responses is the subject's lack of awareness that they are going on. Even when the subject's attention is drawn to them, he does not experience the kinesthetic feedback that ordinarily tells him when he is moving a part of his body. You will recall that it was only when Faraday provided his subjects with visual feedback of the action of their muscles in moving the table that they became convinced that they were the agency through which the table turned. When he provided this feedback, the phenomenon disappeared. In a similar fashion, Carpenter views the water witching situation as one in which the prolonged tension of the arm muscles reduces muscular feedback to almost nothing. Under such circumstances the diviner has no sensory awareness of the action of his muscles in moving the rod. This same lack of feedback prevented Pfungst and other investigators from detecting the implicit cues they were providing for Clever Hans. Only by prolonged and careful observation of *other* subjects did Pfungst discover the muscular movements that he himself was using unconsciously to cue the wonder horse. This lack of feedback occurs in many areas. In baseball, for example, a pitcher can unwittingly tip off opposing batters as to the kind of pitch he is going to throw. Babe Ruth almost had his early pitching career ruined because opposing batters always seemed to know when he was going to throw a curve. Despite the most careful study of himself, he could not discover the clues by which he gave his intention away. The feedback that he needed came about, according to one story, when a fan held a mirror in front of Ruth as he went through the motions of throwing a curve ball. In a flash, Ruth saw what was wrong; whenever he was about to throw a curve, he stuck his tongue out.

IDEOMOTOR ACTION AND SUGGESTIBILITY

Today the evidence is pretty clear that "the idea of a movement is frequently, if not always, followed or accompanied by an incipient movement employing the same muscle groups that are involved in the imagined movement" (Eysenck, 1947). Carpenter tied his concept in with the principle of suggestion by noting that the idea is often implanted by means of a suggestion to the subject. Other investigators have continued this line of thinking, and recently Arnold (1946) and Eysenck and Furneaux (1945) have independently provided evidence that ideomotor action is the basic mechanism underlying the phenomenon of hypnosis.

According to Eysenck (1947) the idea that leads to the ideomotor action and from there to overt movement can be suggested or implanted in various ways. The movement can be directly suggested to the subject by the experimenter; the subject can suggest it to himself either vocally or subvocally; the subject can imagine the movement; he can watch the movement in another person; or he can overhear a discussion of it. In one experiment (Eysenck and Furneaux, 1945) the subjects were given the body-sway test. In this test, the subject stands upright with his hands at his sides and is given the suggestion that he is falling forward. The experimenters found that if the subject gave the suggestion to himself, it proved as effective as having the experimenter make the suggestion. Other experiments have demonstrated that subjects will sway forward by merely imagining that they are falling forward or by seeing another subject fall forward.

Weitzenhoffer (1953) has attempted the most detailed physiological explanation of how the mechanism of ideomotor action operates, especially as the basic principle of hypnotic behavior. Weitzenhoffer begins with the evidence for the existence of ideomotor action and then shows that the basic aspect of hypnosis—homoaction—can be explained in terms of existing physiological knowledge of neuromuscular processes. Homoaction is the process whereby the response to a suggestion alters subsequent responses to that suggestion. Thus, when an experimenter tells a subject, "You are falling forward," the subject's initial response might be an imperceptible tendency to fall forward. This imperceptible response, however, facilitates the subject's next response to the same suggestion. With each repeated suggestion, the responses becomes stronger and stronger until the subject falls forward.

Weitzenhoffer points out that we can account for homoaction by considering ideomotor action in conjunction with the known cumulative changes in nervous and muscular tissues in the presence of a stimulus—these changes gradually accumulating until they manifest themselves in the form of overt muscular contraction. This building-up of small contractions into large sustained contractions, which is known as "neuromotor enhancement," is the basis not only of ideomotor action but, indeed, of all normal muscular action.

Normally, muscular responses associated with thinking can be expected to be minute and not to give rise to overt motion. If, however, it is true that thoughts of muscular action, not specifically directed at producing actual muscular movements, nevertheless do cause the same tissue changes in the muscles concerned as are initiated by voluntary action, then we are led to infer that, under favorable conditions, *the minute responses initiated by thoughts can be built up to relatively huge proportions through neuromotor enhancement* [p. 247].

Weitzenhoffer then goes on to argue that this analysis ties in with the kind of suggestibility that is now believed to underlie hypnotic phenomena, table turning, Ouija boards, pendulum movements, and water witching:

Briefly we may suppose that the initial statement of the suggestion implants or, better, evokes, certain specific thoughts in the subject's mind. Concurrently, small changes occur in appropriate muscle fibers. These changes may be no more than the formation of a local state of excitation, or may consist in an actual propagated state of excitation. Again, a single muscle fiber may be involved, or many. In any event the ground for a contraction has been laid. With subsequent repetitions, the local state of excitation, if one has been produced, builds up until a critical value is reached, whereupon a wave of contraction appears. . . . At first a single nerve impulse, a very small train, or more probably a small volley is initiated. With repetition and/or with increase in intensity of thoughts, the volley grows, and trains either appear or increase (within limits) if already present. In addition, the frequency of impulse also rises. All this leads to greater complexity and magnitude of the induced muscular effects [pp. 247–48].

THE EVIDENCE FOR SUGGESTIBILITY

In this brief sketch of the concept of ideomotor action we have attempted to indicate how the phenomenon of the rod's movement is plausible to us in terms of what we know of how ideas get implanted (suggestion) and how they result in microscopic muscular contractions which may, through enhancement, build up to an overt muscular contraction. The emphasis on ideomotor action resulted in a discussion of what happens *after* the idea is implanted in the subject's mind. The emphasis on *how* the idea is implanted leads directly to a consideration of the nature of suggestion and suggestibility.

The process of suggestion—and of hypnosis, which has been viewed as a special case of suggestion—has been explained in such various ways as "animal magnetism," "ideomotor action," "dissociation of consciousness," "association of ideas," "redintegration," "conditioning," "reduction of determining tendencies," "identification," and "cognitive restructuring" (Allport, 1954). These varying attempts to explain suggestion result from the use of the term to cover a variety of phenomena: the process that leads a mob to act as one person in a lynching, the appeal of rock-and-roll music and dancing, the effects of advertising, the results of hypnosis, etc.

From time to time, critics have questioned whether the various uses of the term "suggestion" in fact refer to the same thing. They have argued that there are many different kinds of suggestion and that these cannot be grouped under a single concept. In the particular case of water witching, this argument has been rephrased to emphasize the uniqueness of the divining process. Thus Kenneth Roberts (1951, 1953) attributes dowsing to an undefined "seventh sense" and vigorously denies that it is related in any way to the Ouija board, table turning, pendulum swinging, and the other phenomena that we have lumped together under the heading of ideomotor action. We have also run across the belief among a few diviners that the ability to use a divining rod is incompatible with the ability to use the pendulum (although the two instruments are quite frequently used interchangeably by many diviners). How do we go about answering such critics? That is, how do we set about to demonstrate the existence of a unitary trait or dimension or tie that underlies the various phenomena that we have described in this and the preceding chapter?

As a matter of fact, there are many lines of evidence that support the contention that a common principle binds together the variety of behavior that we have classified as ideomotor. Here we will illustrate only one kind of empirical confirmation. The experimental approach in this case is to gather together a variety of tasks, each of which is supposed to illustrate response to suggestion or ideomotor behavior. Next a large group of subjects is tested on all the different tasks. If a common principle is behind all the tasks, then we would expect that a subject who is highly suggestible on one task would be highly suggestible on all of the tasks. If there is no common factor involved in the group of tasks, on the other hand, we would expect the subject's performance on one task to be unrelated to his perform-ance on the others.

An illustration of this approach is provided by the experiment of Eysenck and Furneaux upon sixty pa-tients in an Army mental hospital (1945). On the basis of previous work and experimentation in the area of suggestibility and hypnosis, the authors put together a battery of twelve tests including hypnosis, each of which had previously been used as an index of suggesti-bility. Their object was to administer these tests to their subjects to see if they all were measuring the same thing. The twelve tests and brief descriptions are listed below:

Picture Report Test.—The subject is shown a picture (in this case a church interior) for about thirty seconds. He is then asked fourteen "leading" questions concern-ing details in the picture. Five of the questions refer to details that were not actually contained in the picture. A subject's score on this test is in terms of how many of the suggestions contained in the five questions he ac-cepts. A subject who scored 0 would be rated as low on suggestibility; one who scored 5 would be high.

Ink-Blot Test.—The subject is shown a card with an ink blot of undefined shape. The subject is then told that most people thought it looked like a ———. (Here two responses that are typically given by most subjects were suggested; in addition, four inapplicable responses were also suggested.) He is asked to decide whether each of the six responses is appropriate. The subject's score is in terms of how many of the four inappropriate responses he accepts.

Chevreul Pendulum Test.—We have already en-countered the pendulum and have discussed Chevreul's famous experiments with that instrument. In the test for suggestibility the subject is shown a weight suspended from a thread. He is told that if he holds the pendulum over a ruler and stares at it fixedly, he will quickly notice that the bob will start to swing along the ruler, even though he himself remains quite passive and is careful not to move it deliberately. After demonstrating how the pendulum is expected to move, the experimenter hands it to the subject, instructing him to hold it steady and gaze fixedly at the bob. "Continuous strong suggestion was then given to the effect that the bob was beginning to swing, that the swing was increasing, etc." The extent of the swing in inches is taken as the subject's score.

Odor Suggestion Test.—The subject is told that his sense of smell is to be tested. He is confronted with six bottles separately labeled as follows: pineapple, banana, vanilla, rose, jasmine, and coffee. The cork is taken off each bottle in turn, and the bottle is slowly brought closer to the subject's nose from a distance. The subject's task is to report to the experimenter as soon as he can detect the smell. The bottle is held at a distance of two feet and brought slowly closer until the subject reports or until the bottle touches his nose. All but the last three bottles contain the specified essence. The last three bottles contain only water. The subject's score ranges from 0 to 3 depending on how many reports he makes of detecting an odor in the three bottles of water.

Progressive Weights: Impersonal.—The subject is confronted with twelve boxes that are identical in size and shape. The first five boxes increase in weight by gradual increments. The next seven are identical in weight to the fifth box. The subject lifts each box in turn and announces whether it is "heavier" or "lighter" than the preceding box. The subject's suggestibility score is based on the number of boxes in the last seven that he calls "heavier" than their predecessors (minus the number of these that he calls "lighter").

Progressive Weights: Personal.—This is the same test as the preceding one but scored differently. Here the score is the number of times the subject reports the box as either heavier or lighter than its predecessor. The reason for this separate scoring is that the personal suggestion from the experimenter to the subject is merely that the weights differ. If the subject also assumes that they continue to increase in weight, this is an impersonal suggestion derived from the order of the first five boxes.

Heat Illusion Test.—A small heating unit is applied to the subject's forehead. The subject then turns the knob that controls the temperature until he can just detect the first sign of heat. The subject then repeats this performance, but this time the switch has been secretly turned off so that there is no heat in the unit. A score of 1 is given to those subjects who report feeling heat when the switch is turned off.

Body-Sway Test.—The subject stands up, relaxed and with his eyes closed. Verbal suggestions are given to him that he is falling forward, and this is continued for two and a half minutes. His score is in terms of how far he sways in inches. A complete fall is given an arbitrary score of twelve inches.

Press Test.—The subject holds a rubber ball in his hand. The ball is connected by rubber tubing to an instrument that records the amount of pressure the subject is exerting upon the ball. The subject is then given suggestions to the effect that he is squeezing the ball harder and harder. His score is the maximum amount of pressure, over his base pressure, that he exerts.

Release Test.—The subject holds the same rubber

ball, but now he is given suggestions to the effect that his hand is relaxing. His score now is in terms of the amount of pressure reduction.

Hypnotic Susceptibility Test.—The experimenters put the subject through the process of being hypnotized. All subjects go through the same standardized procedure. The subject fixates a bright object and with a constant low sound in the background is given verbal suggestions that his eyes are becoming tired, that they are closing, that he is feeling tired and sleepy, that his arm is rigid, that he will feel no pain, etc. These suggestions are given in a fixed sequence starting with "your eyes are getting tired, you are completely relaxed, you feel incapable of activity, your eyelids are heavy. . ." and ending with suggestions concerning complete catalepsy, inability to hear a buzzer, inability to feel pain, etc. The subject is given a certain number of points for each suggestion he accepts; the points are based upon the number of times such suggestions are accepted by a large number of subjects. Suggestions that the eyes are tired, that the body is heavy, that the eyelids are heavy, that the arm cannot be raised, are accepted by a large number of subjects. On the other hand, posthypnotic amnesia and visual illusions such as a light going on are accepted only by a small proportion of the subjects. From a number of different studies it has been estimated that approximately 85 per cent of the subjects will show some degree of hypnotic susceptibility, and as many as 20 per cent of the subjects will achieve the greatest possible depth of hypnotic trance (Weitzenhoffer, 1953). The subjects in this experiment showed a similar distribution on the hypnotic scale.

Posthypnotic Suggestibility Test.—The subject is told, while in the hypnotic trance, that he will be given a repetition of the Body-Sway Test and that his performance will show greater sway. He is given a few other suggestions. After he is awakened from the trance, the experimenters note how many of these posthypnotic suggestions actually work.

When these twelve tests were administered to each of the sixty subjects, the results showed that if each of these tests is a measure of suggestibility, then the term "suggestibility" must refer to more than one kind of phenomenon. A subject who was high in suggestibility on one of the tests was not necessarily high on all the remaining tests. Although the variation on the tests could not be attributed to one single principle, it looked as if there were two or three underlying factors to account for the interrelationships. In other words, although each test did not correlate with every other test, there were clusters of tests that did go together.

In particular, the authors found that a common factor could account for the performance on the Chevreul Pendulum Test, Body-Sway Test, Press Test, Release Test, Hypnotic Susceptibility Test, and the Posthypnotic Suggestibility Test. The experimenters arrived at this conclusion empirically by a technique known as factor analysis. In principle, a new scale was constructed by giving each subject an average score based on his performances on these six separate suggestibility tests. This new measure was given the name "primary suggestibility" to emphasize the fact that there are other kinds of suggestibility. Each of the six separate tests was then found to be highly related to this over-all index of primary suggestibility, whereas the remaining six tests were unrelated to it. From such evidence the experimenters concluded that the kind of suggestibility exhibited by these six tests was different from that involved in the remaining tasks. The manner in which the experimenters determined the degree of relationship among the tests was by classifying each subject as "high" or "low" on each test and then seeing whether a subject who was high on one test tended to be high on another. The results suggested that the Body-Sway Test is the best single index of primary suggestibility in this experiment, since approximately 87 per cent of the subjects who were high in suggestibility as measured by the Body-Sway Test were also high on primary suggestibility. The weakest measure of primary suggestibility is the Press Test, in which slightly more than 62 per cent of those classified as high on suggestibility were also classified as high on primary suggestibility. There was no tendency for the remaining six tests to distinguish between subjects who were high and low on primary suggestibility.

Eysenck points out that the common feature of the suggestibility tests that involve primary suggestibility is that, in contrast to the remaining tests (which involve perception alone), they all are also illustrations of ideomotor action. "The main feature in the tests which go to define this trait is the execution of a motor movement by subject consequent upon the repeated suggestion by the experimenter that such a movement will take place, without conscious participation in the movement on the subject's part" (Eysenck, 1947). Eysenck reviews the various kinds of evidence concerning the nature of primary suggestibility. Contrary to earlier opinion, it does not seem to be closely related to intelligence, for Eysenck's and Furneaux's subjects were selected for normal intelligence (I.Q. 90–110). Neurotic subjects seem to score higher than normals, but psychotics seem to be less suggestible in the ideomotor tasks than do normals. Further, as already indicated, the effects of primary suggestibility can come about by self-suggestion, suggestion by others, imagination, seeing another person doing the task, or hearing it discussed.

For our purposes, the important consequence of evidence such as this is that it makes our unitary classification of the various phenomena described in the preceding and present chapters more than mere analogy. Such experiments show that primary suggestibility and its manifestation in ideomotor action has a firm empirical basis. The kinds of similarities that we saw in water witching, pendulum swinging, table turning, muscle reading, Ouija boards, and the rest result from a common principle. And this is empirically revealed by the tendency of a subject who is suggestible in one of these tasks to be suggestible in all of them. This refinement of the concept of suggestibility and its connection with the concept of ideomotor action now allows us to give a much more plausible account of why the divining rod moves, and this account need only draw upon concepts already familiar to physiology and psychology.

AN EXPLANATION OF THE ROD'S MOVEMENT

We begin with the naïve observer, Jim Brooks. Jim has heard of water witching before, but he has never seen it work. But now he is among a small group of spectators who have assembled to witness a diviner witch a well for Frank Brown. The diviner grasps the forked twig in the standard grip, forearms tense, head and body leaning forward, eyes fixed upon the butt end of the rod, and proceeds to walk carefully about Frank Brown's property.

Jim watches the trancelike absorption of the diviner with interest. From what we know about implicit muscular responses, we can assume that microscopic muscular contractions are taking place in Jim's forearms as he intently follows the behavior of the diviner. Perhaps Jim's neck muscles and general musculature are tense as he leans forward awaiting the outcome of the diviner's quest for water. Already the idea has been implanted, and implicit muscular responses have occurred. Suddenly the divining rod dramatically springs forward and points down. The diviner stops and looks up as if suddenly awakened from a trance.

The diviner notices Jim Brooks's incredulous gaze. He walks up to Jim and hands him the rod, telling him it will also work for him. As a result of this direct suggestion, Jim's forearm muscles again make microscopic contractions as the idea of duplicating the diviner's performance leads to this imperceptible acting-out. This time we might theorize, on the basis of what we know, that the action potentials in the arms are greater than before and that the initial reaction to witnessing the performance has facilitated the response to the direct suggestion.

Jim grasps the rod in the same grip that he saw the diviner use. His arms tense, his eyes fixed upon the rod's point, he becomes oblivious of the surrounding spectators as he concentrates upon the dominant theme of the rod's actions. The increased tension in his arms and body facilitates muscular response. An impulse that might not lead to overt muscular action in a relaxed muscle may be sufficient to trigger off such action in a tense one. This heightened and prolonged tension, furthermore, masks the neural feedback from his arms and hands. The focusing of his attention on the dominant idea further enhances the effectiveness of the expectation that the rod will move.

Now Jim is nearing the site over which the diviner's rod had dipped. The image of the rod's movements becomes much stronger in the face of the expectancy that it will move. The contractions in the forearm spread to adjoining fibers; the minute contractions begin rallying together. Suddenly the minute contractions—in a great wave of unison—produce a larger muscular contraction. With an almost imperceptible spasm the hands suddenly come closer together and the wrists turn slightly inward. This action upsets the delicate balance of forces existing between Jim's grip and the tensions in the rod. The rod suddenly springs forward with such force that the bark peels off and Jim's hands become painfully scratched. Jim suddenly is aware that the rod has dipped—seemingly of its own accord—over the same spot as it had for the diviner. At first he is at a loss for words. Then he is overcome with a desire to explain to the onlookers that he did not make the rod move; indeed, he was conscious only of an attempt to hold back the rod. He points to the peeled bark and his injured hands as proof. Perhaps the onlookers will believe him; perhaps some will scoff. But Jim has now entered the ranks of the water diviners.

Sometimes the initial experience may result only in a "tingling sensation" when the beginner walks over the site where the rod is expected to turn down. But, with continued practice, the rod's movements become more pronounced, and soon the rod will perform to relatively slight suggestions. This practice effect is entirely in accord with what we know of neuromuscular behavior and ideomotor action.

This account may not be entirely correct in its particulars. Nor does it satisfactorily account for such details as individual differences and the vexing issue of awareness. But the account is sufficiently complete to show that the rod's behavior is a problem for psychology and physiology. To resort to supernatural explanations, to look for new physical forces, or to apply labels such as "seventh sense," "radiesthesia," "cryptesthesia," only complicates and unnecessarily confuses the issue.

This is not to say that there are no unknowns in the story of the rod's behavior. There are sufficient unsolved problems to challenge the physiologist and psychologist for many decades to come. But these problems are not peculiar to water witching. They are problems involving the more general questions of human behavior—problems such as how stimuli initiate sensory and motor behavior, the complicated and elusive problem of consciousness and awareness, and the dramatic manifestations that occur in abnormal and emotional behavior.

CHAPTER 7

Who's Who in Witching

"Blast 'em," he'll roar, "we've been dowsers in my family, man and boy, since the first Pinrose packed up his gear in Cornwall, England, and set sail."

I usually let him get it all out of his system. Maybe it is witchcraft, but Pop's going on to sixty-five, and outside of me and a little scrap of garden patch, he hasn't got much in this world to make him feel important. Even when he does bring in a well, the most he gets is a dozen eggs or a sip of something for snake bite.

HARRIET FRANK, JR., 1955

Mr. G. is a tall, spare gentleman with a sincere expression in his blue eyes. He was born in London eighty-four years ago, but he now is a construction engineer in New Jersey. We have sought him out because he is also a well-known water diviner. We want to learn something about his water witching activities.

Our first question is, "How did you become a water diviner?" In reply, Mr. G. tells us that no one in his family had ever divined. And none of his children do. In fact, his children think it is "a lot of baloney." Mr. G. discovered his talent when he was twenty years old and working for a Montana firm on the west coast of Vancouver Island. While visiting a farmer he witnessed a diviner in action. Mr. G. tried it and, since then, "I never had a failure. I found water all over the West Coast."

"I never charged a cent for finding water," Mr. G. continues. "Water is one essential you must have and I didn't think it was fair to charge poor people. Only money I ever took was when someone would bet me— and I'd take 'em up."

Although Mr. G. is aware that people laugh at his practice, he is not belligerent. "There's no trickery to it," he calmly explains. "You hold my hands, and you'll see I don't move it."

He uses the standard forked twig from an apple, hazel, or maple tree. He sometimes uses a rod fashioned from a copper wire. He holds the rod in the standard palms-up grip in such a way that the rod is under great tension. When he approaches water, "it works and wavers, works and wavers over water." He adds, "Sometimes I can't hold it, and the bark comes off in my hands." He uses his intuition to estimate depth, but he readily admits that he cannot always tell the depth if the land is rocky.

How does he explain water witching? "I can't explain why," he concedes. "It's nothing in the body—no physical sensations—it's just the stick. I don't know why there is an affinity between me and water. I never tried the twig with minerals. I don't know how that would work."

When asked about witching over maps, Mr. G. is quite emphatic. "I don't believe in that. I think it's baloney. You need contact with the body, elbows, and hands."

Mr. G. is but one of a surprisingly large number of active water diviners in this country. Because our survey of divining drew information from counties chosen at random from all the counties with agricultural agents, we can assume that these counties are representative of the total population. On the basis of the number of diviners reported in the sample, then, we can estimate the total number of diviners in the United States as about twenty-five thousand. (Our procedures are explained in detail in Hyman and Cohen, 1957.) If the county agents had been consistent in either underreporting or overreporting the number of diviners, the resulting figure might be as small as fifteen thousand or as large as thirty-five thousand, but these are the outside limits of reasonable variation, and twenty-five thousand remains our best guess.

LEARNING TO FIND WATER

In many ways, Mr. G.'s story is typical of the experience of these American water diviners as a group. For example, the way in which he discovered he could find water is reported again and again. Our files bulge with newspaper clippings, magazine articles, and records of personal interviews with diviners. In all the cases known to us, the diviner discovered his talent not independently but after seeing or hearing about another diviner in action. We have spoken of the experience of Jim Brooks, a beginner at water divining, as an illustration of the theory of suggestion and ideomotor action. Now let us look at the situation as Jim—and the countless Americans like him—might report it themselves.

He saw the rod move in the diviner's hands, and he heard Jeff, the diviner, exclaim that the rod's pull was so great that the bark twisted off in his hands. Still, Jim is puzzled. It just doesn't make sense for a wooden twig to suddenly become alive over underground water. And he has heard talk that this water witching is nothing but superstitious nonsense. Yet Jeff seems like an honest man. He isn't even charging Frank Brown for his services. There is no reason why he would deliberately put on an act. He says he didn't make the rod move. But if Jeff didn't move the rod, what did? Jim finally gets up the courage to express his doubts to Jeff Green. Jeff hands the rod to Jim and says, "Here, try it yourself."

Jim's experience is the kind of personal experience that converts skeptics into diviners. Previously, Jim was willing to believe that the diviner must manipulate the rod. He was skeptical of the diviner's protestations to the contrary. But now that it has happened to him, it is a different story. Now Jim *knows* that the stick moves in his own hands, seemingly of its own accord. Now it is he who has to listen to the skeptical derision of onlookers. The skeptics say that the rod moves because Jim makes it move. They merely smile when Jim denies such a charge. Such doubting makes Jim fighting mad. He knows that the rod moves by itself, and when people say otherwise, they are calling him a liar. And no man likes to be called a liar.

Diviners are people who have gone through an experience similar to Jim's. And, like Jim, each one of them was surprised by the result. In the face of such an inexplicable personal experience, these people have shed their skepticism. When they discover that the horse answers *their* unuttered questions or that the pendulum swings as it should in *their* hands, they become converts to the cause. They become part of the militant band of believers; the smirking skepticism of outsiders irritates them and makes them more convinced of their cause. They know that they are not frauds. Mr. G. expresses the confidence of all diviners when he says, "There's no trickery to it. You hold my hands and you'll see. . . ."

SEX OF DIVINERS

The majority of respondents in our survey report that all the diviners in their counties are men. While men are predominant, however, female diviners are by no means rare; about 42 per cent of the responding counties report that at least one of their diviners is a woman. To this general picture, a certain amount of detail is added by another study whose results are available to us. This material gives us some idea of the proportions of men and women in a particular community and suggests some sex differences in the kind of participation, which may be important in understanding why most diviners are men.

The field experiment conducted in 1949 by the American Society for Psychical Research drew letters from a hundred and thirty Maine diviners, nineteen of whom were women. While there were a few women who suggested in their letters that they did divining on a fairly large scale and at some distance from their homes, the experience of a larger number was apparently confined to working on their own and their neighbors' and relatives' water problems. Examples of the first kind are the following:

I have located three wells for people, two in town and one in my neighborhood. . . .

I am not an expert but have found many wells as a hobby.

Of the latter group, the following are the most articulate letters:

I discovered the forked stick would turn for me more than fifty years ago but never put it to use until 1930, when we bought an acreage and needed a well. I found water and the tally stick said 22 feet and that was right. . . . About eight years ago my daughter-in-law needed more water on her farm. I located it. . . . I also switched for a neighbor and found only fine black sand.

A number of years ago we lived on the edge of a village, had to carry water quite a distance. With an apple tree fork

I found water and we dug a well and found a nice vein. Also when I was a young girl my mother used to carry water up a hill from a well and I found water in the cellar. . . . A year ago in that very dry time we had, . . . one of the neighbors was digging a ditch and down six feet the earth was a dry powder. . . . With the aid of a forked apple tree branch I found water near the cottages. They dug down seven feet and struck water.

In the smaller group of diviners, twenty-seven in all, who were interviewed in the course of this experiment, there were only five women. While this is too small a sample from which to draw reliable conclusions, the interview materials suggest that the activities of the women diviners were more limited than those of the men as a group. Among the men, the records of ten are available; one reported having found a hundred and seventy-five wells and one fifty over a period of years; there were three who had found between ten and twenty, one with a total of seven, and four with one to four. Of the four women whose records are presented, two had found three wells each, and one reported two successes but did not state that this record was complete; one more had found none at all but had simply felt the stick move in her hands. There appears to have been no difference between the sexes in the length of time spent accumulating divining experiences.

Several of the women were hesitant to offer their services for the experiment because, as one of them put it, they were not sure that the experimenters wanted "female help." It would seem from their remarks that female diviners are not only objectively fewer and perhaps less visible than male ones but are also considered somewhat unusual in these New England communities.

We can only speculate about the reasons for this difference between the sexes in divining. Gaston Burridge

(1955) reports in a western journal that he knows of only five women dowsers in all the Southwest—and he claims to know of some hundred practitioners in that area. He suggests that female dowsers are rare not because women lack ability to use the rod but because "the press of other matters" prevents them from doing anything with it.

This seems to us an astute guess. The place of the farm wife has traditionally been in the home; she has had sufficient work to keep her there, what with the housekeeping, the child-rearing, and the barnyard and garden chores. Her schedule has not allowed time for water divining on distant farms, and, furthermore, it probably would have been thought inappropriate for her to do so. Traditionally, it has been the man who goes out into the wider world. Both the small number of women diviners reported and their limited range of activity might be explained in these terms.

AGE OF DIVINERS

While women diviners are an important minority, cases of child diviners are almost unknown; the overwhelming majority of diviners are adults. About 78 per cent of the counties with diviners report that at least one is over sixty-five years of age, but only 2 per cent report any knowledge of diviners under the age of fifteen.

In spite of, or perhaps because of, the rarity of child diviners, an occasional witching prodigy turns up in the press. Recently, for example, newspapers across the nation carried the story of a little girl in South Dakota who found water where others could not. Carol Terbush had discovered that the willow stick worked for her two years earlier, when her father hired a man to find water on his farm.

The so-called "water witch" walked the farmstead and marked the well spot at the point where his willow wand dipped. Mr. Terbush's daughter, Carol, then 9, picked up the willow. She discovered that in her hands it also dipped at the point marked for the well. A neighbor who had witnessed the demonstration asked Carol to try her luck on his farm. The drill promptly hit water at the spot she marked. South Dakotans from a wide area asked help. Carol reportedly succeeded where others failed [*New York Times,* December 3, 1954].

By the time she was eleven, her fame had spread throughout the state, and the State Department of Game, Fish, and Parks hired her to find water for them.

Although the practicing child diviner is something of a curiosity, many diviners report that they first learned they had the "power" in childhood or adolescence. Of the twenty-seven diviners interviewed in the American Society for Psychical Research field experiment reported above, fourteen had first felt the forked stick turn in their hands before they were twenty years old and, of these, eight had had the experience before they were fifteen. In five of these cases, it is impossible to tell from the interview materials whether or not the children became practicing diviners at once; of those remaining, one was an adolescent girl with a record of three successful wells, and eight were adults who stated that their skill remained unused for years after their first experience. The interviewer writes:

After experience in childhood he had no further experience until 1940 [at age 39]. Most of his work in last two years. In last 20 tries successful in all but one.

When 17 or 18, did it with father. Started again in 1931 [at age 50]. Dug 175 wells in past seventeen years.

Stick always worked, even as a boy, but never "proved"

it until 4 years ago . . . [when] he drilled to a vein he discovered on his own property [at age 64].

These remarks suggest that while the rod "works" for children, for some reason they do not often employ their powers until they reach maturity. One of the reasons may be need; some people report that they took up the practice seriously only when, as farm operators, they needed to find water on their own land. Where a diviner branches out into the wider community, we suspect that status is involved; farmers tend to seek out a diviner whom they respect, and they respect mature men, in general, more than children.

EDUCATION

In academic circles, the belief is prevalent that water witching is something that thrives only among the uneducated. Our data supply some justification for this belief; approximately 66 per cent of the counties with diviners report that their "average" diviner has had only a grade-school education or less. While this is a striking fact, it would be wrong to conclude from it that lack of education is a distinguishing characteristic of water witches, for there is contradictory evidence in the remainder of the responding counties. As many as 30 per cent of the counties report that their "average" diviner has a high-school education, and no fewer than 3 per cent of the counties had diviners with college educations. Our acquaintance through correspondence with other dowsers confirms our impression that higher education is no impediment to the practice of water witching.

One might still argue, alternatively, that diviners are less educated, on the whole, than the general population. Here, however, our data give only a part of the story. Water witching is predominantly a rural activity, and it is known that the average educational level of our rural population is lower than that of the urban population. (The 1950 Census reports that the median number of years of school attended by people over twenty-five years of age was 10.1 in urban groups, 8.9 in rural non-farm, and 8.6 in rural farm.) It seems very likely that the distribution of education levels among water witches merely parallels the distribution in the rural counties in which they live. If we could rely on the estimates of education from our questionnaires, we might match these with the county averages and discover whether or not this is the case. However, we feel that the figures are impressions rather than firm facts and as such are subject to the same kinds of reporting bias that we have observed in the case of water witching itself; for this reason, we cannot employ them in this way. We can draw some general support for the hypothesis from the results of our study of the conditions under which water witches are employed (see chap. 8). There we discovered that an original low correlation between high frequency of divining and low average education level all but disappeared when the effects of population, density of population, and amount of urbanization were removed from the consideration by statistical methods.

If some association between relative lack of education and the practice of divining should remain after this rural-urban factor were controlled, we suspect that still another variable would enter to prevent our concluding that relatively little education *in itself* is characteristic of water witches. While data on educational levels of the various age-grades in our population is not available and our own data on age of diviners is imprecise, it still seems possible that diviners, who appear to be largely people of mature years, have had less education than the general rural population simply because they grew up in a time when higher education was much less common than it is today. We would need to control for age, as well, in order to determine the importance of education alone in the total picture.

COMMERCIALISM

We often hear comments to the effect that the diviner is a "fraud" or a "swindler" and that he is out to take money from the "suckers." We have found no justification for such a belief. As far as we can tell, in every case known to us, the diviner is an honest man of recognized integrity. He practices his art out of sincere desire to help his neighbor. One correspondent expresses this attitude in the following way: "I get a big thrill working with the stick, also satisfaction if I help a person get much-needed water easily." Another diviner elaborates on this theme:

When I'm out driving around, lots of times I see men—sometimes women, too—hauling water for a farm. I ask them why they are doing that, and invariably they tell me there isn't any water on the farm. I tell them not to be too sure. Then I cut a stick and usually find a vein for them. . . . To me, this dowsing ability is something which ought to be put to the service of mankind. I'm glad I can do it because I can be of some help to my fellow man by it [*Boston Sunday Herald,* August 29, 1954].

Our data support this impression. Only 2 per cent of our counties report having any diviners who work full time at water witching. And over 60 per cent of these counties with diviners report that they operate on a "non-commercial basis." This usually means that if the diviner charges for his services, he asks only a token fee. Many refuse to accept any fee whatsoever, and the belief among some diviners is that they would lose their power if they accepted remuneration.

Fees, when they are assessed, typically run from five to twenty-five dollars. In a few cases they may go as high as fifty dollars. We have heard reports that in one or two special situations a diviner has received as much as three thousand dollars for his services. Many diviners, especially those charging high fees, work on a money-back guaranty.

The great majority of diviners, then, do their witching as a hobby or, at most, a side line. The occupations in which they earn their livings are of many kinds. Diviners work as real estate agents, electricians, engineers, mechanics, salesmen, forest rangers, miners, masons, housewives, storekeepers, service station operators, construction workers, city employees, clergymen, truck drivers, blacksmiths, carpenters, teachers, mill workers, policemen, barbers, fishermen, druggists, and others.

The five most common occupations from which the diviners come are farmer (reported by 80 per cent of the counties), well-driller (20 per cent of the counties), retired people or pensioners (16 per cent of the counties), rancher (reported in 4 per cent of the counties), and general laborer (7 per cent of the counties).

Not only is the diviner most likely to be a farmer by vocation, but also, if he is a farmer, he is probably a farm owner. Of the counties reporting diviners who are farmers, 73 per cent indicated that they were predominantly farm owners. Farm tenant was checked in only 24 per cent of these cases, whereas farm laborer was checked in 10 per cent of the counties.

ETHNIC GROUPS

The average diviner in the majority of the responding counties was reported to be Protestant; Catholic was checked about half as many times, as would be expected if the distribution of religion among diviners actually reflected that of the general population. The most common ethnic designation was "Old American," with German, Scandinavian, Negro, and American Indian following in that order.

In addition to these groups, our agents checked many other groups as practicing divining. Some of these were: Italian, French, Spanish, Mexican, Portuguese, Mennonite, Pennsylvania Dutch, Slavic, Dutch, Irish, Latter-day Saints, and, in one case, Jewish.

What does this variety in ethnic backgrounds signify? At the very least it tells us that there is no necessary relationship between ethnic origin and the practice of divining. We can find practitioners of witching among almost every group that resides in rural America.

Our data do not allow us to go beyond this simple negative statement. Ideally, we would like to know the answers to such questions as: "Are there some ethnic groups that practice water witching proportionally more than others?" "Is this distribution of ethnic origins among diviners simply parallel to the distribution among the rural population in general?"

Although our data do not allow us to answer such questions definitively, they are suggestive. In addition to asking the agent to check the groups in his county that practice witching, we also asked him to check the groups that are the predominant part of the population of his county. By combining the information from these two questions, we get some information concerning whether the diviner tends to be of the same ethnic origin as the people for whom he works.

The respondents from 181 counties, for example, checked "Old American" as one of the groups that practice witching. And in only 14 of these counties was the category "Old American" not checked as a predominant part of the population. The category "Protestant" was checked as a group that practiced witching in 141 counties; only 8 of these 141 counties did not list "Protestant" as being part of the predominant population. Similarly, Germans were said to be practicing witching in 57 counties in our sample, and the Germans were not a predominant part of the population in only 10 of these counties.

We can examine our data another way to answer our question. We can compare the distribution of groups that are predominant in the counties in our sample with the distribution of groups that practice witching in the counties of our sample. In Table 7, we list, in order, the ten groups most frequently checked.

TABLE 7

Groups Most Frequently Checked for Practice of Witching	Groups Most Frequently Checked as a Predominant Part of the County
Old American	Old American
Protestant	Protestant
Catholic	Catholic
German	German
Scandinavian	Scandinavian
Negro	Negro
American Indian	Italian
Italian	French
French	American Indian
Spanish or Mexican	Spanish or Mexican

Notice that the ten groups most frequently practicing witching in our sample are also the same ten groups that are most frequently the predominant part of the populations of the counties in our sample. And, with a few exceptions, the rank orders are the same.

WHO IS THE DIVINER?—A SUMMARY

The substance of our findings on the American diviner as a person is that he cannot be distinguished from the general rural population by any of the attributes we have investigated. He seems to fit into his community in religion and ethnic affiliation, in education and occupation, and in values regarding neighborliness and economic gain. And he is more likely to be a man than a woman or a child. He may still be different in some way, of course, but our data give us no more clues. The roles of individual life history and personality, for example, in the "conversion" to water witching must be material for another study.

In looking at the diviner as an individual, our emphasis, dictated in part by our interests and in part by our method of study, has been on the sociology of the role of water witch. We can, however, get some idea of the psychology of the role—the needs and satisfactions which make witching worthwhile for the individual dowser—from these same materials. While individual motivation is varied, complex, and often obscure, and there are undoubtedly different reasons why different people take up the practice, our data show certain motives that seem to be widespread among diviners. First, it is very doubtful, from our data, that people go into the business simply to make money. Instead, some take up the practice for the same reason that people hire diviners—they have water problems which the geologists have not solved or cannot solve with precision, and they have heard about or have seen dowsing. Most diviners are not aware that what they are doing differs from their sound techniques for planting, cultivating, and harvesting crops of beans or potatoes.

For some there is evident pride in the accomplishment itself. A dowser reports, "I feel very sure of myself. I have demonstrated in actual tests I can tell the depth to water." Others refer to their records as diviners and recall their successes in a spirit akin to the satisfaction of a craftsman in the evidence of his skill. Others seem to derive much satisfaction from the feeling that they are among a select few who possess the "gift." One such diviner refers to witching as a "miracle" and expresses his feeling about it in somewhat biblical terms: "I am very fortunate in that I have been given the talent to fully understand the underground water fountains or deep springs that casteth forth flowing water."

Some diviners find at least a part of their reward in the apparently mystical experience of dowsing—the feeling of being possessed for a time by a superior and perhaps supernatural power. "I could no more stop the pull than I could reach up and touch a cloud," one dowser recalls. "It was a thrilling experience and I still remember how excited I was." Another diviner attests to the weight of the physical experience when he says that "a day of dowsing leaves him with a strange feeling about the heart that sometimes takes days to recover from."

In divining there is also the satisfaction of giving of one's self to help other people in need—the same satisfaction that is to be found in humanitarian efforts of all kinds. We have seen some of this sense of personal sacrifice for the good of others in Mr. G.'s comment, "I have never charged a cent for finding water. . . . Water is one essential you must have, and I didn't think it was fair to charge poor people," and in similar remarks of others. The other side of the helping process—the gratitude and respect of the beneficiaries—would seem to be another important recompense for the diviner. He gains prestige in his community through his good works. A man who knows where to find water underground is useful to the people of his community. They seek him out for advice and help, and they speak of him with respect and admiration. As would be expected, diviners do not acknowledge this as a factor in their motivation, but we can assume on the basis of our knowledge of human behavior that this is a powerful incentive.

When we come to possible unconscious motives behind the use of a divining rod, we must anticipate that the psychoanalysts would find the obvious symbolism of the rod, its attraction to water and to Mother Earth, tempting soil for the kinds of speculations in which they so frequently indulge. And our search of the psychoanalytical literature eventually uncovered just such an attempt (Servadio, 1935). Of course, the witching performance is seen as a sexual act. The rod allegedly symbolizes the penis or clitoris. Its motion is like an erection and is often accompanied by emotions akin to sexual excitement. The object of the act—the penetration and exploration of the earth—is interpreted as a symbolic penetration of the mother (with which the earth has been universally identified by analysts). The whole experience is seen as an acting-out, by means of symbolic manipulations, of the unconscious desire to return to the womb. The plausibility of such a hypothesis depends upon one's acceptance of psychoanalytical thinking. The psychoanalysts themselves have presented no evidence, and we can find only the most fragmentary kind of supporting evidence for such an argument. In the Ozarks, "there is a very general notion that virility has something to do with this 'power.' . . . 'A feller has got to be a whole man,' one old gentleman said, 'if he aims to take up witch wigglin'.' He meant that a water witch must be normal sexually; a man who has anything wrong with his genitals can never locate wells with a witch stick" (Randolph, 1947). For the most part, however, the sexual connotation of water witching seems to reside in the obvious analogy of the rod to a penis. If any deeper connections exist, they will have to be uncovered by more experimental investigation.

Finally, our inquiry into contemporary divining has led us to believe that, for some diviners, there is deep satisfaction in what they see as a triumph of common sense over scientific knowledge. Modern man is living in a world which he can no longer order or comprehend without special training—a world in which a man must spend twenty or more years in school to master one small area of specialization and no longer considers the possibility of ever becoming familiar with more than a fraction of the world's knowledge. The physicist now describes a table not in terms of its shape, hardness, or function, all of which are perceptible to us, but rather in terms of atoms moving, invisibly, at incredible speeds. The ordinary man lives in a world whose complexity he is aware of but can only dimly comprehend. In such a world, the appeal to common sense, the adherence to the technique which "works" in spite of the inability of science to explain it, may well be a comforting defense. In this one area, at least, says the diviner, I know more than the scientist. As one diviner expresses it, "There are so many things the scientists, the doctors, and everybody could learn if they would try . . . instead of making fun of it and just saying it isn't so." In other words, through the practice of divining, some diviners may be symbolically saying to the scientist, "There are more things in heaven and earth, Horatio, than are dreamt of in your philosophy."

CHAPTER 8

For Whom the Witch Tells

The sciences seek to determine the precise condi-
tions under which events come into being and
continue to exist.

ERNEST NAGEL, 1954

A major goal of our nationwide survey was to discover the conditions under which water witching is practiced. Are we more likely to find divining in particular geographical regions? Is the practice related to the average educational level of a county? Is it more likely to be found where water is easy to find or where it is difficult to find?

Before we undertook our survey of county agricultural extension agents, we examined many individual case histories of water witching to see if they would provide us with clues. These instances suggested that people turn to water witching for a variety of reasons and under many different conditions. The following cases illustrate some of the situations that involved the use of a water diviner.

On Sunday, October 14, a drama was enacted on Maple Hill in Plainfield, Vermont. A small drama in the eyes of the world perhaps, but a drama nevertheless. It came about in this way.

Farmer Merton Potter needed water, and to find it he had searched his lands fruitlessly for weeks; finally he had to admit that he needed help. But to help him he called no plumbers, no geologists, nor scientific water experts. He sent for a dowser, a man who has the uncanny ability to locate underground water with the aid of only a forked stick. The dowser he sent for was a simple man, a farmer also, from neighboring West Hill. For him this was to be an everyday occurrence, for he had located many hundreds of springs and wells in the past. For Farmer Potter to call him was only natural, for everyone had always called him when they needed water [Reed, 1953].

In this account we are told that Farmer Potter sent for a dowser because it "was only natural"; in that community it was the thing to do. Perhaps Potter did not have any available alternatives or did not know that more reliable techniques exist. But such explanations will not account for the next case.

We know of a geologist, a ground-water specialist, who recently moved into a house in California that faced upon the grounds of a public school. He was surprised when he saw that the school had employed a water diviner to solve its difficulties in obtaining sufficient water. When the diviner's designated site failed to yield water, the geologist went before the school board and offered his services, free of charge, to help locate an adequate site for the well. The school board did not reply to his offer. Instead, a week later, the geologist looked out his window and was dismayed to see that the school had hired another diviner to locate the needed underground water. Here we see that witching was employed by the school authorities even when they were aware that scientific help was available at no cost. We must assume, lacking further details, that the authorities in this situation chose water witching because they believed it could do a better job than a competing technique of a trained scientist.

Sometimes a diviner is employed for reasons extraneous to whether it is the only alternative or whether it is the most valid technique. In one case, a well-driller in Minnesota uses water witching frequently. This driller does not believe in the practice but uses it as a device for keeping "trade secrets." He explains that when a well is drilled, the driller must file an extensive report with the state giving complete details about how the site was chosen and the cues that were employed. The drillers have discovered that they can avoid giving such a detailed report (apparently they feel that their "secrets" of water-finding are their own affair) if they employ a diviner, for then they simply have to report that the well was witched.

In another instance, a man in Vermont encountered an apparent witching "closed shop." When he called in a local driller, the man refused to drill a well unless the site were first witched. Outraged, he called upon other well-drillers in the community but got the same response from each. Finally, he had to give in, and he hired a diviner to select a site and thereby obtained his well.

In this last case the diviner was employed against the better judgment of the employer. The Bonds, whom we encountered in the first chapter, also had no intention of hiring a dowser. They regarded water witching as a lot of superstitious nonsense. But under extraordinary circumstances, in extreme desperation, they finally turned to Henry Gross and his divining rod.

Cases such as these warn us that no single reason will account for all occurrences of water witching, and suggest that the practice will be found under a wide variety of conditions. In some instances the crucial factor seems to be a lack of information concerning better alternatives. In other situations the explanatory factors seem to involve the educational level, the climate, the difficulty or ease of finding water, or the degree of urbanization.

But the fact that many different conditions can lead to water witching does not rule out the possibility that, as a general rule, certain conditions tend to favor the practice more than others. Indeed, prior to conducting our own survey, we had both theoretical and empirical grounds for suspecting that the occurrence of water witching was closely tied up with the problems of obtaining adequate water. Vogt (1952) referred to the practice as a "ritual pattern" and suggested that its occurrence is closely tied to the difficulty and uncertainty of finding underground water.

Consequently, in the design of our survey, we focused primarily upon the relationship of water witching to problems in finding water. Our procedure was to classify each county in our sample in terms of how much water witching occurred and also in terms of ground-water problems. Then—after making appropriate adjustments for such factors as educational level, population density, precipitation—we examined the relationship between divining and ground-water problems. We looked for three possible outcomes.

Water witching is unrelated to ground-water problems. If the incidence of water witching could not be predicted from the severity of ground-water problems, then this would considerably weaken the case for classifying the practice as a ritual that occurs under conditions of uncertainty and anxiety in coping with the environment. We would have to look elsewhere for factors that are conducive to the practice.

Water witching is negatively related to ground-water problems. If water witching tended to flourish under conditions where it is *easy* to find underground water, this would directly contradict the anthropological characterization of the practice as a form of ritual. Yet such a possibility was consistent with a reason that was frequently advanced to us for the persistence of the practice. This notion (or what we prefer to call the "They can't go wrong" theory) proposes that witching survives in communities where water is easily accessible because the consumers never realize that they could be just as successful in locating water without the aid of the diviner.

Water witching is positively related to ground-water problems. If water witching tended to flourish in counties where finding water was difficult, then this would be consistent with Vogt's theory that the practice was analogous to the magical rituals of primitive societies (1952). Such a relationship, although consistent with the theory, does not necessarily validate the theory. The relationship could, of course, arise for other reasons. One such reason was frequently advanced by our informants, and we have labeled it the "nothing to lose" theory. This theory states that people turn to water witching because they have no better alternative and because they have little to lose (if witching is invalid) and everything to gain (if witching is valid).

A HYPOTHETICAL EXPERIMENT

Our empirical survey, then, had as a major objective the task of deciding which of these three possible relationships between divining and ground-water problems best described the situation as it currently exists in the United States. Because we had to study counties as they actually exist, our procedures for collecting and analyzing our data were necessarily complex. We had to employ statistical tools that would enable us to compare counties that differed in important respects (see Hyman and Cohen, 1957). But before we describe what we actually did, let us describe a hypothetical and idealized experiment which will clarify what we were trying to do.

Imagine that we are able to find or construct two communities that are identical in size, topography, climate, natural resources, and other geological and geographic features, with one important exception. Community A has a fairly level water table, and any well will produce adequate water if it is drilled to a depth of fifty feet. Community B has a water table that is highly irregular. A well may have to go down to a depth of only twenty feet to hit an adequate flow; or it may have to go down to over two hundred feet. The surface features in Community B yield no reliable cues to whether a site will produce a good well at a reasonable, or at an excessive, depth.

To complete this ideal, controlled experiment, imagine that we have access to a sample of people with a common ancestry, folklore, education, and heritage. We randomly split this sample in two and populate Community A with half our sample and Community B with the other half. We then sit back for ten years and await the outcome. During this period we can expect that the people in both communities will develop similar customs. We can assume that they will have equal needs for ground water and that they will develop approximately the same number of wells. What we are interested in counting is the proportion of wells that have been witched in each of the communities.

If we discover that the proportion of wells that have been witched in each community is the same, we would conclude that there is no relationship between groundwater problems and water witching. But if we discover that Community A has more water witching than Community B, we would conclude that there is a *negative* relationship between water witching and ground-water problems. Such a relationship, if discovered, would naturally lead to speculation about why it exists. The attempt to interpret observed relationships is the theoretical (and often the controversial) aspect of the scientific procedure. In this illustration, for example, we might explain the results in terms of the "They can't go wrong" theory. If, on the other hand, we discover that Community B has more water witching than Community A, we would conclude that there is a *positive* relationship between water witching and ground-water problems. Then we might interpret this relationship in terms of the ritual theory, the "nothing to lose" theory, or some other theory depending upon other information and previous theoretical orientation.

Even if we wanted to conduct it, such an experiment is beyond the realm of possibility. But we have described it because the ideal of having communities matched on every important variable except water witching and uncertainty of water table is what we were striving for when we collected and analyzed our data. In reality, we could only approximate such control by the manner in which we collected our data and used statistical manipulations. Our procedure was to order the 358 counties that participated in our survey in terms of amount of water witching activity. We then examined this ordering in relation to ground-water regions and in relation to such variables as population density, degree of urbanization, level of education, amount of precipitation, and difficulty in finding water. By using correlational techniques with these relationships we were able to statistically equate the counties for certain variables and compare them on others.

AN INDEX OF WITCHING ACTIVITY

Our first problem was to measure the amount of water witching taking place within a county. Each responding agent sent us an estimate of the number of water diviners he believed were practicing in his county. But the actual number of diviners in a county is not sufficient. A total of eight diviners in a sparsely settled region means something different from the same total in a more densely populated county. And more important than the actual number of diviners is the proportion of wells that are divined.

Consequently, we developed two separate indexes of water witching activity. The first one is the number of diviners per 100,000 people. Such a ratio helps us to equate counties for differences in population size. It may be, for example, that there is a high number of diviners in Marion County, Indiana, simply because there are more people in this county than there are in a county such as McKinley, New Mexico, which has only three diviners.

This ratio index tells us that, for the United States as a whole, there are about 18 diviners per 100,000 persons. But of more immediate interest to us is the great variation from county to county in concentration of diviners. The range in our sample of 358 counties is from 0 to 643 diviners per 100,000 population. The highest concentration is found in a county in southwestern Kansas.

Our other measure is the percentage of drilled wells that are divined. (We also attempted to get a similar index on hand-dug wells, but, according to our informants, such wells very rarely are sunk today.) Again we find a considerable variation from county to county. The range is from 0 per cent to 100 per cent—the 100 per cent reported from a county in southern Nevada.

These two indexes need not be highly correlated. A county could have a lot of diviners, but each might have very little work to do. Another county might have almost all of its wells divined but have only one diviner or drill only one or two wells per year.

Fortunately, as it turned out, the two indexes are highly intercorrelated. Statisticians have developed ways of expressing the degree of relationship between two variables in terms of a number called a "correlation coefficient." This coefficient came out to be .88 between our two indexes. We can convey some idea of what this means by the following example. Suppose that we divide the counties on each index into two equal groups such that 50 per cent are above the average on that index—call these "high"—and 50 per cent are below the average—call these "low." Then, if for simplicity we assume 100 "highs" and 100 "lows" on each variable, a correlation of .88 would give us Table 8. As can be seen,

TABLE 8

ASSOCIATION BETWEEN NUMBER OF DI-
VINERS PER 100,000 AND PROPORTION
OF WELLS THAT ARE WITCHED

(Corresponding to a Correlation of .88)

NUMBER OF DIVINERS PER 100,000	PROPORTION OF WITCHED WELLS	
	High	Low
High............	85	15
Low............	15	85

the correspondence between the two measures is high but not perfect. Approximately 85 per cent of the counties that are high on one index are also high on the other index. The lack of perfect agreement, however, does not mean that the two indexes are measuring different things. When we consider that each index has a margin of error attached to it, then this degree of association is quite high.

The county agricultural agents found it much easier to estimate the number of diviners in their counties than to tell us what proportion of the drilled wells were divined. In fact, the number of agents who refused to estimate the percentage of wells divined was greater than the number who refused to estimate the number of diviners. This suggests that at least one of these indexes could not be too reliable, and, in consideration of non-perfect reliability, the correlation of .88 between the two indexes indicates that for all practical purposes they can be considered equivalent. Consequently, we decided that we need use only one of these indexes as our basic measure of witching activity. Because more agents answered the question about the number of diviners, and because this measure appeared to be the more reliable, we employed the number of diviners per 100,000 as our basic index.

WITCHING IN THE TEN MAJOR GROUND-WATER REGIONS

To begin our analysis we grouped the counties into two classes, urban and rural. All counties with 50 per cent or more of their population classified as urban by the U.S. Census were put into the urban stratum. All others were classified as rural. We were able to make a separate estimate of the proportion of diviners for the urban and rural strata. As Table 9 indicates, the number of diviners per 100,000 persons in our population is about 18. But for the urban counties, this index is about 8 diviners per 100,000, as contrasted to 35 diviners per 100,000 persons in the rural counties. We did not try to group the urban counties by ground-water regions because they were so few.

We further classified the rural counties into ten strata

according to which of ten major ground-water regions each fell into (see Fig. 1 for a map of these regions; also cf. Thomas, 1952). As Table 9 reveals, there seems to be considerable variation among the ten ground-water regions in proportion of diviners, the range being from about 20 to 70 diviners per 100,000 persons.

There is a high concentration of water diviners operating on the Columbia Lava Plateau, on the Great

TABLE 9

NUMBER OF DIVINERS PER 100,000 PERSONS AS
ESTIMATED FOR EACH STRATUM
IN OUR POPULATION

Counties in Sample	Number of Diviners per 100,000
Urban counties	7.7
All rural counties	35.3
Columbia Lava Plateau	70.1
Great Plains	60.0
Colorado Plateau	55.4
Unglaciated Central	48.0
Glaciated Central	44.6
Western Mountain Ranges	30.6
Unglaciated Appalachian	29.7
Arid Basins	24.2
Coastal Plains	21.5
Glaciated Appalachian	19.5
Entire population	18.1

Plains, on the Colorado Plateau, and in the Unglaciated Central region. We would like to consider the geology and ground-water problems of these regions and see what bases they indicate for this concentration.

The Columbia Lava Plateau includes the "extensive high, rather dry dissected plateaus underlain by lava rocks in eastern Washington and Oregon and southern Idaho. . . . There is great promise for development of ground water from some of the productive lava-rock aquifers." But "this is one of the most imperfectly known ground water regions in the country. Its promise can never be realized until both the general principles

of the hydrology of lava rocks and the details of occurrence of water in each part of the region are better
understood" (Thomas, p. 31). In this region then there
emerges a correlation between divining activity and an
unsure water supply.

How about the Great Plains? These are "extensive
semiarid to subhumid plains and plateaus east of the
Rockies, extending from South Dakota to western Texas
and eastern New Mexico. The region is underlain mainly by consolidated sedimentary rocks, covered by alluvial outwash from the Rockies. . . . The region is one
of prevailing water deficiency, under existing conditions
of development" (Thomas, p. 40). Again the impression
one has is that water diviners would be employed in
this region.

The Colorado Plateau is made up of "extensive dissected arid and semiarid plateaus underlain by stratified sedimentary rocks in the 'Four State' region of
Utah, Arizona, New Mexico, and Colorado, and also in
Wyoming." We all know this region produces lots of
uranium, but water is another matter. "Its need for
water is greater than its ability to produce water. . . .
Because of generally deficient rain and snowfall and of
scarcity of productive aquifers and great depth to some
beneath the plateau surfaces, there is lack of adequate
water supplies even to support grazing, to say nothing
of irrigation agriculture," reports Mr. Thomas (p. 35)
of this region. Here, too, there emerges a pattern of
inadequate water supply and heavy reliance upon water
witching.

In the Unglaciated Central region, there are "interior
plains and low plateaus extending from the Great Plains
or Rocky Mountains on the West to the Appalachian
region on the East, north of the Gulf Coastal Plain and
south of the glaciated area. . . . It is characterized by

aquifers of rather low productivity. . . . The water problems of the region are those of general inadequacy for all uses at reasonable cost" (Thomas, p. 45). Our impression is that there are enough problems to keep the water diviners in business.

How about the regions where we find a low concentration of water diviners? These are the Glaciated Appalachians (including New England and parts of New York, Pennsylvania, and New Jersey), the Coastal Plains, the Arid Basins, and the Unglaciated Appalachians.

In the case of the Glaciated Appalachians, "characterized by hilly or mountainous terrain, with thin glacial drift on the uplands and thicker drift in the valleys," the region "is one of relatively abundant supplies of water of good quality," reports Thomas (p. 63). So despite all the famous literature on water witching from New England, it appears that there are actually fewer diviners and fewer problems here than in many regions of the United States.

The Coastal Plains region "extends from Long Island and the sandy islands and capes of Massachusetts clear to Texas, and includes the Mississippi Embayment as far north as Cairo, Illinois. . . . Except in its extreme western part in Texas, the region most abundantly endowed with water of all those in the United States" (Thomas, p. 65). It is certainly no accident that we find only 21.5 diviners per 100,000 population in this well-watered region.

"But the Arid Basins," the reader will ask, "won't this region present an exception to this line of reasoning?" Mr. Thomas (p. 22) tells us that "the Arid Basins are the alluvial basins that flank the mountain ranges of the West. . . . As the moutains are the great sources of water in the West, so the alluvial basins are the great receivers and storers of the water. . . . The region is far ahead of all other regions in ground water development." So, despite the aridity of this region, good ground water is found, and in some quantity.

Finally, the Unglaciated Appalachians are described as "characterized by mountains and hilly uplands separated by broad valleys. . . . The region is one of generally high rainfall and runoff, and rather well-sustained stream flow resulting from evenly distributed rainfall. . . . Small, reliable supplies of water are generally easy to obtain except on hill and mountain tops. . . . Here again, water problems are less serious than in some other regions" (Thomas, p. 60).

This leaves two regions, the Glaciated Central and the Western Mountain Ranges, to be considered. Here we find that concentration of diviners is intermediate, and ground-water problems appear to be intermediate. Of the Glaciated Central, we find that "water problems, on the whole, are not as serious as in some other regions" (Thomas, p. 51); the Western Mountain Ranges are "the great rain catchers or water collectors of the West. Because of the tightness of the rocks of which they are built and of their rather thin mantle of weathered rock and soil, they do not store ground water in great quantity, or for long" (Thomas, p. 16).

This comparison of ground-water regions suggests that those regions with severe ground-water problems have more water witching than those regions with few ground-water problems. But the findings from these comparisons can only be suggestive rather than conclusive. For one thing, the number of regions is quite small. Each region covers a lot of territory and includes many counties, and these counties vary greatly in witching activity. Also, these ground-water regions vary in other ways that must be taken into account. The Columbia

Lava Plateau and the Great Plains not only have a high proportion of diviners but are the least heavily populated and urbanized; the Glaciated Appalachian and the Coastal Plains, both low on witching, are very densely populated. It could very well be, as someone might argue, that the amount of water witching is simply a function of the population density or degree of urbanization rather than of ground-water problems.

Obviously, what we need is a way to compare regions that is unaffected by differences in uncontrolled variables such as population density and degree of urbanization. To find such a way, we abandon the comparisons among ground-water regions and look, rather, at the variations among counties within these regions.

THE CORRELATION OF WITCHING WITH OTHER VARIABLES

Our procedures for studying and controlling variability among the counties within regions are based on what is called partial correlation theory. Although the theory and its application are highly technical (see Hyman and Cohen, 1957), we can convey some idea of what we did. Within each ground-water region we calculated the correlation between pairs of measures on which the counties varied. Only the four largest ground-water regions had sufficient counties for this purpose (Unglaciated Central, Glaciated Central, Coastal Plains, and Unglaciated Appalachian). From the pattern of such correlations we were able to group the various indexes into four clusters or major factors.

One set of variables had to do with population characteristics of each county, all of which were obtained from the 1950 Census. A combination of the variables population density, population, percentage of urban population, and percentage of population increase (1940 to 1950) comprised a factor that we labeled "tendency toward urbanization." Within a ground-water region, the proportion of diviners was negatively related to this factor (the correlation between diviner density and this factor was —.37). Such a relationship merely reiterates what we have already learned from our comparison of urban with rural strata. But we had to calculate this correlation because our statistical technique demanded that we do so if we wanted to adjust other relationships so as to be unaffected by "tendency toward urbanization."

A second factor was defined by two variables having to do with the educational level of the community— percentage of adult population with five or more grades of schooling and percentage of adult population with at least high-school education. These two variables combine to define a factor we have labeled "amount of schooling." Water witching is negatively, but slightly, correlated with this factor (—.22). Although this correlation is quite low, we nevertheless adjusted other correlations to be free of the influence of "amount of schooling."

A third factor was defined by three rainfall variables —January precipitation, July precipitation, and annual precipitation. None of these three variables correlated with the proportion of diviners in a county.

A fourth factor consisted of four indexes that we used as measures of the degree of uncertainty and anxiety attached to the attainment and maintenance of adequate water—range in depth of drilled wells, lack of ground-water information, percentage of wells resulting in dry holes, and problem score. The index "range in depth" was simply the difference between the shallowest and the deepest well that one might find in a county. We assumed that, in general, the greater this range, the greater the uncertainty one had as to how deep he might have to drill before he encountered water. The index "lack of ground-water information" was based on the agent's assessment of the adequacy of available information concerning the ground-water supply. The "percentage of dry holes" was simply the proportion of well-sinkings that ended up as dry holes.

Of particular importance was our "problem score" index which was a specially constructed scale to measure the severity of ground-water problems based on how the respondent rated the degree of importance for his county of these issues: "may get a dry hole"; "may get too little water"; "may not be able to find water where wanted"; "may cost a great deal"; "may have to drill to a great depth."

Not only did proportion of diviners correlate positively with each of these four indexes, but it also correlated significantly and substantially (.59) with the factor composed of these indexes ("severity of ground-water problems"). The degree of this relationship becomes even more meaningful when we note that it exists *after* we have equated the counties for ground-water region, "tendency toward urbanization," "amount of schooling," "precipitation," and number of wells sunk each year (see Hyman and Cohen, 1957).

For those readers who are unfamiliar with the concept of correlation, some feeling of the degree of this relationship between proportion of diviners and "severity of ground-water problems" can be conveyed as follows. Imagine that we arrange two hundred counties, first, in order of incidence of divining and, second, in order of severity of ground-water problems. Then, if we arbitrarily classify the highest one hundred counties in proportion of diviners as "high" on this variable and the remaining one hundred counties as "low" on divining; and, if we similarly classify the one hundred highest counties in severity of ground-water problems as "high" on this latter variable and the remaining one hundred as "low," then the correlation between the two variables of .59 can be depicted by Table 10.

When the counties are classified in this manner we see that the relationship is such that 70 per cent of the

TABLE 10

DEGREE OF ASSOCIATION BETWEEN NUM-
BER OF DIVINERS PER 100,000 AND
SEVERITY OF GROUND-WATER PROB-
LEMS*

(Corresponding to a Correlation of .59)

NUMBER OF DIVINERS PER 100,000	SEVERITY OF GROUND-WATER PROBLEMS	
	High	Low
High.............	70	30
Low.............	30	70

* After counties have been made statistically equal on the factors "tendency toward urbanization," "amount of schooling," and "amount of precipitation."

counties "high" on witching activity are also "high" in severity of ground-water problems.

Thus we conclude that there is a substantial tendency for the incidence of water witching to be positively related to the severity of ground-water problems.

SUMMARY

Our survey shows, first, that water witching is more common where there is little tendency to urbanization; thus, the more rural the locality, the greater will be the proportion of diviners to the population. Less decidedly, for there are many exceptions which keep these correlations small, it shows that water witching is more frequent in communities where the average number of years of schooling is low. Most significantly, it demonstrates that water witching is employed more where water is difficult to find; the greater the problems involved in finding good underground water, the greater the number of diviners per 100,000 people. The relationship between water problems and divining is so strong that it remains even when the supporting effects of low tendency to urbanization and low education are removed; in general, where two communities are equally rural and equal in educational level, the one in which ground water is more difficult to find will have the greater proportion of diviners.

There are exceptions to this tendency, as the lack of perfect correlation indicates. A few counties with severe water problems have no diviners, and a few counties with no problems have many diviners. But the over-all tendency for the incidence of witching to be higher where ground-water problems are severe is consistent with expectations based on the ritual theory and also on the "nothing to lose" theory. Such an interpretation of the observed relationship, however, takes us beyond the data and into the realm of scientific speculation. The theoretical significance of our findings and the question of what they mean will occupy us in our last chapter.

CHAPTER 9

Water Witching as Magical Divination

The last lesson we would attempt to gather from the divining rod is this: once let a superstitious practice start, there is no telling how or when it will end.

LEE F. VANCE, 1891

We have reached the conclusion that water witching does not work as a reliable empirical technique to locate underground water. It is more like the belief that you should plant root crops, like potatoes, in the dark of the moon (Passin and Bennett, 1943) than it is like using fertilizers to increase the size and number of your potatoes after you have planted them. No connection can be demonstrated, using scientific methods, between the phases of the moon and a crop of potatoes. But a direct and effective connection can be scientifically demonstrated between the use of fertilizers and a potato crop.

This observation has led more than one observer, like Mr. Vance, writing on "Three Lessons in Rhabdomancy" in the *Journal of American Folklore* almost seventy years ago, to conclude that water witching is all superstition. In fact, many of our rural sociologists and government agricultural experts act as if water witching and similar practices had already been replaced by scientific methods in rural America, for, despite the continuing prevalence of these practices, it is rare to find any mention of the problem in their books and reports. When they do consider the matter, practices like water witching, planting by the moon, and castrating calves by the signs of the zodiac are usually treated as super- stitions that survive only among unenlightened back- country farmers. And they go on to argue that science will soon cause the disappearance of these superstitions from the rural American scene. In the words of one of these observers:

The magical mind, rather than the scientific attitude, tends to prevail in rural America. . . . This is an emotional and unreflective attitude which does not clearly perceive the steps between thoughts and actions. . . . Expressions of magical mindedness are seen in numerous superstitious be- liefs and practices in regard to harvesting and planting. . . . The impress of science is already marked and the agencies carrying it to the farmers persistent. . . . With much prestige already established for this method, there is every reason to think that fairly rapid headway will be made in the immediate future. To the degree such progress is made, the magical mindedness will disappear [Sims, 1929].

There is certainly a grain of truth in this kind of ex- planation of water witching, for it *is* a superstitious practice from the point of view of the detached scien- tific observer. But does it persist *merely* because back- country farmers are lacking in education and are "magi- cal minded"? As we indicated in the last chapter, the difference in educational levels in various regions of the United States does not begin to account for all the vari- ations we have discovered in the practice of water witching. It is clear that water witching persists even in rural regions where the educational level is relatively high. Furthermore, while the general growth of science has been impressive in the United States in the thirty years since Sims wrote, our data indicate that water witching has continued to flourish.

We therefore conclude that water witching is a clear-cut case of *magical divination* in our culture which persists because there are potent psychological and social reasons for it. In plain language, the practice does something important for the farmer who hires a water witch. He does not define it as magical divination but thinks rather that the technique is as valid as planting potatoes, hoeing out the weeds in the crop, and adding fertilizer to increase the yield.

In explaining our conclusion, we shall define "divination" as "the art or practice of foreseeing or foretelling future events or discovering hidden knowledge, often accompanied by rites" (*Webster's New International Dictionary*). This covers a great deal of human activity, including the activities of scientists like meteorologists who predict in daily reports what the weather will be like tomorrow, the day after tomorrow, or next week. They are foreseeing the weather. It also covers the activities of geologists who by studying the surface of the earth, the layers of rocks in canyons and on the sides of mountains, and the sands, gravels, and rocks that are bailed out of wells, can provide us with knowledge of the earth that is ordinarily hidden from us who walk around on its surface. There is undoubtedly a deep and enduring human propensity to engage in divination that will translate the unknowable into the knowable, the uncertainties into certainties, and this divination is engaged in by curious scientists and by rural water diviners alike in their search for knowledge of what lies beneath the surface of the ground.

The concept of divination covers a wide variety of human activity which ranges from the omens and oracles of the ancient Greeks to the tests of modern psychologists. We use divination because we expect that a sign will be followed by a certain outcome. If the weatherman says that it will be sunny this coming week-end, we behave as if it will be sunny—we plan our picnic or make reservations at the seashore, etc. We do this despite the fact that the weatherman's predictions are not always correct. Yet, in using these predictions as a basis for action, we say that we are acting rationally. We are acting rationally because there is a scientific, if not certain, connection between the weatherman's signs and the future behavior of the weather. This connection is far from perfect, but we can show that we will be correct more often if we follow the weatherman than if we employ some other device for anticipating the weather. When we use the outcome of a psychological test to select people for college, to take another example, we are using the test score as a valid sign of the ability of the examinee to succeed in college. Again, we know the sign is far from perfect. We know that many predictions of success will be followed by actual failure in college. But still we say we are behaving rationally because scientists have demonstrated a correlation between test score and future success. By using the test we know that our predictions of future success will be correct much more often than if we tried to make our selections without the test.

Thus, we see that one aspect of all divination is that it can never be perfect. No form of divination known to science can anticipate the future with 100 per cent accuracy. All we demand of a divination device is that it predict outcomes better than chance and better than alternative forms of divination. When it has been scientifically established that there is a correlation between signs and certain outcomes, then the use of these signs for divination is considered "rational," "sensible," "scientific," etc.

There exist today many forms of divination in which such a connection between signs and outcomes has never been demonstrated. Astrology, palmistry, tea leaf reading, numerology, and other forms of soothsaying belong to this class. Yet these various systems provide guides for the behavior of millions of people. We call all systems of decision-making in which the signs have no demonstrable connection to the anticipated outcomes "magical divination." And because the use of water witching belongs to this category, we classify it as a form of "magical divination."

We hasten to add that the appellation "magical divination" does not imply that the use of water witching is indefensible. Nor do we wish to put water witching into the same class with the hocus-pocus of the sleight-of-hand artist. By our criteria, water witching is "irrational," but as students of modern decision theory know, the definition of rational is quite arbitrary; what is rational on one set of assumptions becomes irrational with another set of assumptions.

A PSYCHOLOGICAL RATIONALE FOR WATER WITCHING

As a matter of fact, there are many situations in which we must act, but we cannot act rationally even if we want to. Such is the case when we have insufficient information by which we can decide whether our actions are based on scientific criteria. This, of course, is precisely the situation in which many individuals in search of underground water find themselves. They need to act now. At the time of decision they are in no position—either by training or through available information—to make a sensible judgment about a reasonable way to choose a well-site. Yet they have to choose. In such situations, as we have seen, many people resort to water witching. They need some sign or guidepost, so they follow the signs created by a diviner.

There are other reasons why we must not be too hasty in ridiculing someone for resorting to water witching. The decision to drill a well is an important one and one that will be made by an individual only once or, at most, a few times during his lifetime. The concept of "rational behavior," on the other hand, comes to us by way of economics and mathematical probability and applies specifically to decisions that are repeated over a large number of similar situations. The rational man of classical economics is one who acts so as to maximize his benefits when these benefits are averaged over a large number of decisions. To illustrate what we mean, imagine a situation in which you are given a choice between the following two alternatives: (*a*) you will receive $1,000 a week for the rest of your life, or (*b*) at the end of each week a coin will be tossed; if it lands "heads" you will receive $10,000, but if it lands "tails" you will receive nothing. The rational choice, according to classical economic theory, is alternative *b*. On some weeks, it is true, you will be unlucky and receive nothing. But on other weeks you will be lucky and receive $10,000. Since this is a recurring event, you will be lucky on approximately half the coin tosses, and, thus, your average income from alternative *b* will be $5,000 per week as compared to a steady income of $1,000 per week from alternative *a*.

The key feature of this picture of rational man is that we assume the decision he is making is one that is to be repeated over a large number of trials. And, in this way, it becomes meaningful to speak of his *average* gain from *repeated* events over the *long run*. But what happens to our hypothetically "rational" man when his decision is restricted to one event? That is, imagine that his two choices are between these two alternatives: (*a*) he will receive $1,000 for sure, and (*b*) he will receive $10,000 if a toss of a fair coin is "heads," otherwise he will receive nothing. Just what is a wise or "rational" decision in this case (frequently called a "payoff matrix")? Classical economic theory would advise, "Choose the second alternative, for it has the greater expected value—in the long run." But our rational man can correctly point out that he is not interested in the long run; he can make this decision only once. As Bruner, Goodnow, and Austin (1956) and others (Savage, 1954; Luce and Raiffa, 1957) have pointed out, it is not obvious that a theory based on a series of instances is applicable to decisions about a particular instance. In such cases, what is a wise choice will vary from individual to individual and from circumstance to circumstance. It will depend upon idiosyncratic features and subjective values. An individual who is financially secure, for example, may regard the gain of $1,000 with indifference, but the opportunity to acquire $10,000 would very likely appeal to him. If this is so, alternative *b* would seem to be the wise choice. Another individual, on the other hand, may need exactly $1,000 for an operation to restore his vision. For him, the alternatives take on the meaning of (*a*) getting back his sight for certain, versus (*b*) a fifty-fifty chance of getting back his sight (plus some additional cash). The wise decision here appears to be alternative *a*.

This distinction in kinds of decisions corresponds with Cronbach and Gleser's (1957) dichotomy of institutional and individual decisions:

Institutional decisions such as selection of employees may be distinguished from individual decisions such as choice of a vocation. In the typical "institutional" decision, a single person makes a large number of comparable decisions. The "individual" decision is one in which the choice confronting the decision maker will rarely or never recur.

The classical theory of "rational behavior" is mainly concerned with maximizing gain over several decisions and applies to institutional decisions.

In the institutional decision, we may think of the decision maker as trying to maximize the benefit from a whole series of similar decisions. That is, he seeks a policy which will work best "on the average" over many decisions about admission or job assignment or therapy. Since each decision involves the same set of values, he can combine different decisions and strike some type of statistical balance which gives the best overall outcome.

As an example of an institutional decision, let us imagine a company that is going to drill a large number of wells over a wide area. From past experience it knows that a witched well is successful about 50 per cent of the time, whereas a well chosen by a trained geologist is successful 60 per cent of the time. Let's say that the company estimates it loses $1,000 for every well that is a "failure," but every successful well is worth $2,000. If the company hires a diviner to locate a hundred wells, it can expect to fail in approximately fifty of them (total loss, $50,000) and succeed in fifty of them (total gain, $100,000), resulting in a net gain of $50,000. If it hires the geologist, on the other hand, it can expect to fail in about forty wells (loss of $40,000) and succeed in sixty (gain of $120,000), resulting in a net gain of $80,000. Clearly, the "rational" decision in this case is to choose the geologist, because the company can expect a greater income from that decision. The consideration in this choice is the fact that the company will average its losses and gains over a large number of similar decisions.

One very important characteristic of institutional decisions is pointed out by Bruner, Goodnow, and Austin (1956). In what they call "series decisions" (and what we call "institutional decisions"), "an individual may make decisions or categorizations which carry little chance of immediate success but promise to yield considerable subsequently relevant information. This expectation of recouping, of being able to nullify past errors or losses, is one of the most comforting and significant features of series decisions."

But the man who is going to make his decision once or at most a few times cannot find the comfort that comes from the expectation of recouping, of averaging losses with gains. And this is, of course, the more typical situation in well-drilling; a man in search of underground water is going to sink one or two wells over a finite span of time. The promise of a probability or the expectation of what will happen over several similar decisions may or may not be a "rational guide" for such an individual decision. Considerable controversy exists among theoreticians in this area (cf. Savage, 1954, and Luce and Raiffa, 1957). As Cronbach and Gleser (1957) phrase it:

The individual decision is often unique. The choice may occur only once in a lifetime. Even where the decision can be "remade" at a later time if the first course of action works out badly, the original decision has an uncancellable influence on the welfare of the individual. A poor choice of curriculum at the outset of a student's college education will continue to handicap him long after he has discovered his error and changed to a more suitable curriculum. It is meaningless to speak of "averaging his risk," since he makes only a few such decisions at most.

Cronbach and Gleser conclude that individual decisions

must be made on highly personal bases. What is "rational" for one person may not be for another.

Water witching, from the scientist's viewpoint, is "irrational" divination. This is because the scientist's view is institutional; he is evaluating a large series of outcomes from water witching. But from the viewpoint of an individual consumer making an individual decision it is perhaps meaningless to call water witching "irrational." At least, if we do so label it, we must be careful to specify precisely in what way we are making the transition from the institutional to the individual situation.

Another feature of the decision to sink a well is the pressure of time. Quite frequently such a decision is made only as the result of an immediate and pressing need. Under such conditions the emphasis is placed upon immediately accessible cues—even those of questionable validity—rather than upon more valid cues that would be obtained only after undesirable delay and greater effort. The pressure of time leads to a search for cues that have salience (Bruner, Goodnow, and Austin, 1956). Contrast the clear-cut indications of the rod with the vague suggestions of the scientific geologist. The rod's message is decisive and unambiguous. The diviner says, "Dig here," and pinpoints the site precisely. The geologist supplies general information but leaves the pinpointing to the consumer. The scientist supplies guidance alone; the diviner relieves the consumer of all responsibility for choice.

The action of the rod also provides reassurance at a time when the anxious seeker for water most needs it. The scientist, ever honest and ever aware of the fallibility of his method, qualifies his judgment and does not guarantee success. The water diviner goes about his business with the certitude that comes from blind faith.

The scientist's cues may ultimately have a more valid connection with the presence of underground water, but at the moment of decision the decisiveness of the rod's action supplies the greater emotional relief.

That the result of a well-sinking may often be learned only after considerable delay further emphasizes these immediate benefits of a method that is clear-cut in its guidance. Sometimes it may be weeks or months after the initial selection of a site before the venture can be classified as a success or failure. And often a well that is initially classified as a failure becomes mysteriously productive after a span of time, whereas one that looked good suddenly goes bad. Up to now, we have over-simplified our problem by talking as if it were a relatively simple matter to decide whether a witched well is a success or a failure. In fact, the outcome of a well-drilling is often so ambiguous that debate rages for years over whether it was successfully or unsuccessfully divined (cf. Roberts, 1951, 1953, 1957). This ambiguity enables Kenneth Roberts to argue, for example, that Henry Gross's divining rod infallibly reacts to underground "flowing water" and, at the same time, to report many cases in which clients charge Henry with failure. He argues that these apparent "failures" really do not demonstrate the fallibility of the divining rod but rather the bungling of well-drillers whose dynamiting techniques or heavy tractors crush or deflect the delicate water veins from their natural course. He reports on many cases where a well that was at first thought to be a failure later turns out to yield an adequate supply of water. (It should be mentioned that seasonal variations and other factors can produce tremendous variability in the flow of water at a particular site.)

Gross was hired, for example, to divine a well for the archaeological camp at the ancient Mayan city of Tikal in Guatemala. (For different accounts cf. Roberts, 1957; Shook, 1957; our information comes in part from personal communication with E. M. Shook.) Gross designated three different sites that he said would produce water within depths ranging from 286 feet to 499½ feet and "all this water good to drink and flowing." The archaeologists drilled at one of the sites selected by Gross to a depth of 520 feet with no sign of water. They regarded the effort as a failure. But Roberts maintains that certain features of the situation argue against classing this as a failure for Gross. He adduces four rationalizations. In the first place, he argues that the drilling equipment at Tikal could not go deeper than 520 feet (neglecting to emphasize that Gross's estimate of the bottom depth was much less than this figure); second, the hole was drilled without a casing, which would prevent surging (this still neglects the fact that no water was found); third, the drill had encountered a thick layer of clay ("Henry described this clay as 'a brown slime that my rod won't read.' . . . His rod had, he told me, been unable to read some 400 feet of that 'damned brown slime.' Now he was sure, the water was down about 720 feet"); and, finally, Henry Gross, on his second trip to Tikal became "panicky." "He apparently tried to think his way out of the failure of the drill to encounter water at the depth his rod had first given him. This is fatal, because a dowsing rod can't think." Because of such ambiguities in the definition of "success," Roberts is able to maintain consistently his belief that witching in Gross's hands is infallible in spite of many claims by clients to the contrary.

Although the employment of a water witch is something that any one person will consider only a few times in his life, he will be aware of numerous case histories in his neighborhood. And because in many of these accounts the action of the witch was followed by success, or what can be construed as success, the decision to use the diviner will have added attraction. Of course, he may very well be aware of failures that have resulted from water witching.

Certainly we know from studies of aspiration level that degree of confidence is based on a general summary of success and failure in situations seen as comparable to the present one being faced, and, more immediately, upon the success or failure of recent performance. Indeed, then, confidence can be increased by a tendency to emphasize or remember selectively one's successes and also by the tendency to see a present task as similar to past tasks on which one has used a cue successfully. There seems to be evidence, moreover, that past success has the effect of increasing confidence more than past failure reduces it [Bruner, Goodnow, and Austin, 1956].

We cite these characteristics because they make plausible our assertion that water witching can be a form of magical (irrational) divination and still be an understandable and psychologically defensible form of action. Because the decision to drill a well is unique and calls for immediate action, emphasis is placed upon those cues that are immediately available, that provide specific guidance, reduce ambiguity, supply emotional reassurance, and lead to decisive action in a moment of anxiety and concern.

WATER WITCHING AS A CULTURAL PATTERN

What we have said gives a plausible, psychological justification to the persistence of water witching. Justification can also be made from the viewpoint of the anthropologist and sociologist. To explain this we need to look a little more deeply into the situation in which man finds himself on this earth. As we look around the world and study both the histories of modern nations and the cultures of primitive peoples, we see that human beings have developed all kinds and varieties of ways of exercising and extending their control over the natural environment. Eskimos manufacture excellent bone harpoons which efficiently kill seals and walruses, and they have an immense amount of sound knowledge about the habits of these animals and the environment in which they live. The Hopi Indians of Arizona are masters of the technique of planting and growing corn in the arid Southwest. The Trobriand Islanders know how to plant and grow yams efficiently and how to build canoes to enable them to fish productively in the inner lagoon of their South Sea island. Twentieth-century Americans, with a high degree of scientific development and probably more kinds of machines than any other people in the world, are well along the road to almost complete control of many aspects of life as we know it.

But with all this accumulation of sound knowledge there continue to exist everywhere situations beyond the range of man's techniques and knowledge. The seals and walruses may not be found where the Eskimo looks for them on a given day, and his family goes hungry. The summer rains have an exasperating way of not starting on time in the Southwest, or of not coming at all some summers, and, despite all the Hopi's hard work, the corn crop fails. The Trobriand Islanders do well fishing in the inner lagoon, but when they put out into the open sea to catch larger fish, they sometimes run into a tropical storm and do not come back. Our American science does not tell us with exactness the path of a tornado, and our technology gives us little control over it when it strikes.

All these situations cause anxiety and concern. We

feel frustrated, and we also feel a deep need to make some kind of intellectual sense out of why it has to be this way. And the significant thing is that we human beings do not just take it on the chin and do nothing about the problem. Instead, we always develop and maintain some kind of activity which makes us feel that we are doing something about the problem and makes us think we have an explanation of why it had to happen in the first place. This activity, from the point of view of the observer of the scene, is called a "magical" practice (Malinowski, 1925; Homans, 1941; Parsons, 1944). The Eskimos manipulate amulets and charms, and their *angakoks,* or shamans, make what they believe to be journeys to the bottom of the sea to placate the Sea Goddess who controls the seals and walruses—all with the firm conviction that these ritual activities will increase their chances of finding and killing the sea mammals on which they depend for food (Rasmussen, 1929). The Hopis have an elaborate set of masked *kachina* dances for rain making. The *kachinas* are thought of as ancestors who return with clouds and rains that help the community. They normally come in groups to dance in the plaza and are impersonated by the men wearing different types of masks (Titiev, 1944). The Trobriand Islanders surround their open sea fishing with magical rituals. In discussing the role of magic in their culture, Malinowski writes:

While in the villages on the inner lagoon fishing is done in an easy and absolutely reliable manner by the method of poisoning, yielding abundant results without danger and uncertainty, there are on the shores of the open sea dangerous modes of fishing and also certain types in which the yield varies according to whether shoals of fish appear beforehand or not. It is most significant that in the lagoon fishing, where man can rely completely upon his knowledge and skill, magic does not exist, while in the open sea fishing, full of danger and uncertainty, there is extensive magical ritual to secure safety and good results [1925, p. 32].

Even more dramatic are the magical rituals that have emerged in the often frustrating contact between the primitive peoples of the world and the expanding European cultures. An example is the Ghost Dance, which spread like a grass fire among the Plains Indians, especially the Sioux, in 1889–90. This ceremony was adopted by the Sioux at a time when the buffalo had vanished, the Indians had been confined to a reservation for some years, and the United States government was attempting unsuccessfully to make farmers out of these erstwhile buffalo-hunters. It was believed that the dance would not only cause return of the dead Sioux, driving immense herds of buffalo, but would also lead to the annihilation of the white people through a great landslide that would cover them up forever. During the dance, the Sioux wore "ghost shirts" cut in Indian style, which were believed to be bulletproof (Mooney, 1896). Here again we see a people faced with frustration and uncertainty who adopt and elaborate a set of magical rituals that they confidently believe will remove the source of the frustration and provide them once more with a way of life they understand.

Let us see if there is anything about the underground water situation in the United States which bears any resemblance to these other situations. We have presented ample evidence to show that the exact location of shallow underground water supplies is uncertain in many parts of this country and that finding a good well is, for countless rural dwellers, a matter of great emotional and practical urgency.

For most regions of the United States a competent

ground-water geologist can provide (with sufficient study of the surface outcroppings and of the sands, gravels, and rocks bailed out of previously drilled wells) a sound *general* description of the water resources. But, unless there is time and money to sink test wells at close intervals, even the most careful geological mapping leaves much doubt as to the depth and amount of ground water available in any *particular* location where a well is needed. The knowledge of particular small areas remains as hidden from geological divination as from any other procedure, and the situation is one in which we would expect some kind of magical divination to be used.

To illustrate these statements, let's turn for a moment to a rural village of two hundred people in the arid Southwest where one of us recently spent eighteen months living and studying the history and life of the community (see Vogt, 1955). This small community, Fence Lake, was established by families from Texas (a number of them from a town called Cotton Center, Texas) and Oklahoma, who settled on homesteads in western New Mexico in the 1930's. These people started raising crops of pinto beans on dry-land farms in this area, where the old-time ranchers scoffed at them and asserted that the land was only good for grazing cattle and sheep.

The natural environment is unusually uncertain for dry-land farming. The soil is excellent for beans, but the necessary ninety-day growing season is often cut short by late spring frosts or early fall frosts at this elevation (7,000 feet). But the basic problems turned out to be those of inadequate and fluctuating rainfall and the development of water resources for livestock and household use. Annual precipitation averages 12.5

inches, but it varies from 6 to 19 inches, and sometimes the summer rains do not come at all.

When these homesteaders first arrived in 1930 and 1931, they found it necessary to haul water in barrels by team and wagon from a lake located three miles from the center of the community. When the lake went dry in a drought after a year or so, they hauled water from a spring seven miles away. If a bean farmer had livestock, it meant that he had to haul water at least every other day.

A few farmers tried drilling wells in those early years, but it was soon discovered that, although in some places water was struck at shallow depths (80–100 feet), in others dry holes were the only result after drilling over 500 feet. At a cost of one dollar to three dollars a foot (depending upon how hard the rock was that the well driller had to penetrate), few of the homesteaders were willing to take the risk.

Some geologists from the Soil Conservation Service began to visit the community and to make certain recommendations on the location of wells. They told the people that their community was on top of the Mesa Verde formation (made up of sandstone and shale), which had been cut into channels and ridges during Tertiary times and then later partly covered up by sands and gravels. Still later, lava flows came in on top of the Tertiary sands and gravels. And, a further complication, there were a number of faults and at least one syncline which affected the buried rock strata. Water, they said, could be found in the Mesa Verde formation or in the Tertiary sands and gravels at the bottom of one of the old buried channels. But when it came to declaring the depth and amount of water that might be found at a *particular* well site, they could answer only in general terms.

It was in this situation that Fritz Jacoby, a bean farmer of German ancestry from Texas, suddenly "discovered" that he had the "power" to witch for water. As a young boy he had seen water witching done in Texas. So one day he simply cut a forked stick from his wife's peach tree, tried out the technique as he remembered it, and it "worked." That is, the stick pointed down over two "water veins" near his farmhouse. He traced the veins to a point where he said they crossed each other and had a successful well drilled at this spot at a depth of 230 feet.

Fritz rapidly achieved community-wide reputation as a water diviner and "successfully" dowsed eighteen wells in the next eighteen years. Six wells were dowsed by a second man, who came to the community later, making a total of twenty-four wells located in this manner.

During the same period, however, Fritz dowsed five well sites that were completely dry holes, and he often missed calculating the depth by as much as 200 to 400 feet. And during the same eighteen years, from 1933 to 1951, twenty-five wells were successfully drilled without benefit of dowsing of any kind; and seven dry holes were drilled in locations that were not dowsed. Lee Bell, the local driller, who is a complete skeptic about dowsing, was already drilling in water-bearing formation on two occasions when Fritz appeared with his forked twig. Fritz announced (after dowsing around the immediate area of the well rig) that Lee had best move his rig, since he would never hit water in the holes he was then drilling.

As time went on, Fritz practically killed his wife's lone peach tree by cutting witching sticks from it; so he had to shift to using forked twigs from piñon trees which he found "worked" just as well. He came to explain his "power" in terms of "electricity," and he usually attributes his errors to the presence of iron—like a knife in his pocket which he forgets about or an old piece of farm machinery in the vicinity—which "short-circuits the electric current."

What was happening in Fritz's case is very clear in geological terms. When he dowsed his own well, he was over an area where the Tertiary sands and gravels were close to the surface, and water was found at 230 feet. The other wells which he "successfully" dowsed were either drilled into the Tertiary formation or the farmers were willing to drill to greater depths and reach the Mesa Verde formation. The dry holes were located either where Tertiary sands did not exist and the farmer was unwilling to go deep enough to strike the Mesa Verde formation or over the Tertiary sands but in places where buried channels or the syncline made the depth to water greater than the wells were drilled. The same geological facts account for the successful wells and dry holes that were not dowsed.

This looked like a case where magical divination was being used in a situation of uncertainty and anxiety, where geological divination could not provide answers for particular well-sites. Since we knew that many of the families came from the Texas Panhandle, especially from the area around Cotton Center, Texas, we decided to find out what life was like in Cotton Center. Wilfrid C. Bailey, a colleague then teaching at the University of Texas, was persuaded to make a study of this Panhandle community. He studied carefully the ground-water conditions on those flat Texas plains and discovered that the average annual rainfall is almost twice as great (22 inches) as it is in Fence Lake and that the ground-water table stands at a nearly constant level, 125 feet below the surface of the plains. Wells are located where it is most convenient to drill them. Bailey's field notes clearly indicate that water witching is widely known but almost never practiced. He classifies it as an "unused skill" in Cotton Center (Bailey, 1951).

Now the case began to be even more exciting. There appeared to be a real connection between the uncertainty of locating wells in the arid Fence Lake environment (with its complicated geology) and the flourishing of water witching. This conclusion was fortified by the fact that the same kinds of people living in Cotton Center (with its simple geology and level water table) did not use water divining, but when they migrated to Fence Lake the unused skill was activated and flourished within two years after their arrival (Vogt, 1952).

These conclusions can now be applied to the United States as a whole because of the strong correlations we reported in the last chapter between water witching and ground-water problems as measured by "problem score for drilled wells," "range in depth of drilled wells," "percentage of wells resulting in dry holes," and "lack of ground-water information."

Additional evidence comes from a recent survey of farmers in Ohio. Rogers (1958) classified water witching as a form of "agricultural magic" along with such practices as planting crops, castrating or dehorning livestock, or cutting weeds by the "signs of the moon." Each farmer was scored on an Agricultural Magic Scale according to the degree to which he agreed with the following two statements:

1. There are some things about farming where signs of the moon are important.

2. When a farmer wants to drill a well he should first witch for water.

Approximately 34 per cent of the farmers agreed with the first statement, and about 39 per cent agreed with the second one. Because Rogers found evidence that belief in planting by the moon frequently went along with belief in witching, he combined the two beliefs into one measure of agricultural magic.

After analyzing the data from personal interviews with a random sample of 104 farm operators and 88 farm housewives, Rogers concludes:

Magical beliefs are more likely to be used in decision-making situations where a high degree of risk and uncertainty are involved. Farmers who relied upon agricultural magic were more resistant and less likely to adopt new technological farming practices. Many respondents, however, saw no ideological conflict between magical beliefs and science.

Rogers' use of the term "agricultural magic" seems to coincide with our term "magical divination." And his finding of a connection between such magic and risk and uncertainty agrees with our results on the distribution of water witching.

Witching, then, in the U.S.A. seems to persist where the location of an adequate water supply is attended by anxiety and uncertainty, and this is precisely what our magical ritual theory predicted. From this viewpoint, water witching is a way of coping with nature in a situation where the outcome is important but uncertain. It is a form of magical divination that functions, like the magic in primitive societies, to reduce anxiety.

The magical ritual theory stresses the non-rational factors behind water witching, but, as we have indicated, many users of the practice try to make out a rational case for their choice. This rational case tends to coincide with what we have called the "nothing to lose" theory. The argument emphasizes the fact that in many situations expert advice is lacking or inadequate because of peculiar geological factors. The person in search of water turns to the diviner because, even if witching is invalid, the witch's judgment cannot be worse than his own. So he has little to lose (if there is nothing to witching) and a lot to gain (if there is something to witching). As one Nebraska agent put it, "Farmers drilling an irrigation well feel that the 5 to 25 dollar fee is so small compared to the 3,000 to 15,000 dollar investment that they do it even though they aren't sold on it."

Perhaps to some extent then, both theories are correct. It may even be that they are opposite sides of the same coin. The motivating factors of anxiety and uncertainty combine, according to the ritual theory, to create a need for clear-cut, anxiety-reducing responses. And water witching, as we have argued in detail, provides just such a salient response. On the other hand, one of the important contributing factors to the prevailing uncertainty is the lack of scientific ground-water information, and this enables the man who turns to the diviner to rationalize his behavior in terms of the "nothing to lose" theory.

GAINS AND COSTS OF WATER WITCHING

All of this leads up to our final word on water witching. We take the view that water witching is a form of magical divination. We do not feel, however, that it is "superstitious nonsense" that should be stamped out at all costs, because, like other magical practices in our own and other societies, it does something important for people in uncertain situations that are, as yet, beyond the control of science.

Perhaps the most important thing it does is to provide *certain* and very *specific* answers which tend to relieve the farmers' anxiety about ground-water resources and to encourage them to go ahead and drill the well. We are certain that Fritz Jacoby's dowsing of wells in Fence Lake encouraged a number of farmers to go ahead and drill and get on with the business of developing their homesteads, instead of continuing to haul water by team and wagon for seven miles. If they drilled deep enough, they all struck water whether the well-site was dowsed or not, but the very act of dowsing was important in tipping the scales in favor of going ahead with the drilling.

But it is equally clear that the practice involves certain fundamental costs in the long run. Energy and resources are invested in a technique that does not provide any better information about the location of shallow underground water supplies than does the good judgment of individual farmers who have lived in an area for a long time and made common-sense observations of the surface geology and of the successes and failures of nearby wells. It is often the case that a dowsed well will be located at sites that are inconvenient and inefficient for the most economical operation of the house or farm. We know of some farmhouses in Fence Lake that have been built in inaccessible places on the sides of hills "because that is where the water witch found the water."

In so far as the adherents of dowsing also believe they are really being "scientific" about locating underground water, these attitudes detract from the efforts to obtain more precise geological information. Even if the scientific method does not give the farmer an accurate estimation of the depth of water in a given location, it is at least a more promising long-range approach to the development of water resources for the United States.

WATER WITCHING AND EDUCATION

How much effect would more and better education have upon the persistence of water witching and other magical practices in our society? Our data indicate that education per se has little if any relation to the existence of water witching. Our files contain many instances of college graduates and even men with Ph.D.'s and M.D.'s who either practice or firmly believe in water witching. And we have already expressed pessimism concerning the elimination of water witching merely by spreading the word that it "doesn't work."

But this does not mean that belief in water witching is independent of education. The recent awareness and national focus upon our educational system (*Life*, March 24, 1958) has brought to light deficiencies which have long vexed those of us who deal with students at the undergraduate and graduate levels in colleges. We are told that only 25 per cent of our high-school students study physics, but even more surprising is the number of college graduates and Ph.D.'s who manage to complete their formal education without being exposed to a course in science or mathematics. We even find many graduates openly boasting about their cleverness in avoiding laboratory courses. Today we live in a culture whose technology is based upon, and whose potential survival may depend upon, the achievements of the scientific method. And yet this method of seeking "truth" is omitted from many educational programs.

This "divorce of science and culture" is a relatively recent feature of our educational philosophy. According to Bertrand Russell (1958):

The separation of science from "culture" is a modern phenomenon. Plato and Aristotle had a profound respect for what was known of science in their day. The Renaissance was as much concerned with the revival of science as with art and literature. Leonardo da Vinci devoted more of his energies to science than to painting. The Renaissance architects developed the geometrical theory of perspective. Throughout the eighteenth century a very great deal was done to diffuse understanding of the work of Newton and his contemporaries. But, from the early nineteenth century onwards, scientific concepts and scientific methods became increasingly abstruse and the attempt to make them generally intelligible came more and more to be regarded as hopeless. The modern theory and practice of nuclear physicists has made evident with dramatic suddenness that complete ignorance of the world of science is no longer compatible with survival.

One can argue that the inclusion of scientific courses in the curriculums of grammar and high schools will not lessen the impact of pseudo science. There will always be those compelling social and psychological reasons for choosing water witching that we have already examined. But it seems to us that we should at least offer in our schools a set of standards with which to evaluate the seductive appeals of the various pseudo sciences. We cannot turn everyone into a Newton, a Darwin, an Einstein, or a Pavlov; but at least we can make everyone aware of the pitfalls of accepting desired conclusions without patient investigation.

Instead of treating the glaring boners of men like Blondlot as skeletons in our closets, we should present these cases as outstanding examples of how sincere and dedicated men can go wrong. A careful analysis of the factors that led such outstanding scientists into what turned out to be errors is one of the most effective ways of alerting us to the precautions that are necessary to pursue truth unfettered by our prejudices. Instead, we find that the theory of unconscious muscular action to account for the rod's movement, first put forth by Schott and Kircher in the middle of the seventeenth century, had to be worked out anew by Faraday and Chevreul in the middle of the nineteenth century to explain the movement of rods, pendulums, and turning tables. Now, in the middle of the twentieth century, we discover that many geologists, laymen, and others—unaware of the work of Faraday and Chevreul—find themselves baffled by the rod's behavior and unable to find an explanation. It is necessary to teach people from scratch what has been known for centuries.

Recently, a book entitled *The Search for Bridey Murphy* became a nationwide best seller. It was about a woman who, while in a hypnotic trance, allegedly became possessed by another personality who had existed many years before. The twin appeals of hypnotism and reincarnation made the book a "publishing phenomenon" (Breen, 1956). Within two months of its initial publication on January 6, 1956, the publishers printed 170,500 copies. Arrangements were made to serialize the book in thirty-nine newspapers; an abridged version appeared in *True* magazine; a recording of a session with Bridey Murphy sold 30,000 copies at $5.95 within a few months; a movie was made from the book; and sales of other books on hypnotism and the occult suddenly soared.

People speculated about why this particular book on the supernatural was so much more successful than the hundreds of others that have been published. Perhaps one reason was that its author, Morey Bernstein, was an amateur writer and new to the field. The book is an autobiographical account of his conversion, first to the reality of hypnotism, and then to the world of the supernatural. After using hypnotism to treat cases of stuttering, insomnia, migraine headache, hysterical paralysis, and excessive smoking (Bernstein is not a medical doctor), Bernstein tried an age-regression experiment with an especially good subject whom he called Ruth Simmons. Under hypnosis he instructed her to go back in time—to a time before she was born. Reacting to this suggestion, Ruth Simmons suddenly took on the role of Bridey Murphy, who lived in Ireland in the early nineteenth century. She developed an Irish brogue, performed jigs, and gave facts, names, and places to help establish her identity in her previous existence.

Perhaps the most curious aspect of the book is its author's and publisher's failure to check into the background and childhood of its principal witness—Mrs. Ruth Simmons. Instead the book gives us page after page about Bernstein's background and philosophy. Yet the whole case for reincarnation rests entirely upon the assumption that Mrs. Simmons, in the role of Bridey Murphy, is spouting facts and doing things beyond the knowledge of her present existence. Instead of the obvious search into her background, a reporter was sent to Ireland to painstakingly match the facts in the Bridey Murphy account to whatever facts could be unearthed in official documents in Bridey Murphy's alleged existence. The result was a syndicated series of articles coming to no clear-cut conclusion.

Almost without exception the reviewers of the book pointed to the obvious lack of information about Mrs. Simmons. Again and again they suggested that the key might be found in the childhood of Mrs. Simmons. A typical comment was:

The story of Bridey Murphy is in large part the story of the childhood of Ruth Simmons. Who can check back on every experience, book, movie, conversation, and stimulation to which a single child may have been exposed? And who, after studying the vagaries of the human mind, can deny the possibility that one such mind can create dozens of Bridey Murphys? The Bridey Murphy story is just another fascinating episode in the endless creativity of the human psyche. To us whose business is the study of human behavior *The Search for Bridey Murphy* is but another addition to anecdotes concerning memory and forgetting. It is also a chapter in the history of man's wants and aspirations, of how man's need for a purpose in life—his desire to have concrete proof of an existence after death—can cause him to ignore the obvious, in favor of the more desirable explanation [Ray Hyman in the *Boston Sunday Globe*, May 13, 1956].

The Search for Bridey Murphy suddenly disappeared from the best-seller lists when reporters from the *Chicago American*, with the help of the pastor of the church to which Mrs. Simmons went as a little girl in Wisconsin, were able to get the facts of Ruth Simmons' childhood and publish them serially in the Hearst newspapers beginning on June 11, 1956, and ending on June 21. In the book, Bridey Murphy speaks with an Irish dialect, dances a jig, gets spanked for scraping paint off a metal bed, has a baby brother who dies, has an "Uncle Plazz," recites Irish folklore, likes the "Londonderry Air" and potato pancakes, and has red hair. In real life, Ruth Simmons as a child recited monologues in Irish dialect, danced jigs, got spanked for scraping paint off a newly painted metal bed, had a baby brother who died, had an "Uncle Plazz," was taught Irish folklore by a relative, loved the "Londonderry Air" and potato pancakes, and touched up her brown hair with henna in an effort to convince herself and others that it was really red. The reporters uncovered many more such details out of which the fictitious Bridey Murphy had been created.

Again, the question arises whether proper education

could have dampened the Bridey Murphy hysteria. In the first place, the Bridey Murphy story has been repeated over and over again in previous times. An early example was an illiterate servant girl who, while in a feverish delirium, spoke phrases in flawless Hebrew, ancient Greek, and Sanskrit. And, as usual, there were those onlookers who eagerly jumped to the conclusion that she was temporarily "possessed" by a being of superior intelligence. But others, rather skeptical, patiently investigated the girl's background and discovered that she had worked for a scholarly clergyman as a child. He would parade back and forth outside the window of the room in which she was working, reading aloud passages from ancient Greek, Hebrew, and Sanskrit. In this way the emphasis shifted from reincarnation to subconscious memory.

The classic study in this strange land of "retro-history," or of people who take on the personalities of previous existences, is that of the Geneva shopkeeper Helene Smith (Flournoy, 1900). At first Mrs. Smith would enter into a trance and emerge as Marie Antoinette; in another period she became a lady from the planet Mars; and finally she was the daughter of a fourteenth-century Arab chieftain. Here was living proof, or so thought many eager believers of reincarnation. But the psychologist Flournoy carefully observed and studied Helene Smith in all her phases over a long period of time. He noticed that as Marie Antoinette she accepted cigarettes until it was pointed out to her that cigarettes were unknown in those days. Her Martian language turned out to be of exactly the same grammatical structure as French (the only language known to Mrs. Smith), and the historical facts that she described in her "Hindu Cycle" were found to have come from a book whose information (and therefore Mrs.

Smith's information) subsequently turned out to be false. After his patient study of Mrs. Smith, which is a model investigation of multiple-personality, matching the thoroughness of Pfungst's investigation of Clever Hans, Flournoy concluded, "For me, it is only a question of memories of her present life; and I see nothing of the supernormal in that."

The cases of Helene Smith and of Bridey Murphy reflect the strong effect that our beliefs about and our desires for immortality can have upon our powers of reasoning. Yet we feel, at least in some instances known to us, that a prior acquaintance with the facts and a penetrating analysis would have lessened the impact and the false logic of the Bridey Murphy hysteria. We also feel that knowledge of Chevreul's classic study of the pendulum, Faraday's ingenious investigation of table turning, and Pfungst's painstaking exposure of Clever Hans would alert people to look before they leap to conclusions about the divining rod, the pendulum, the doodlebug, and other devices dependent upon involuntary motor action that still engage the energies and passions of a large portion of our "educated" population.

Postscript 1978

While the subject of water dowsing has continued to be of interest to scientists and laymen alike, no hard evidence has appeared in the past two decades to cause us to change our minds about the basic conclusions we reached when this book was published in 1959—i.e., that water divining is not an empirically reliable technique for locating shallow underground water, but rather a form of magical divination.

There has been, however, an interesting series of responses to our book which we would like to describe. The book was widely reviewed in both professional and more popular journals, and, to the best of our knowledge, all but four were generally favorable. These were, significantly enough, the *American Journal of Psychical Research*, the *Journal of Parapsychology*, the *Journal of the British Society of Dowsers*, and the *Quarterly Digest of the American Society of Dowsers*. We also received dozens of letters from individuals, for the most part either dowsers or "believers" in the practice of dowsing. These were virtually all in the nature of uncontrolled case history experiences of the type we have already described in chapter 3. It is worth providing a couple of examples. One man wrote from North Carolina:

I am afraid you have run into a lot of fakers or the equivalent of same.

I thought this ability to witch water was just Old Wives tales until we bought a small acreage in Alameda, Texas, near Houston. Merely through curiosity my wife and I visited the land and cut a forked stick and having already decided the approximate site of the house we intended to build, I grasped the stick in the approved fashion and started walking.

The drag down of the point of the stick away from me was decidedly strong at one point. We stopped and put a peg down. . . .

The well driller struck a good flow of sweet water at approximately eighty feet where the peg had been placed.

A woman wrote from Oregon as follows:

I am a grandmother of eighty four years. I discovered the forked stick would turn for me more than fifty years ago but never put it to use until 1930, when we bought an acreage and needed a well. I found water and the tally stick said 22 feet and that was right. They could hear water running before they struck it. It was a dug well.

About eight years ago my daughter-in-law needed more water on her farm. I located it and the taly was around 55 feet, I don't remember the exact number. Water was found there and it has furnished water for farm use as well as the house which is modern with bath and everything. I also switched for a neighbor and found only fine black sand which the assayer said there was a trace of gold but not enough to bother with. Others who used the divining rod could find nothing so I wondered why as the tally went to the sand. To me there is no witching or magic about it: I think it is just electricity. When you hold a forked stick one prong in each hand I have heard that referred to as forming a circuit. I don't know anything about the working of currents, but there must be a pull from somewhere to make the stick turn, and I can feel a sensation in my arms when it begins to turn. When my husband put his hand on my shoulder the stick would not turn; when he removed his hand and stepped back it worked.

A major development in the world of dowsing in the United States has been the founding of the American Society of Dowsers in 1961, just two years after our book appeared. We cannot be certain that the founding of the Society was really in response to our book, but we suspect there may have been some connection since on page 24 we had commented, "European diviners are better organized than their American counterparts. They form societies, sponsor journals, and hold international congresses." We know that the founders of the American Society of Dowsers were familiar with *Water Witching U.S.A.* Indeed, one of the early issues of the *Quarterly Digest of the American Society of Dowsers* carried a review of our book which stated that our failure to recognize the validity of dowsing constitutes "a road block [to the acceptance of dowsing], contributing to the malnutrition, if not death by starvation for human beings, depriving them of water in drought stricken areas." Shortly after the American Society of Dowsers was founded in Danville, Vermont, one of us (Vogt) promptly joined the society, and, after the first membership list was published, received an irate letter from a dowser, asking, "What are you doing as a member of our American Society of Dowsers?" Not to be intimidated by such letters, Vogt, with the assistance of Linda K. Barrett, a research assistant of the Department of Anthropology at Harvard, undertook a three-year study of the Society. The study included making three field trips to the annual convention (held in Danville) in 1965, 1966, and 1968; interviewing 40 members from various regions of the United States; and analyzing the results of a pretest and test questionnaire returned by 134 members and the *Quarterly Digest* of the Society. Our conclusions were related in an article, by Linda K. Barrett and Evon Z. Vogt, "The Urban Dowser," published in the *Journal of American Folklore*, 82, No. 325 [July–Sept. 1969], 195–213. The following facts are drawn from that article; readers desiring more details should look at the original article.

We discovered that the American Society of Dowsers (ASD) had approximately one thousand members in the mid-1960s, and that, surprisingly, there was no overlap between the twenty-five thousand rural dowsers in the United States and the members of the ASD. The ASD members are living in cities, for the most part; hence our designation of them as "urban dowsers." To be more precise: While the rural dowsers reside in or near communities of populations less than five thousand and do not belong to the ASD, nearly 80 per cent of the members of the ASD live in communities of over five thousand, and of this group, 66 per cent live in metropolitan areas of over fifty thousand. The rural dowsers have a grade school education or less and pursue farming as a primary means of earning a livelihood. By contrast, 86 per cent of the urban dowsers have finished high school, 33 per cent have finished college, and only 5 per cent are farmers or retired farmers. Most are white collar workers with mid-1960s average annual family incomes between $7,000 and $14,000, but with 18 per cent having incomes over $14,000. (Recent information indicates that the ASD has grown to a membership of over eighteen hundred members.)

While the talents of the rural dowser are focused on the problem of locating water, the urban dowser has found new "uses" for his divining: the location of underground objects placed there by man (water and gas pipes, telelphone cables, sewers, and graves); the location of lost objects (golf balls, mislaid rings, watches, coats, runaway pets, and missing persons); medical dowsing (detection of disease, determining which organ is infected, and predicting the sex of fetuses); the prediction of future events (the date a new car will be delivered, whether or not a business deal is wise, and the winners of the Kentucky Derby); the analysis of personal character (determination of honesty and dishonesty).

The failure of dowsing to validate itself under

conditions of controlled tests and experiments and the ensuing scientific skepticism have precipitated a number of reactions among the organized, urban dowsers. The first of these is a deep-seated mistrust of the scientific community and the feeling that science has ignored dowsing because of its a priori conviction that there "couldn't be anything to it." Others are disillusioned with the basic tenets of the scientific method and claim that because dowsing is subjective in nature, science cannot validate it.

The urban dowser is much concerned with terminology. For example, although "witching" is the name most commonly used by the rural dowser, it is both avoided and denounced by his city counterpart because of its occult connotations and implications of witchcraft and sorcery. Instead, the practice is referred to as "dowsing," "divination," or sometimes by the European name "radiethesia."

In contrast to the rural practitioner, the urban dowser is organization conscious. A number of members of the ASD belong to the British Society of Dowsers, and to such associations as the American Society for Psychical Research. Further, while the rural dowser is part of a local, oral tradition in which beliefs concerning divining are passed along by word of mouth, the urban dowser learns about the phenomenon in various publications. Over 75 per cent of the ASD members joined the society as a result of reading about it in various magazines. For example, 44 per cent of the members first learned of the ASD through *Fate Magazine*, a periodical concerned without occult and supernatural matters.

Practically every ASD member has some sort of explanation as to why the rod moves and how dowsing works, and this is one of the richest aspects of dowsing folklore. A great many of the urban practitioners maintain that dowsing is an aspect of extrasensory perception which may be either a "God given" gift, or the product of a highly developed body or mind. Other theories envisage invisible rays or waves as creating an affinity between the dowser and an object. Sometimes called "matter-rays," these may be magnetic, electromagnetic, radiational, or cosmic. Either Nature or the hand of Providence has imbued all elements with such rays; however, their intensity, frequency, or wave length varies from one element to another. Each item has its own code, the belief goes, and is recognizable by the dowser, who may sense and detect them like a Geiger counter confronted with radioactivity, or whose body may emit its own rays which forcefully react with those of the element being dowsed, generating the movement of the dowsing instrument. Still other theories see electricity as the means of communication between the dowser and an object, or liken dowsing to the homing instinct of pigeons and the ability of lost dogs and cats to find their way back over great distances to their owners' homes.

There is agreement among urban dowsers that an individual must be in good health, both physical and spiritual, in order to perform successful dowsing. Lack of physical health is the result of disease or injury, or of immoderate eating, drinking, or smoking; lack of spiritual health is due to lack of faith in God and insufficient prayer.

Many urban dowsers, like the famous Henry Gross described in Kenneth Roberts's books, engage in map and photograph dowsing. It is believed that the location of any underground item can be divined on a map by a process referred to as "telesthesia." The dowser simply moves his rod or pendulum over a map or photograph of the area until it indicates a particular spot.

Medical dowsing—more common in Europe than in

the United States—is familiar to all of the ASD members though not practiced by all. The divining may be done over the patient to locate a diseased organ, or it may be done over a few drops of saliva, blood, or urine.

We also discovered that the conventions of the American Society of Dowsers are devoted to papers describing various experiences with dowsing, to demonstrations of various kinds of divining, and to symposia and discussions concerning how and why dowsing works!

We began the first edition of this book with a number of questions. The preceding accounts of the American Society of Dowsers and the urban dowser serve to update our answers to two of them: What is divining and who practices it? We should now like to review our conclusions on two of the others: Does it work and what makes the rod or pendulum move?

On the question of what makes the rod or pendulum move, our reading of the dowsing literature indicates that more and more of the writers on dowsing agree with the theory put forth in our book. That is, almost all the defenders of dowsing now admit that the rod or pendulum moves as a direct result of muscular reactions and serves to amplify such reactions. Many proponents even agree with us that the muscular reactions, in turn, are set off by nervous impulses originating in the diviner's unconscious processes.

It is at this point that skeptic and believer part company. The believers argue that the impulses that set off the "dowsing reaction" are somehow responses to information that originates in the dowsing target. When the dowser is on a site, this information may be in the form of very low frequency electromagnetic radiation that is perturbed by the object of search. Other theorists argue that the radiation has to be high frequency radiation in the microwave part of the spectrum. Both theories have serious flaws. The low frequency waves cannot carry enough information to account for the alleged feats of detection. But the high frequency waves do not have sufficient energy or penetrative powers to be detected by systems with even the most highly developed sensitivity imaginable.

The attempts to find some form of radiation to account for the dowsing reaction emanate from those investigators who want to find a scientifically acceptable basis for dowsing. However, the proponents of such radiation theories frankly admit that the evidence of successful map dowsing and other forms of distance divining seems about as good as that for on-site dowsing. And if map dowsing is to be admitted, this effectively rules out any form of radiation theory. The alternative would be some form of extrasensory perception, and this, in turn, would mean that if dowsing works, it must do so according to some paranormal principle.

The various theories put forth to account for dowsing are clearly presented in Francis Hitching's *Dowsing: The Psi Connection* (Garden City, N.Y.: Doubleday/Anchor Press, 1978). Hitching, who is a proponent of dowsing, does an excellent job of presenting the pros and cons of the various theories as well as setting forth the sorts of evidence that might support them.

Hitching also does a reasonably balanced job of presenting the empirical evidence in favor of, as well as against, the validity of divining. One of us (Hyman) has carefully evaluated the major studies of divining that have appeared since the publication of our book, and has discovered that the new evidence is consistent with what we have already reported. It is still the case that controlled scientific studies show no validity to divining. And the often striking stories in support of dowsing still emerge only from anecdotal and case history accounts. Hitching is surprisingly candid in agreeing with our position. He admits in several places in his well-written and encyclopedic book that by scientific standards there just is no case for dowsing. In a chapter provocatively entitled "Dowsing versus Science," he writes:

Looking at the history of tests of dowsing ability held under controlled experimental conditions, it is clear that none of them has unambiguously proved dowsing to be a repeatable faculty to be summoned at will. Once you depart from the kind of anecdotal case-history recounted so far in this book, you move into a treacherously sticky area of claim and counter-claim, proof and half-proof. Trying to demonstrate dowsing by statistical methods is like trying to photograph a ghost—you may see it, but the moment you try to operate the camera, the shutter jams and the ghost disappears. (Therefore, a scientist would say, there wasn't a ghost.) Maddeningly for dowsers—even those with years of experience—theirs seems to be a slippery and elusive gift that wilfully slides away at the moment they would most like to show it. [pp. 99–100].

Later in his book, Hitching tries to imagine an encounter between a psychic and a scientist.

The psychic finds it impossible to verbalize his personally felt experience and instinct; the scientist, searching to explain the symmetries of natural law, can only do so through mathematical theorems and formulae. Seeking to prove his point, the psychic might say, "I feel it, therefore it is"; the scientist, "it can't be measured, therefore it isn't." [p. 211].

In these words Hitching vividly portrays the very same dilemma that we have described in our chapters on whether witching works. We can sympathize with the believers whose personal experiences have persuaded them that dowsing is a reality. They *know* it works. Yet they are constantly frustrated in their attempts to convince the scientific skeptics. As soon as the scientist appears on the scene with an objective comparison, the much vaunted powers of the dowser melt away. The dowser behaves just like any other random instrument.

Hitching points out that for the scientist, if it can't be measured then it doesn't exist. It is tempting at this point to paraphrase one of the axioms that used to be attributed to psychoanalysis (in a satirical vein). "If it can be measured, then it must be something else." It seems to us that this latter proposition more closely captures the dowser's reponse to an unsuccessful scientific test than the one Hitching uses. In many of the experiments set up to test dowsers (and reviewed by Hitching), the dowsers had agreed ahead of time to the conditions and even helped in the design of the experiment. Many of them stated in advance that they were confident that the scientists' measurements would reveal the truth of dowsing. Only after the results were announced and the dowsers had clearly failed did they raise questions about what the scientist had measured.

One might think that a completely rational dowser would look at the evidence as assembled by ourselves or by Hitching and at least raise the possibility that maybe he or she has been wrong in believing dowsing works. After all, if a system is claimed to work so reliably and accurately in finding the depth and amount of underground water, locating missing persons, and answering almost any conceivable question with unerring success, shouldn't it be able to show even partial success under scientific observation? Isn't it strange that a practice that has been with us for over five hundred years has consistently been unable to justify itself according to scientific standards? And doesn't it strongly suggest a pseudoscientific faith when every negative finding is explained away as being irrelevant? Shouldn't our rational diviner begin to get suspicious that he is dealing with a nonfalsifiable system?

But we would be naive and unworldly to expect such reactions on the part of committed dowsers. The personal experiences are vivid, real, and compelling. The scientific evidence is abstract, artificial, and comprehensible only to the initiates. As social scientists we may be dismayed, but certainly not surprised, to find that the proponents of dowsing do not accept scientific evidence when it fails to back up their personal convictions. In fact, as Hitching points out, some become antiscientific. They attack science as being not only "irrelevant," but actually harmful. Others simply give up trying to convince scientists.

The most disturbing reaction, however, is one strongly implied by Hitching and actually spelled out by many authors on dowsing. This reaction goes something like this: By currently accepted scientific standards dowsing cannot be demonstrated. But, since dowsing is valid (according to the proponent), there must be something wrong with scientific method as applied to dowsing. Therefore, scientists should bend the rules or change the standards in order to allow dowsing to pass muster. In other words, science should make an exception for dowsing.

Such a plea (or demand) for special dispensation misses the whole point of what science is about. As we tried to point out earlier in the book there probably is no such animal as "*the* scientific method." But there are sets of procedures, safeguards, and controls that have been developed through experience, in various areas of scientific inquiry, as ways to correct for the fallibility of our unaided intuitions and personal convictions. As we pursue particular lines of inquiry in more and more detail, we find that we have to supplement or correct our normal modes of perceiving, calculating, judging, inferring, remembering, and other mental ways of knowing in order to remove biases and self-deceptive tendencies.

It is not that personal judgments and intuitions are always wrong. They sometimes are surprisingly correct and insightful. The problem is that they just as often, if not more often, are strikingly in error. Unfortunately the strength of the personal experience, intuition, or compelling insight is no indication of its potential truthfulness. One function of scientific method is to help us sort out those personal convictions that are true from those that are false.

Many of the proponents of dowsing, like many of the proponents of occultism and mysticism, mistakenly, in our judgment, draw a dichotomy between scientific and other ways of knowing. Hitching and many dowsers, for example, seem to argue that science is just one way of knowing and that there are other and equally valid ways of knowing. And dowsing, according to them, is true by one of these alternative ways of knowing. This is a very confused and misleading fiction that Bertrand Russell and others have long been trying to correct. Scientists, in fact, employ all ways of "knowing" available to them in generating their theories, hypotheses, and explanations. They differ, to the extent they do differ, from nonscientists in putting whatever it is they have come to "know" to rigorous and objective tests. This is the only way as far as we know that exists to separate myth from reality. In asking us to make exceptions for dowsing, the proponents are asking us, in effect, to give up the only way available to us to separate sense from nonsense.

Evon Z. Vogt
Ray Hyman
October, 1978

Letter of Explanation and Dowsing Questionnaire Mailed to County Agricultural Extension Agents

February 11, 1956

Attention: County Agricultural Extension Agent

DEAR SIR:

We are conducting a study on the practice of "dowsing"— the location of underground water with a forked stick or pendulum. As the County Agent, we feel that you are the ideal person to contact for such a study. Because you have the extensive knowledge necessary to be able to deal with this topic, we need your cooperation in answering the enclosed questionnaire.

We are studying this technique of locating water from an historical viewpoint, tracing the use and the spread of specific practices from county to county. We are not interested in proving or disproving the efficacy of the method, but we are concerned with the factors associated with its use, such as the groups engaging in the practice, the techniques used, and the explanations offered for the practice. "Dowsing" has many different names; it is called "water-prophesying," "water-divining," "water-witching," and a host of other terms. For this study, we define a dowser as one who:

1) uses or has used a forked stick, wire, or pendulum to locate underground water and
2) as a result of his activity a well has been dug or drilled on the site he indicated.

Whether water is found is not necessary for our definition.

The significant criterion is that a well is dug or drilled following from the actions of the dowser.

We cannot overemphasize the importance of your filling out this questionnaire. In the sample we have devised it is imperative that we have 100% response if our data are to be significant. We realize that some of the questions may be difficult to answer, but an estimated answer is, for our purposes, superior to no answer. If there are no dowsers in your entire county, mark that on the form because the absence of dowsers in an area is as important as their presence.

At the end of the questionnaire there is space for general comments or criticisms. We encourage you to write your reactions to the questions themselves, and to add any ideas you have which we may not have covered. May we repeat that the information which you can give us will be invaluable, and we would appreciate your filling out the form as soon as possible.

Your anonymity will be respected in any published reports; if we wish to use a quote your permission will be asked in advance. After the project is completed we will be glad to send you a published report of our results.

Sincerely yours,

Evon Z. Vogt
Associate Professor of Anthropology

Ray Hyman
Assistant Professor of Psychology

DOWSING QUESTIONNAIRE

(Please do not leave any questions blank; if you
do not know an answer, write in "I don't know.")

Name: ——   County: ——   State: ——
Length of time you have been county agent: ——

1. Is dowsing practiced in your county? Yes ☐ No ☐

2. If your answer to question No. 1 is *Yes,* skip this question and answer *all* the remaining questions beginning with No. 3. If your answer to question No. 1 is *No,* please answer the following:

a) Was dowsing practiced in your county in the past?
Yes ☐ No ☐

b) Is it possible that dowsing is practiced in your county now and that you would not know about it?
Yes ☐ No ☐

c) Please answer questions 9, 10, 11, 12, 16, 18.

3. How certain are you that dowsing is practiced in your county?
Check *one:*

   a) I've heard or read reports about it being practiced in my county, but *I haven't seen* it practiced.——

   b) I've seen it practiced.——

   c) I've seen it practiced and I've heard or read reports about it being practiced in my county.——

4. Please indicate the number of practicing dowsers in your county that *you know* about.——
Please estimate the total number of dowsers that you *think* are practicing in your county.——
If you can't estimate the number, give the range. From —— to ——

5. Is it possible that there are other dowsers in your county that you would not know about? Yes ☐ No ☐

6. Are there dowsers in your county who are female?
Yes ☐ No ☐

7. Are there any dowsers in your county who are under 15 years old? Yes ☐ No ☐

8. Are there any dowsers in your county who are over 65 years old? Yes ☐ No ☐

9. What percentage of wells in your county are drilled, bored or driven? —— Dug by hand? ——

10. Approximately how many new wells are opened each year in your county? ——
Approximately how many dry holes result from drilling and digging for wells each year? ——

11. What is the average cost per foot of each of these kinds of wells including the casing?
Drilled wells ——
Hand dug wells ——
Hand driven wells ——

12. What is the average depth and range at which water is found in:

	Average Depth	Range of Depth
Drilled wells	——	——
Hand dug wells	——	——
Hand driven wells	——	——

13. Among wells drilled (bored or driven) each year, what percentage are dowsed? ——
Among wells dug by hand each year what percentage are dowsed? ——

14. In your county, has the percentage of wells dowsed in the past ten years (*a*) increased ☐ or (*b*) decreased ☐ or (*c*) stayed the same ☐?

15. How much do dowsers charge for locating wells? ——

16. In your county how important are each of these problems to a man when he decides to dig or drill a well. (Please check appropriate boxes for both dug and drilled wells.)

	IMPORTANCE FOR HAND DUG WELLS			IMPORTANCE FOR DRILLED WELLS		
	Great	Some	Little	Great	Some	Little
May get a dry hole						
May cost a great deal						
May have to drill to a great depth						
May get too little water						
May get poor quality water						
May not be able to find water where he wants it						

Comments: ——

17. How is the use of dowsers' services distributed throughout your county?
    a) Concentrated in certain areas ☐
    b) Evenly scattered ☐
    If concentrated in certain areas, what or where are these areas? ――――

18. In your opinion how good is the available geological ground-water knowledge in your county?
    a) Adequate for the whole county ☐
    b) Adequate for certain regions only ☐
    c) Inadequate ☐

19. Please estimate the percentage of practicing dowsers for whom dowsing is a full time or major occupation. ―――― per cent.

20. If dowsing is not a full time occupation, what are the occupations of the dowsers? ――――

21. If some dowsers are farmers, are they most likely to be: (*a*) farm owners ☐ or (*b*) farm tenants ☐ or (*c*) farm laborers ☐?

22. How much education does the average dowser have: (*a*) grade school ☐ or (*b*) high school ☐ or (*c*) college ☐?

23. What is the name of "dowsing" in your county? ――――
    a) What are the most common dowsing techniques used? ――――
    b) How is depth estimated? ――――
    c) How is rate of flow estimated? ――――
    d) If a stick is used, does it point up or down to locate water? ――――
    e) What is the most common explanation of the *action of the forked stick or pendulum?*
       (1) by dowsers: ――――
       (2) your own theory: ――――

24. What are common sayings about *those who have the ability* to locate water (e.g., some say it is hereditary;

some say only men can do it; some say that only one person in a family can do it)?

25. Please check the groups in your county that practice dowsing:

☐ Old American   ☐ Protestant
☐ German   ☐ Catholic
☐ Italian   ☐ Jewish
☐ French   ☐ Other (please specify)
☐ Negro
☐ Scandinavian
☐ American Indian   Any other groups:——
☐ Spanish (or Mexican)

26. Please check the groups that are the predominant part of the *rural* population in your county:

☐ Old American   ☐ Protestant
☐ German   ☐ Catholic
☐ Italian   ☐ Jewish
☐ French   ☐ Other (please specify)
☐ Negro
☐ Scandinavian
☐ American Indian   Any other groups:——
☐ Spanish (or Mexican)

Comments: ——

Water-Well Location by Scientific Divination*

H. E. THOMAS

I take my cue for the title of this appendix[1] from the statements by Professors Vogt and Hyman (pp. 193–94, above) that ". . . one aspect of all divination is that it can never be perfect. No form of divination known to science can anticipate the future with 100 per cent accuracy. All we demand of a divination device is that it predict outcomes better than chance and better than alternative forms of divination. When it has been scientifically established that there is a correlation between signs and certain outcomes, then the use of these signs for divination is considered 'rational,' 'sensible,' 'scientific,' etc."

The petroleum industry, which has developed methods of scientific divination to a high degree (without, however, adopting the term "divination" as pertinent to those methods) has conclusive evidence that those methods produce a higher proportion of successful wells than are obtained by alternative methods. In the decade 1946–55, about 55,000 new-field wildcats (holes in unproved areas) were drilled in the United States (Moody, 1957). Of those located by scientific techniques 12.3 per cent were successful; the proportion rose to 15.5 per cent for those using geological, geophysical, and geochemical techniques to the utmost. By contrast, only 4.1 per cent of the holes located on nonscientific bases were successful. From this record it is easy

[1] Publication approved by the Director, U.S. Geological Survey. The author is Branch Area Chief, Pacific Area, Ground Water Branch, Water Resources Division, U.S. Geological Survey, Menlo Park, California.

to see why 19 out of 20 wildcats for oil are now located on the basis of scientific "signs."

As to ground water, there are no comparable data to show the relative success of scientific divination, magical divination, and other means of locating wells. Water is a far more abundant resource than petroleum, and we have come to expect a far higher proportion of successful wells in unproved areas than the one in nine that is the over-all average for oil wildcats. Of the millions of wells that have been dug or drilled in the United States, probably the great majority have yielded water in quantities sufficient at least for rural and domestic use. Nevertheless, good aquifers are clearly in the minority among the rock materials that one is likely to encounter in the upper few hundred feet of the earth's crust, which is the zone that is penetrated by most water wells. Gravel and sand, plus such consolidated rocks as sandstone and limestone, make up probably less than 10 per cent of the total; the other 90 per cent include clay and shale, which are notoriously poor producers of water, and crystalline rocks, in which water is obtained only from cracks and crevices. Considering the large number and wide distribution of successful wells and the large proportion of rock materials that do not yield water readily to wells, it appears that mankind has long been exercising some form of divination to obtain greater success than would be possible by purely random selection of places to seek water under ground.

It is commonplace to find variations from well to well in the type of rock material penetrated, the depth to water, the rates at which water can be withdrawn, and the quality of that water. These variations are indications of the uncertainty that accompanies underground exploration. The scientist, confident that these variations have a natural explanation, endeavors to marshal the documented experience of mankind in the hope of reducing that uncertainty. Established principles of geology, physics, and chemistry are fundamental to his interpretation of the specific conditions in the area he is investigating.

DATA FROM EXISTING WELLS

The scientific methods of water-well location are dull and prosaic in comparison with the flashy job that can be done by a dowser. I felt this particularly years ago as a scientific rookie, plodding from farmhouse to farmhouse, asking whether there was a well, how deep it was, might I see the log, and might I make various tests—a far cry from my conception of a water "expert." But this routine work does provide a background of past experience as a basis for "predicting outcomes better than by chance." Well-drillers, water witches, and others in the community who are interested in ground water have of course developed a similar backlog of experience, consciously or unconsciously. If someone needs a new water supply, an established well-driller can offer the benefit of his drilling experience in the area, in addition to his capability in operating his rig; and although a water witch might not recognize it, I suspect that his rod may develop a flip of experience after he has seen the results of drilling at previously "witched" sites. Thus it is logical for anyone desiring a new well to seek out the specialist having a long record of successful wells in the vicinity, whatever his explanation for this success. Although for each client the well location is an individual decision, it may approach an "institutional" or "series" decision (pp. 196–98, above) for the well-driller of long experience.

A corollary to the advantage of long individual experience in well location is the advantage of combining and integrating the experience of all who have worked in the region, thus providing a still broader basis for predicting the probability of obtaining water at an untried site. In more than a dozen of the states that have laws pertaining to ground water, one objective of those statutes has been to increase the public information concerning the ground-water resource. The data commonly demanded of either the well-owner or the well-driller include the well location, depth, diameter, log (showing rock materials penetrated), description of casing and equipment, purpose of use, chemical analysis, depth and temperature of water, and quantity produced. Progressive well-drillers have come far from the attitude of yesteryear that such information should be a "trade secret." With stabilization of the industry, and possibly with an assist from drillers' associations where they can talk over mutual problems, there is increasing realization that pooled information helps each one to minimize the uncertainty that is inherent in each job. Hence the recent legislation in several states calling for more data concerning water wells has had strong support from the drillers.

So far we have emphasized fact-finding and data collection. These are essential parts of the scientific method, and quite meritorious, but to me they are very much like haying. A farmer can cut the right grass at the right time, collect it, and haul it to some place where it is readily available. But so far as the general public is concerned, that hay is valuable only after it has been worked upon by specialists, who convert it into milk, or perhaps beef. Similarly, massed water data of themselves are not of much use to the general public, but with the right sort of data a specialist can decipher the occurrence of ground water in an area far more extensive than the immediate vicinities of the wells from which his data were obtained.

A report by Goldthwait (1949), based on analysis of drillers' records of 1,600 wells in New Hampshire, offers the kind of information that can help prospective well-owners make quasi-institutional decisions rather than individual decisions in their search for water. He points out the over-all uncertainty of obtaining water in the tight crystalline rocks (granite and schist) tapped by these 1,600 wells: water exists only in joints and other crevices, and there is no true water table; water flow and water level may vary greatly from crack to crack in a few tens of feet, so that one well may get water only a few feet down while a deeper well a few feet away may be dry. The report includes considerable discussion of probabilities, with graphs showing various relations such as those between yield and depth of well, depth to water, and depth of mantle rock. An important conclusion is that "Convenience is the best guide to location if contamination is not nearby. . . . Whether you strike the flow you required or not is a matter of chance—77 chances in 100 if you want a supply of 3 or more gallons per minute, 22 in 100 if you require a large supply for cooling or camp needs of 12 gallons per minute or more" (p. 20).

In a report on an area in the Piedmont of North Carolina, Mundorff (1948) covers another area in which crystalline rocks predominate, and in which there is, similarly, a considerable variation in the yield of wells. He finds significant differences in the average yields of wells in the various rock units and points out that wells in the valleys and draws yield more than those on slopes and far more than those on hilltops. Since most of the existing wells are in the less productive rock types, and most are also in the less favorable topographic locations, it is evident that if such a scientific analysis had been made long ago its benefits would have exceeded its cost many fold through the years.

DATA FROM GEOLOGIC STUDIES

What of the areas where no one has drilled wells and where, therefore, one can call on neither voice of experience nor record of success in ground-water development? Such areas are diminishing in the arid western United States with the rapid increase in population and water requirements in recent years, but there are still many unexplored localities; and there are still a good many such areas in the more humid eastern part of the country, especially where surface water has been sufficient for the small requirements of the past, so that there has been no urge to develop ground water.

In such unexplored areas a man may logically draw upon his experience in other areas, particularly if there is any basis for analogy with the unexplored area, and look for cues that may be indicative of water. For example, some plants are indicators of water at relatively shallow depths, and they may also be indicators of the quality of the water. Areas of natural ground-water discharge—springs, seeps, swamps, some lakes, and perennial streams—give important clues concerning the location of ground-water reservoirs. Commonly the most valuable clues are geological and come from the rocks that appear at the surface and from the geomorphology and structure that can be discerned by geologic studies. The geologic history of a region may include such processes as weathering, erosion, sedimentation, compaction, volcanism, glaciation, and mountain-making; and each of these may affect the storage and movement of ground water.

Maps can be very important sources of information, and I would not belittle Henry Gross's use of his rod on a map until I was assured that his map could not possibly have given any information concerning ground water. A field inspection of a large area can be more confusing than enlightening, unless and until the significant features are depicted on a map. Topographic maps provide invaluable aid, by showing such water features as swamps, lakes, springs, and the perennial portions of streams, as well as by showing physiographic features. Geologic maps go further, by depicting the framework in which ground water can move and be stored: they show the areas of outcrop of various rock units and such structural features as folds and faults, and they provide the means by which the trained user can visualize the underground relationship of rock bodies which may serve as conduits for or barriers to the movement of water. In some areas supplemental information is available from geophysical surveys that have been made during exploration for petroleum or other mineral resources; these may indicate the depth of rock materials that may be water bearing.

There is probably less uncertainty in Louisiana than in any other state about the outcome of drilling for water at any specified site. This is partly because the geology is simple, for the Gulf Coastal Plain is underlain by strata which are of relatively consistent thickness, attitude, texture, and water-bearing properties over fairly extensive areas, and partly because it is well known through petroleum exploration. The remaining uncertainty has been reduced by the efficient collection and analysis of data from water wells and oil wells as part of the co-operative ground-water program of the U.S. Geological Survey and the Louisiana Departments of Conservation and Public Works. Now, for most of Louisiana, if you specify a certain location, you can be furnished information on the depth at which you will find water, the quality of that water, and the yield you can expect.

STUDIES OF GROUND-WATER HYDROLOGY

The two preceding sections, on data from wells and geologic studies, are concerned primarily with finding water of economic value—that is, of suitable quantity and quality for the use intended—but with only slight rewording they could be applied to any mineral resource, such as petroleum, diamonds, or metallic ores. Characteristically these other resources occur in finite quantities which have remained underground for a long time and will remain indefinitely unless taken out by man; but once extracted they are gone, and there is no replenishment. In exploratory digging or drilling for water, as for these other resources, the prime concern of course is to find suitable water; but once that has been found the well-owner expects, or at least hopes, that his well will not go dry. In other words, he expects renewability of the resource. Thus to a greater extent than for other resources, the water-seeker is concerned with the source of water.

We have ample evidence that practically all the potable water on all continents is of meteoric origin;[2] or, more

[2] It has long been recognized that some waters within the earth are of non-meteoric origin. Such waters would include water that is in, or is derived from, lava near the surface or molten rock at greater depth (some of this may be "juvenile" water appearing at the earth's surface for the first time); and water released by compaction of sediments, or by compression and recrystallization of minerals under pressure. Characteristically, however, the waters known to be of non-meteoric origin are small in quantity, and invariably they are too highly mineralized to be potable.

broadly, it is part of a vast circulatory system—the hydrologic cycle—which includes vapor, surface-water, soil-moisture, and ground-water phases; and involves the processes of precipitation, infiltration, percolation, seepage, and evapotranspiration, by means of which water moves from one phase to another of the cycle. Renewability of the water resource is inherent in the hydrologic cycle, in which the fresh water on the continents—whether in the soil, in ground-water reservoirs, or in lakes or streams—receives increments periodically from precipitation. Increased storage as a result of precipitation is shown by higher lake levels, higher water levels in wells, and increased soil moisture; eventually there is increased discharge of water by evaporation and transpiration from the soil, by spring flow or seepage to streams from ground-water reservoirs, and by greater runoff in streams. In rainless periods there is a decrease of storage in the soil, in lakes, and in ground-water reservoirs, or a decrease in the discharge of water from them, or both. Thus, there is an over-all balance in nature between the "income" and the "outgo" of water. This balance is indicated by the hydrologic equation, which states that for any area the total water received (by precipitation plus inflow of surface and ground water) is balanced by the discharge (by evapotranspiration plus outflow of surface and ground water), with necessary corrections for changes in storage during the period.

Studies of the hydrology of ground water, and its relation to precipitation, streamflow, lake and reservoir storage, and soil moisture, provide important clues to the most likely locations for productive wells, when used in conjunction with studies of data from existing wells and of the geology of the area. More important, hydrologic studies provide the answer to the question, "Now that I have it, how much can I take, and for how long?"

Some of the earliest studies of ground-water hydrology were made in arid basins of the West more than fifty years ago—long before there was intensive pumping for irrigation and when there were few wells (Mendenhall, 1905; Meinzer,

1911, 1912). The reports of these studies told where ground water had been found, at springs and seeps and the few wells existing at the time; and then, on the basis of studies of the geology and hydrology, they told how the water got there, where to look for additional supplies, and in general how much could be expected. A report on the Mojave Desert of California (Thompson, 1929) is still the basic document on ground water in one of the most arid regions in the United States but a region that is becoming increasingly attractive to Los Angelenos who are allergic to smog or bumper-to-bumper traffic. These arid basins are by no means places where water is assured at any point; random drilling would result in a high proportion of dry holes, holes of excessive depth, or wells yielding water unfit for use. The low incidence of water witching in many of the arid basins (p. 181, above) is probably due, at least in part, to the availability of reconnaissance reports on ground-water hydrology.

The time allowed for a scientist to evaluate the possibilities of obtaining a successful well at a particular site may range from that required for a short visit to the site and a brief ride around the vicinity to a period of several weeks, permitting field investigation and collection of all scientific data that may be available and pertinent. In on-the-spot analyses he must necessarily fall back upon his past experience; training in geology and hydrology—both by education and by field experience—tells him what to look for and how to evaluate his findings on the basis of sound scientific principles. Of course, any such scientific education would be of benefit in similar situations to a well-driller, or to a dowser and his divining rod. Hence, many drillers have taken courses in geology, several geologists have become well-drillers, and several of the larger drilling companies have geologists on their staffs. The U.S. Geological Survey for several years has carried on a program of spot analyses for well-location in some of the least populated areas in the country—the western grazing lands administered by the Bureau of Land Management—undertaken as part of that agency's Soil and Moisture Conservation program. Under the direction of Harold V. Peterson, the program has resulted in a high proportion of successful wells in very unprepossessing places—in desert foothills, in alkali-floored valleys, and near the shores of Great Salt Lake, for instance. Spot analyses in areas where there is a deficiency or lack of geologic and hydrologic data, however, are poor substitutes for a comprehensive study of the area, and they are justified only in cases of urgency where no more satisfactory basis exists. Although on the surface the spot analyses appear to be more economical, because less time is consumed, they provide predictions that have less assurance of success, and they must be undertaken for each new development.

The value of a comprehensive regional study of groundwater hydrology was clearly shown in the Navajo and Hopi Indian Reservations, which cover an area of about 25,000 square miles (more than three times the size of New Jersey) in northeastern Arizona and adjacent parts of New Mexico and Utah. The area is arid, and there are few perennial streams, except for the San Juan and Colorado rivers, which form the north and northwest borders of the reservation. About two hundred wells had been drilled on the reservation prior to 1949, of which about 75 per cent were successful (yielded supplies sufficient for domestic and stock use), 15 per cent were dry holes, and 10 per cent yielded impotable water. In 1950 the U.S. Geological Survey commenced a comprehensive study of the geology and ground-water hydrology of the entire area of the reservation. The first job was spot analyses of ten specific areas where water supplies were urgently needed for villages or for proposed schools; successful wells were obtained at each of the eight sites recommended for drilling.

The comprehensive investigation included geologic mapping of the entire area, and delineation of the stratigraphy and geologic structure (Harshbarger, Repenning, and Callahan, 1953). These studies showed that there were seven water-bearing formations in the reservation, mostly sandstone but including some limestone, and that these formations made up 30 per cent of the total thickness of 8,000 feet of sedimentary rock. In the water-bearing formations, the contained water is probably less than 25 per cent of the gross volume of the rock, and only a minor fraction of this—perhaps a fourth—could be withdrawn by wells. Water-bearing formations do not underlie every part of the Navajo country, and this fact reduces further the water-supply capabilities. From one place to another the water-yielding capability of the underlying rocks differs widely, and at some places it is essentially zero. Thus, the potentiality for ground-water yield at any site depends upon an interplay between variable geologic and hydrologic factors. An important part of the study, therefore, was the identification and evaluation of these factors so as to permit accurate prediction of conditions in any part of the reservation. Since the completion of the study, the Geological Survey has acted as consultant to the U.S. Bureau of Indian Affairs and to the Navajo Tribal Council in well location. Of 375 holes drilled, 350 have been successful, 10 had insufficient water to meet the requirement at the site, 3 had impotable water, and 12 were dry holes.

To sum up, studies of ground-water hydrology may be broadly classified as exploratory or reconnaissance, systematic areal, and detailed quantitative. Exploratory investigations are made where there has been little or no ground-water development, generally by geologists experienced in ground-water work. They may be undertaken in a small area as a basis for selection of a site for a single well or they may constitute a reconnaissance over a broad region to classify various subdivisions according to relative prospects for productive wells. Conclusions are based largely on studies of stratigraphy and geologic structure and, particularly, of the geologic formations that appear to be permeable enough to permit storage and movement of ground water.

Systematic ground-water surveys are generally made where the number of wells is sufficient for a better understanding of the framework through which ground water moves—the geology of aquifers and acquicludes—than is possible in a reconnaissance. Geophysical prospecting, supplementing the data from wells, may provide information about the distribution and total volume of water-bearing materials. Much is learned about the water also. Measurements of water levels in wells lead to delineation of the form and position of the water table or of the piezometric surfaces, which indicate the direction of movement of ground water, and perhaps also the areas of recharge and natural discharge. Detailed records of fluctuations of water levels in individual wells show the effects of the forces acting upon the ground-water reservoir: some fluctuations are caused by changes in pressure—atmospheric, tidal, earthquake, or other superimposed load—others by recharge to or discharge from the aquifer. Chemical analyses show the variations in dissolved matter in the water of different aquifers and also the changes in dissolved materials as the water moves through an aquifer. Similarly, measurements of the temperature of water from wells and springs provide information on the movement of water in the ground-water reservoir, as well as on the usefulness of the water itself for cooling or other heat-exchange processes. Inventories of wells show the extent and pattern of the ground-water development. A systematic areal survey requires the talents of hydraulic engineers, chemists, and geophysicists as well as geologists. The results are largely qualitative: identification of the areas of recharge and discharge, and direction of ground-water movement, in each water-bearing formation; evaluation of the relative importance of the various means of recharge and discharge; and correlation of ground-water data with data concerning other phases of the hydrologic cycle.

Detailed quantitative investigations lead to a continuing inventory of the quantity and quality of water in a ground-water reservoir. For such an inventory it is necessary to know the physical characteristics of the aquifer (determined in part by means of pumping tests) so that the quantity and rates of movement can be computed. The discharge from the reservoir by all natural means and by wells is determined as accurately as possible; recharge is similarly computed; and changes in storage are calculated on the basis of the volume and storage coefficient of the part of an aquifer that is saturated or unwatered. Where an aquifer is recharged from various sources, the chemical and physical characteristics of the water may aid in determining the proportionate contribution from each source. The development and use of water may cause profound changes in the chemical or bacteriological quality of ground water, which is shown by periodic analyses of water from individual sources. A continuing inventory, showing the ground-water resources at any desired time, requires continuing records not only of pertinent ground-water data (water-level fluctuations, amount of water discharged, etc.) but also of other related phases of the hydrologic cycle. Where these records have already been collected for several years, the inventory can be projected back to show the effects of major climatic variations and of chronologic changes in development and use of water. Quantitative determinations call on the best efforts of the hydraulic engineer, geologist, geophysicist, chemist, and meteorologist.

In conclusion: The scientist can see no farther below the ground than the next person. To minimize the uncertainty about what will be found in drilling for water, he utilizes the disciplines of several sciences—geology, physics, chemistry, hydrology, meteorology, and even biology. And if this appears to be a formidable array, it amounts only to organizing and marshaling the pertinent experience of mankind, rather than merely his individual experience, for the task. The scientist, being human, is undoubtedly gratified, as is the dowser, when his predictions are borne out by the test of drilling; but as a scientist he is also committed to the method of "trial and error," and thus to recording his failures as well as his successes, for the reason that they also lead to fuller understanding of ground water.

REFERENCES TO APPENDIX II

GOLDTHWAIT, R. P. 1949. *Artesian Wells in New Hampshire.* (New Hampshire State Planning and Development Commission, Mineral Resources Survey, Part XI.) Concord, N.H. Pp. 20.

HARSHBARGER, J. W., REPENNING, C. A., and CALLAHAN, J. T. 1953. "The Navajo Country, Arizona–Utah–New Mexico," in *Subsurface Facilities of Water Management and Patterns of Supply–Type Area Studies,* pp. 105–29. (U.S. Congress, House Committee on Interior and Insular Affairs, *Physical and Economic Foundation of Natural Resources,* Vol. IV.) Washington, D.C.

MEINZER, O. E. 1911. *Geology and Water Resources of Estancia Valley, New Mexico.* (U.S. Geological Survey Water-Supply Paper 275.) Washington, D.C. Pp. 88.

———. 1912. *Geology and Water Resources of Sulphur Spring Valley, Arizona.* (U.S. Geological Survey Water-Supply Paper 320.) Washington, D.C. Pp. 231.

MENDENHALL, W. C. 1905. *The Hydrology of San Bernardino Valley, California.* (U.S. Geological Survey Water-Supply Paper 142.) Washington, D.C. Pp. 124.

MOODY, G. B. 1957. *Exploratory Drilling in 1956.* (American Association of Petroleum Geologists Bulletin, Vol. 41, No. 6.) Tulsa, Okla. Pp. 996.

MUNDORFF, M. J. 1948. *Geology and Ground Water in the Greensboro Area, North Carolina.* (North Carolina Board of Conservation and Development, Division of Mineral Resources Bulletin 55.) Raleigh, N.C. Pp. 108.

THOMPSON, D. G. 1929. *The Mojave Desert Region, California.* (U.S. Geological Survey Water-Supply Paper 578.) Washington, D.C. Pp. 759.

Bibliography

AGRICOLA, GEORGIUS. 1556. *De re metallica*. Translated from the first Latin edition by H. C. HOOVER and L. H. HOOVER. New York: Dover Publications, 1950.

ALLPORT, GORDON W., and POSTMAN, L. 1947. *The Psychology of Rumor*. New York: Henry Holt & Co.

ALLPORT, GORDON W. 1954. "The Historical Background of Modern Social Psychology," in *Handbook of Social Psychology*, ed. G. LINDZEY. Vol. I. Cambridge, Mass.: Addison-Wesley.

ARNOLD, MAGDA B. 1946. "On the Mechanism of Suggestion and Hypnosis," *Journal of Abnormal and Social Psychology*, **41**, 107–28.

BAILEY, W. C. 1951. *A Study of a Texas Panhandle Community: A Preliminary Report on Cotton Center, Texas*. Unpublished manuscript, Laboratory of Social Relations, Harvard University.

BARRETT, SIR WILLIAM. 1911. "The So-called Divining or Dowsing Rod," in *Psychical Research*, pp. 167–86. ("Home Library Series.") London.

BARRETT, SIR WILLIAM, and BESTERMAN, THEODORE. 1926. *The Divining Rod: An Experimental and Psychological Investigation*. London: Methuen & Co.

BEARD, GEORGE M. 1877. "Physiology of Mind Reading," *Popular Science Monthly*, **10**, 459–73.

BEAUSOLEIL, BARONESS DE. 1640. *La restitution de Pluton*.

BERNSTEIN, M. 1956. *The Search for Bridey Murphy*. New York: Doubleday & Co.

BERRIEN, F. K. 1952. *Practical Psychology*. Rev. ed.; New York: Macmillan Co.

BESTERMAN, THEODORE. 1938. *Water-Divining, New Facts and Theories*. London: Methuen & Co.

BOND, NANCY EWART. 1956. "We Witched Water, and What Do You Know? It Worked!" *Woman's Day*, **35** (May), 99–103.

BREEN, H. 1956. "Bridey Murphy Puts Nation in a Hypnotizzy," *Life*, March 19.

BRONOWSKI, J. 1953. *The Common Sense of Science*. Cambridge, Mass.: Harvard University Press.

BRUNER, J. S., GOODNOW, JACQUELINE J., and AUSTIN, G. A. 1956. *A Study of Thinking*. New York: John Wiley & Sons.

BURRIDGE, GASTON. 1955. "Does the Forked Stick Locate Anything? An Inquiry into the Art of Dowsing," *Western Folklore*, **14**, 32–43.

CAMPBELL, N. 1952. *What Is Science?* New York: Dover Publications.

CARPENTER, W. B. 1852. "On the Influence of Suggestion in Modifying and Directing Muscular Movement, Independently of Volition," *Proceedings of the Royal Institution of Great Britain*, **1**, 147–53.

——. 1874. *Mental Physiology*. London: C. Kegan Paul & Co.

——. 1877. *Mesmerism, Spiritualism, &c.* New York: D. Appleton & Co.

CHEVREUL, MICHEL EUGÈNE. 1833. "Lettre à M. Ampere sur une classe particulière de mouvements musculaires," *Revue des deux mondes*, **2**, 258–66.

——. 1834. *De la baguette divinatoire, du pendule dit explorateur et des tables tournantes*. Paris: Mallet-Bachelier.

CHRISTOPHER, MILBOURNE. 1955. "Animal Wonders," *M.U.M.*, **44**, 471–75.

COLVILL, HELEN HESTER. 1909. *Saint Teresa of Spain*. New York: E. P. Dutton & Co.

COOVER, J. E. 1917. *Experiments in Psychical Research*. Stanford, Calif.: Stanford University Press.

CRONBACH, L. J., and GLESER, GOLDINE C. 1957. *Psychological Tests and Personnel Decisions*. Urbana: University of Illinois Press.

DALE, L. A., *et al.* 1951. "Dowsing: A Field Experiment in Water Divining," *Journal of American Society of Psychical Research*, **45**, 3–16.

"The Divining Rod," *American Journal of Science,* **2,** (1826), 201–12.

ELLIS, ARTHUR J. 1917. *The Divining Rod: A History of Water Witching.* (U.S. Geological Survey Water-Supply Paper 416.) Washington, D.C.: Government Printing Office.

EMERSON, RALPH. 1821. "On the Divining Rod, with Reference to the Use Made of It in Exploring for Springs of Water," *American Journal of Science,* **3,** 102–4.

EVANS, BERGEN. 1954. *The Spoor of Spooks and Other Nonsense.* New York: Alfred A. Knopf.

EYSENCK, H. J. 1947. *Dimensions of Personality.* London: Routledge & Kegan Paul.

EYSENCK, H. J., and FURNEAUX, W. D. 1945. "Primary and Secondary Suggestibility: An Experimental and Statistical Study," *Journal of Experimental Psychology,* **35,** 485–503.

FARADAY, MICHAEL. 1853. "Experimental Investigation of Table Turning," *Athenaeum,* July, pp. 801–3.

FLOURNOY, T. 1900. *From India to Planet Mars.* New York: Harper & Bros.

FOSTER, W. S. 1923. "Experiments on Rod Divining," *Journal of Applied Psychology,* **7,** 303–11.

FRANCE, HENRY DE. 1948. *The Elements of Dowsing.* London: G. Bell & Sons.

GARDNER, MARTIN. 1952. *In the Name of Science.* New York: G. P. Putnam's Sons.

———. 1957. *Fads and Fallacies in the Name of Science.* New York: Dover Publications.

GREGORY, J. W. 1929. "Water Divining," in *Smithsonian Institution Annual Report, 1928,* pp. 325–48. Washington, D.C.: Government Printing Office.

HAKE, H. W., and HYMAN, RAY. 1953. "Perception of the Statistical Structure of a Random Series of Binary Symbols," *Journal of Experimental Psychology,* **45,** 64–74.

Handbuch der Wünschelrute: Geschichte, Wissenschaft, Anwendung. 1931. Berlin: R. Oldenbourg.

HILDEBRAND, J. H. 1957. *Science in the Making.* New York: Columbia University Press.

HOMANS, GEORGE C. "Anxiety and Ritual: The Theories of Malinowski and Radcliffe-Brown," *American Anthropologist*, **43**, 164–72.

HYMAN, RAY, and COHEN, ELIZABETH G. 1957. "Water Witching in the United States," *American Sociological Review*, **22**, 719–24.

HYMAN, RAY, and JENKIN, NOEL S. 1956. "Involvement and Set as Determinants of Behavioral Stereotypy," *Psychological Reports*, **2**, 131–46.

HYMAN, RAY, and VOGT, EVON Z. 1958. "Some Facts and Theories on Water Witching in the United States," *Geo Times*, **2**, No. 9 (March), 6–15.

HYMAN, RAY, and VOGT, EVON Z. "Water Witching: An American Paradox," *Scientific American* (in press).

JACOBSON, EDMUND. 1932. "The Electrophysiology of Mental Activities," *American Journal of Psychology*, **44**, 677–94.

———. 1938. *Progressive Relaxation.* 2d ed.; Chicago: University of Chicago Press.

JAMES, WILLIAM. 1948. *Psychology.* New York: World Publishing Co.

JASTROW, JOSEPH. 1935. *Wish and Wisdom.* New York: Appleton-Century-Crofts.

KATZ, EDWARD, and PAULSON, PETER. 1948. "A Brief History of the Divining Rod in the United States, I," *Journal of the American Society for Psychical Research*, **42**, 119–31.

———. 1949. "A Brief History of the Divining Rod in the United States, II," ibid., **43**, 3–18.

KIRCHER, ATHANASIUS. 1645. *The Magnet, or Concerning the Magnetic Art*, Book 3, Part 5, chap. 3. Rome.

KLINE, M. V. (ed.) 1956. *A Scientific Report on "The Search for Bridey Murphy."* New York: Julian Press.

LANG, ANDREW. 1908. *The Origins of Religion and Other Essays*, pp. 55–62. London: Watts & Co.

LEET, L. DON. 1953. Review of Kenneth Roberts, *The Seventh Sense, American Scientist*, **41**, No. 4 (October), 652–56.

LEVINSON, H. C. 1950. *The Science of Chance.* New York: Rhinehart & Co.

LOVIBOND, S. H. 1952. "The Water Diviner's Frame of Reference," *Australian Journal of Psychology*, **4**, 62–73.

LUCE, R. D., and RAIFFA, H. 1957. *Games and Decisions.* New York: John Wiley & Sons.

MABY, J. C., and FRANKLIN, T. B. 1939. *The Physics of the Divining Rod.* London: G. Bell & Sons.

MAGER, HENRI. 1931. *Water Diviners and Their Methods.* London: G. Bell & Sons.

MALINOWSKI, BRONISLAW. 1925. "Magic, Science and Religion," in *Science, Religion, and Reality,* ed. JAMES NEEDHAM. New York: Macmillan Co.

MATTHEWS, RONALD. 1952. "Radiesthesia: An Old Hoax or a New Science?" *Realities*, **18** (May), 31–35, 72.

MAX, L. W. 1937. "Experimental Study of the Motor Theory of Consciousness. IV. Action-Current Responses in the Deaf during Awakening, Kinaesthetic Imagery and Abstract Thinking," *Journal of Comparative Psychology*, **24**, 301–44.

MEYERHOFF, HOWARD A. 1953. "Can a Water Witch Really Find Water?" *Popular Science*, **163** (October), 99–102, 304.

MOONEY, JAMES. 1896. *The Ghost Dance Religion.* ("Fourteenth Annual Report of Bureau of American Ethnology, 1892–93.") Washington, D.C.: Government Printing Office.

MURCIA VIUDAS, ANDRES. 1953. *Aguas subterraneas, prospección y alumbramiento para riegos.* ("Manuales Técnicos," Serie I, Numero 18, Publicaciones del Ministerio de Agricultura). Madrid.

ONGLEY, P. A. 1948. "New Zealand Diviners," *New Zealand Journal of Science and Technology*, **30**, 38–54.

PARSONS, TALCOTT. 1944. "The Theoretical Development of the Sociology of Religion," *Journal of the History of Ideas*, **5** (April), 176–90.

PASSIN, H., and BENNETT, J. W. 1943. "Changing Agricultural Magic in Southern Illinois," *Social Forces*, **21**, 98–106.

PEIRCE, C. S. 1955. *Philosophical Writings*. New York: Dover Publications.

PFUNGST, OSKAR. 1911. *Clever Hans*. New York: Henry Holt & Co.

Radio-Perception: Journal of the British Society of Dowsers, **12**, No. 90 (December, 1955), 321.

RASMUSSEN, KNUD. 1929. *Intellectual Culture of the Iglulik Eskimos.* (*Report of the Fifth Thule Expedition, 1921–24,* Vol. 3, Part 1.) Copenhagen: Gyldendalske Boghandel, Nordisk Forlage.

RAYMOND, ROSSITER W. 1883. "The Divining Rod," *Transactions of the American Institute of Mining Engineers,"* **11**, 411–46.

RECHTSHAFFEN, A., and MEDNICK, S. A. 1955. "The Autokinetic Word Technique," *Journal of Abnormal and Social Psychology,* **51**, 346.

REED, VERNER Z. 1953. "Water Dowser," *Vermont Life,* **7**, 46–51.

REICHENBACH, H. 1951. *The Rise of Scientific Philosophy.* Berkeley: University of California Press.

RHINE, J. B. 1950. "Some Exploratory Tests in Dowsing," *Journal of Para-psychology,* **14**, 278–86.

RHINE, J. B., and RHINE, LOUISA E. 1929. "An Investigation of a 'Mind-reading' Horse," *Journal of Abnormal and Social Psychology,* **23**, 449–66.

RICHET, CHARLES. 1923. *Traité de Métapsychique.* Paris.

RIDDICK, THOMAS M. 1951. "Dowsing Is Nonsense," *Harper's Magazine,* **203** (July), 62–68.

———. 1952. "Dowsing—an Unorthodox Method of Locating Underground Water Supplies or an Interesting Facet of the Human Mind," *Proceedings of the American Philosophical Society,* **96** (October), 526–34.

RINN, J. F. 1950. *Sixty Years of Psychical Research.* New York: Truth Seeker.

ROBERTS, KENNETH. 1951. *Henry Gross and His Dowsing Rod.* New York: Doubleday & Co.

———. 1953. *The Seventh Sense.* New York: Doubleday & Co.

———. 1957. *Water Unlimited.* New York: Doubleday & Co.

ROGERS, EVERETT M. 1958. "Agricultural and Technological Change." Paper presented to Ohio Valley Sociological Society, May 3.

RUSSELL, BERTRAND. 1958. "The Divorce of Science and 'Culture,'" *UNESCO Courier,* 2 (February), 4.

SAVAGE, L. J. 1954. *The Foundations of Statistics.* New York: John Wiley & Sons.

SEABROOK, W. 1941. *Doctor Wood.* New York: Harcourt, Brace & Co.

SERVADIO, E. 1935. "La baguette des sourciers: Essai d'interprétation psychanalytique," *Revue français de psychanalyse,* **8,** 488–500.

SHOOK, E. M. 1957. "The Tikal Project," *University Museum Bulletin* (University of Pennsylvania), **21** (September), 37–52.

SIMS, N. LeR. 1929. *Elements of Rural Sociology.* New York: Thomas Y. Crowell Co.

STOUFFER, S. A. 1950. "Some Observations on Study Design," *American Journal of Sociology,* **55,** 355–61.

STRATTON, G. M. 1921. "The Control of Another Person by Obscure Signs," *Psychological Review,* **28,** 301–14.

SWIFT, JONATHAN. 1710. *Virtues of Sid Hamet the Magician's Rod.* London.

THISTLETHWAITE, D. 1950. "Attitude and Structure as Factors in Distortion of Reasoning," *Journal of Abnormal and Social Psychology,* **45,** 442–58.

THOMAS, H. E. 1952. *The Physical and Economic Foundation of Natural Resources. III. Groundwater Regions of the United States—Their Storage Facilities.* (Interior and Insular Affairs Committee, House of Representatives, United States Congress.) Washington, D.C.: Government Printing Office.

TITIEV, MISCHA. 1944. *Old Oraibi: A Study of the Hopi Indians of Third Mesa.* ("Papers of the Peabody Museum of American Archaeology and Ethnology," Harvard University, Vol. 22.) Cambridge, Mass.

TROMP, SOLCO W. 1949. *Psychical Physics: A Scientific Analysis of Dowsing, Radiesthesia and Kindred Phenomena.* Houston, Tex.: Elsevier Press.

TYLOR, E. B. 1883. "Anthropology II," *Nature,* **28,** 55–59.

VANCE, LEE F. 1891. "Three Lessons in Rhabdomancy," *Journal of American Folklore,* **4,** 241–46.

VOGT, EVON Z. 1952. "Water Witching: An Interpretation of a Ritual Pattern in a Rural American Community," *Scientific Monthly,* **75** (September), 175–86.

———. 1955. *Modern Homesteaders: The Life of a Twentieth Century Frontier Community.* Cambridge, Mass.: Harvard University Press.

———. 1956. "Interviewing Water Dowsers," *American Journal of Sociology,* **62,** No. 2 (September), 198.

VOGT, EVON Z., and GOLDE, PEGGY. 1958. "Some Aspects of the Folklore of Water Witching in the United States," *Journal of American Folklore,* **71,** 519–31.

WARD, L. KEITH. 1946. *The Occurrence, Composition, Testing, and Utilization of Underground Water in South Australia, and the Search for Future Supplies.* (Department of Mines, Geological Survey, South Australia, Bulletin No. 23.) Sydney.

WATSON, J. B. 1924. *Psychology from the Standpoint of a Behaviorist.* 2d ed. Philadelphia: J. B. Lippincott Co.

WEITZENHOFFER, ANDRE. 1953. *Hypnotism: An Objective Study in Suggestibility.* New York: John Wiley & Sons, 1953.

WILLIAMSON, PAUL B. 1938. "A Reply on Dowsing." New Orleans. (Mimeographed.)